D0840730

JOHN BUNYAN

Born at Elstow, near Bedford, in 1628, the son
of a brazier. Served in the Civil War on the Parliamentary side. Became a preacher in 1657; and
pastor of a congregation in Bedford, 1671. Inter-
mittently imprisoned for unlicensed preaching
from 1660 to 1672, and again in 1675. Died in
London on 31st August 1688.

JOHN BUNYAN

Grace Abounding
&
The Life and Death of
Mr Badman

INTRODUCTION BY
G. B. HARRISON

DENT: LONDON
EVERYMAN'S LIBRARY
DUTTON: NEW YORK

All rights reserved
Made in Great Britain
at the
Aldine Press · Letchworth · Herts
for
J. M. DENT & SONS LTD
Aldine House · Albemarle Street · London
This edition was first published in
Everyman's Library in 1928
Last reprinted 1969

Published in the U.S.A. by arrangement
with J. M. Dent & Sons Ltd

No. 815   Hardback ISBN 0 460 00815 3
No. 1815 Paperback ISBN 0 460 01815 9

INTRODUCTION

In the Bedford congregation which Bunyan joined in 1655 it was a rule that new members, before they were formally admitted into full fellowship, should make a public declaration of the workings of Grace in their souls. Many accounts of conversion and spiritual experience were recorded during the seventeenth century, and a number have survived in print; of these John Bunyan's *Grace Abounding to the Chief of Sinners* is the best known. It was written in 1666 when Bunyan had already endured six years of imprisonment for his principles.

Apart from what Bunyan has told in *Grace Abounding*, some details of his early life survive. He was baptised in the parish church of Elstow, a village near Bedford, on 28 November, 1628, his father being Thomas Bunyan, a brazier; John Bunyan was the first child of his father's second marriage. In November 1644 he was imprested as a soldier in the Parliamentary army, and served until July 1647. In 1655 he joined the congregation which had been founded at Bedford by John Gifford some five years before.

John Gifford had been a major in the king's forces during the Civil War and had taken a prominent part in the desperate fighting at Maidstone in 1648. He was captured and condemned to death, but with the aid of his sister he managed to escape on the night before his execution. Thence he had made his way to Bedford, where he set up as a doctor. At first Gifford was noted for his dissolute living, but after some months he became converted, and was the leading spirit in bringing together into a small congregation of believers some of those at Bedford who shared his views. Only one relic of Gifford's teaching remains, the very beautiful letter which was copied into the *Church Book of Bunyan Meeting*; it shows that he was a man of high spiritual quality, and it is not surprising that he was a considerable influence in Bunyan's life at its most critical period.[1]

After Gifford's death the congregation began to keep a record of their doings in the *Church Book*, which is still preserved at Bunyan Meeting at Bedford. In the list of members therein recorded Bunyan's name is twenty-sixth. He is first mentioned on 28 June, 1657, and thereafter he takes a prominent part in the affairs of the congregation.

After joining the Bedford congregation Bunyan had quickly made himself felt and soon began to be well known locally as a preacher. In the following year (1656) he was disputing actively with the Quakers, which led him to publish his first book, *Some Gospel Truths Opened*. Two other books, which were founded on his sermons at this time, were published shortly afterwards, *A Few Sighs from Hell* (1658), and *The Doctrine of the Law and Grace Unfolded* (1659).

With the death of Oliver Cromwell in September 1658 and the collapse of his system, the re-establishment of the monarchy seemed to be the only way to end a state of chaos. King Charles the Second was restored to the throne in May 1660, and, in the autumn following, the persecution of Nonconformists began. Considering the upheavals of the last twenty years, the Royalists were comparatively tolerant; in Bunyan's case, for instance, it is clear from his own account that he was given every opportunity of conforming; but it is not surprising that so stanch a believer should have refused the slightest compromise on principles, which might in any way weaken the faith of those whom he had converted by his preaching. For some months after his first appearance before the magistrate his name occurs in the entries in the *Church Book*, but after October 1661 it disappears for seven years. No meetings of the congregation are recorded between March 1664 and October 1668, when the persecutions were hottest.

Being thus prevented from preaching, Bunyan occupied himself with writing. He was released for some months in 1666 but soon rearrested as he persisted in preaching. It was at this time that he wrote *Grace Abounding to the Chief of Sinners*.

[1] See *Grace Abounding*, § 77.

Such is a brief outline of Bunyan's life up to 1666 from external sources. Naturally there are many gaps, which can, to some extent, be filled from *Grace Abounding*; but *Grace Abounding* is not, and was not intended to be, an autobiography. Bunyan wrote the book as a record of his own spiritual experiences, to encourage his fellow-saints whose faith was weakening under persecution, and to show them that he too had endured temptations, far fiercer than theirs. Hence he was not so much concerned with the outward facts of his own life as with tracing the steps by which he came to be the spiritual father to the saints at Bedford. Much therefore is omitted which most readers would like to know.

Bunyan says nothing, for example, of his mother, and very little of his father; and yet to one or both of them must presumably have been due the religious ideas, which reappeared in the terrible dreams of his childhood, and those fundamental intuitions which enabled him to resist all the assaults of doubt and unbelief. He does not record the name of his first wife, nor her death, nor his second marriage. Yet both his wives appear to have been women of considerable character; and to the first, more than to any other human being, he owed his conversion.

Again, his military service which lasted for two and a half years was omitted altogether from the first edition of *Grace Abounding*, for the incident recorded in §13 was added later as an afterthought.

These omissions and many others are due to Bunyan's purpose in writing the book. He was not writing about himself but about God's dealings with him, and, however much the biographer may regret Bunyan's silence, it is in the circumstances justified. To have recorded the multitude of incidents which made up his life would have been to reduce the magnitude of his spiritual struggles. This can be seen by comparing the later additions, telling of his trials and imprisonment, with the earlier account of his conversion. The conflict is on a lower plane; the worst threats of Mr. Wingate, or Judge Keeling, or the well-meant casuistry of Mr. Cobb were feeble compared with the audible assaults and promptings of Satan himself who had tormented Bunyan as he walked alone on the road between Elstow and Bedford.

Grace Abounding was published in 1666; other editions
followed to which Bunyan made many additions, the
most important being the account of his escapes from
danger (§§ 12–14); the bell-ringing incident (§§ 32–6); the
Ranters (§§ 43–5); Luther's *Commentary* on Galatians
(§§ 129–31); and the indignant repudiation of the charges
of immorality (§§ 301–17), probably added after certain
venomous rumours had been circulated by his enemies
in 1674. The *Continuation* of Bunyan's life (p. 130) was
added in 1692; the *Relation* of his imprisonment (p. 103),
usually printed with *Grace Abounding*, was not published
till 1765.

Bunyan published nothing after *Grace Abounding* for
five years. He remained nominally a prisoner between 1666
and 1672, but it is clear from the entries in the *Church
Book* that he was allowed considerable liberty, and he
was able to take the lead in the reorganisation of the
congregation which had been scattered during the times
of persecution.

At the end of 1671 the congregation elected him as their
pastor. A few weeks later Charles the Second issued the
Declaration of Indulgence, and Bunyan was formally
licensed as a preacher in May 1672. He was now writing
busily again; two works, important for the understanding
of Bunyan's theology, appeared in 1675, *Light for them
that sit in Darkness*, and *Instructions for the Ignorant*. These
were followed by *The Straight Gate* and the first part of
The Pilgrim's Progress. In 1676, Bunyan had again been
in prison for six months and during this time the Dream
had come to him, but it was not published until 1678.
The allegory was so enthusiastically received that two
further editions, considerably enlarged, soon followed.

Bunyan was now forty, and *The Pilgrim's Progress* was
his twenty-fourth book. Its success prompted him to show
the opposite side of the picture in *The Life and Death of
Mr. Badman* (1680).

Both *The Pilgrim's Progress* and *Mr. Badman* largely
owe their vitality to the fact that Bunyan was drawing
on his own very vivid experiences of all sorts and conditions
of men, but the contrast between the two books shows
Bunyan's great skill as an artist. In the Pilgrim's passage

to the Heavenly City, experience is sublimated into allegory and symbol; in Mr. Badman's descent to destruction,
Bunyan tells the story as an actual happening, and the
excellence of the book lies in its vivid realism; "yet have
I," says he, "as little as may be, gone out of the road of
mine own observation of things."

Bunyan chose the dialogue form for *Mr. Badman*, in
this following Arthur Dent's *Plain Man's Pathway to
Heaven* which had exercised considerable influence over
him in the early stages of his conversion.[1] By choosing
this form and telling the story as a conversation between
Mr. Wiseman and Attentive, he was able to digress quite
naturally to denounce those failings which were most conspicuous in his own congregation. Badman himself is a
composite character, but many of his particular sins were
not unknown to some of the individual members of Bunyan's flock as a study of the *Church Book* shows; and
not only is the picture of Mr. Badman and his circle true
to life, but the two speakers themselves illustrate very
clearly the attitude of the believer towards the "carnally
minded."

At first sight there is not much in common between
Grace Abounding and *Mr. Badman*, yet the two books
supplement each other. *Mr. Badman* being concerned with
the temptations of the world and the flesh, *Grace Abounding*
with the assaults of the devil. *Grace Abounding* is the
record of the inner spiritual experience which turned an
unlearned artificer into a leader of the saints, a true and
steadfast "professor"—to use the word used by Bunyan
and his fellow-believers; without such an experience Mr.
Wiseman's attitude would have lacked all sincerity. *Mr.
Badman* shows the professor faced by the ordinary problems
and temptations of everyday life, and, as Bunyan very
truly realised, the devil tries a man just as hard in his
daily business as in his faith or his lusts, and not the
least of the religious man's difficulties is to keep a high
standard of honesty against unscrupulous competition. But
even the professor is in some danger when he contem-
plates the sinner too closely, for, though neither Mr. Wiseman nor Attentive is likely to lapse with Mr. Badman,

[1] See *Grace Abounding*, § 15.

they are not always free from the fault of gloating over muck-heaps.

Mr. Badman has not been a favourite book with Bunyan's most zealous disciples, who are somewhat offended by its lurid truthfulness; but it is scarcely an exaggeration to call it the first modern English novel, and as a picture of the trader in a small county town it is invaluable.

After Bunyan had been elected pastor of his congregation at Bedford, and especially after *The Pilgrim's Progress*, his reputation both as a preacher and a writer spread widely. "When Mr. Bunyan preached in London," wrote Charles Doe, his first editor, "if there were but one day's notice given, there would be more people come together to hear him preach than the meeting-house would hold. I have seen to hear him preach, by my computation, about twelve hundred at a morning lecture, by seven o'clock on a working day in the dark winter time. I also computed about three thousand came to hear him one Lord's-day, at London, at a town's end meeting-house; so that half were fain to go back again for want of room, and then himself was fain, at a back door, to be pulled almost over people to get upstairs to his pulpit."

Bunyan continued to write and to preach for the rest of his life. *The Holy War* was published in 1682, the second part of *The Pilgrim's Progress*, telling how Christiana and her children followed Christian, in 1685, seven years after the first part. Bunyan died in London on 31 August, 1688, and was buried in Bunhill Fields.

Bunyan left over sixty books, some of which were published posthumously. Many have little interest to-day, though more of them are worth reading than is usually supposed. *The Pilgrim's Progress* is accepted among the dozen greatest books in the English language; and neither *Grace Abounding* nor *Mr. Badman* will be neglected by anyone who cares to understand English puritanism at its greatest. Nor must it be forgotten that, though few great English writers have been puritans, puritanism is one of the strongest and most fundamental traits in the English character. John Bunyan was both puritan and artist, and in both of the greatest.

G. B. HARRISON.

SELECT BIBLIOGRAPHY

SEPARATE WORKS. *Some Gospel Truths Opened*, 1656; *A Vindication of Some Gospel Truths Opened*, 1657; *A Few Sighs from Hell*, 1658; *The Doctrine of Law and Grace Unfolded*, 1659; *Profitable Meditations*, ?1661; *I Will Pray with the Spirit*, 1663; *Christian Behaviour*, 1663; *A Map Shewing the Order and Causes of Salvation and Damnation, c.* 1664; *One Thing is Needful*, 1665; *The Holy City*, 1665; *Prison Meditations*, 1665 (a broadsheet in verse); *The Resurrection of the Dead and Eternal Judgement*, 1665; *Grace Abounding*, 1666; *A Confession of My Faith*, 1672; *A Defence of the Doctrine of Justification by Faith in Jesus Christ*, 1672; *Differences in Judgement about Water-Baptism no bar to Communion*, 1673; *The Barren Fig Tree*, 1673; *Peaceable Principles and True*, 1674; *Light for them that Sit in Darkness*, 1675; *Instruction for the Ignorant*, 1675; *The Strait Gate*, 1676; *Saved by Grace*, 1678 (lost); *The Pilgrim's Progress* (Part I), 1678; *Come and Welcome to Jesus Christ*, 1678; *A Treatise of the Fear of God*, 1679; *The Life and Death of Mr Badman*, 1680; *The Holy War*, 1682; *The Greatness of the Soul*, 1683; *A Case of Conscience Resolved*, 1683; *A Holy Life*, 1684; *Seasonable Counsel*, 1684; *The Pilgrim's Progress* (Part II), 1684; *A Caution to stir up Watch against Sin*, 1684 (broadside); *A Discourse Upon the Pharisee and the Publican*, 1685; *Questions about the Nature and Perpetuity of the Seventh-Day Sabbath*, 1685; *A Book for Boys and Girls or Country Rhymes for Children*, 1686; *Good News for the Vilest of Men*, 1688; *The Advocateship of Jesus Christ*, 1688; *The Work of Jesus Christ as an Advocate*, 1688; *A Discourse of the Building, Nature, Excellency, and Government of the House of God*, 1688; *The Water of Life*, 1688; *Solomon's Temple Spiritualized*, 1688.

POSTHUMOUSLY PRINTED. *The Acceptable Sacrifice*, 1689; *Mr Bunyan's Last Sermon*, 1689.

The following were left in manuscript at Bunyan's death and were printed in Charles Doe's Folio of 1692: *An Exposition of the First Ten Chapters of Genesis; Of Justification by Imputed Righteousness; Paul's Departure and Crown; Of the Trinity and a Christian; Of the Law and a Christian; Israel's Hope Encouraged; The Desires of the Righteous Encouraged; The Desires of the Righteous Granted; The Saint's Privilege and Profit; Christ a Complete Saviour; The Saint's Knowledge of Christ's Love; Of the House of the Forest of Lebanon; Of Christ and His Ruin.*

A Relation of the Imprisonment of Mr John Bunyan, 1765.

COLLECTED WORKS. 1692 by Charles Doe (6th edition, 1771); 1853, 1862, by G. Offor; 1859 by H. Stebbing.

BIOGRAPHIES, COMMENTARIES, ETC. Robert Southey, *A Life of John Bunyan*, 1830; Lord Macaulay, *John Bunyan*, 1850; J. A. Froude, *Bunyan* (English Men of Letters), 1880; John Brown, *John Bunyan: His Life, Times, and Works*, 1885, etc., edited with addenda and notes by F. Mott Harrison, 1928 (the standard biography); C. H. Firth, *John Bunyan*, 1911; Gwilym O. Griffith, *John Bunyan*, 1927; G. B. Harrison, *John Bunyan: a Study in Personality*, 1928; Henri Talon, *John Bunyan: The Man and His Works*, 1951 (contains a useful bibliography).

The Church Book of Bunyan Meeting was reproduced in facsimile in 1928.

GRACE ABOUNDING. R. Sharrock (ed.) *Grace Abounding to the Chief of Sinners*, 1962.

CONTENTS

CONTENTS

GRACE ABOUNDING TO THE CHIEF OF SINNERS;

OR, A BRIEF RELATION OF THE EXCEEDING MERCY OF GOD
IN CHRIST, TO HIS POOR SERVANT, JOHN BUNYAN

A PREFACE, OR BRIEF ACCOUNT OF THE
PUBLISHING OF THIS WORK

WRITTEN BY THE AUTHOR THEREOF, AND DEDICATED TO
THOSE WHOM GOD HATH COUNTED HIM WORTHY TO
BEGET TO FAITH, BY HIS MINISTRY IN THE WORD

CHILDREN, grace be with you, Amen. I being taken from you
in presence, and so tied up, that I cannot perform that duty
that from God doth lie upon me to youward, for your further
edifying and building up in faith and holiness, etc., yet that
you may see my soul hath fatherly care and desire after
your spiritual and everlasting welfare; I now once again,
as before, from the top of Shenir and Hermon, so now
from the lions' dens, from the mountains of the leopards
(Song iv. 8), do look yet after you all, greatly longing to see
your safe arrival into the desired haven.

I thank God upon every remembrance of you; and rejoice,
even while I stick between the teeth of the lions in the
wilderness, at the grace, and mercy, and knowledge of Christ
our Saviour, which God hath bestowed upon you, with
abundance of faith and love. Your hungerings and thirstings
also after further acquaintance with the Father, in his Son;
your tenderness of heart, your trembling at sin, your sober
and holy deportment also, before both God and men, is
great refreshment to me; "For ye are my glory and joy"
(I Thess. ii. 20).

I have sent you here enclosed, a drop of that honey, that
I have taken out of the carcase of a lion (Judges xiv. 5-9).
I have eaten thereof myself also, and am much refreshed
thereby. (Temptations, when we meet them at first, are as
the lion that roared upon Samson; but if we overcome them,
the next time we see them, we shall find a nest of honey
within them.) The Philistines understand me not. It is
something of a relation of the work of God upon my own

3

soul, even from the very first, till now; wherein you may perceive my castings down, and raisings up; for he woundeth, and his hands make whole. It is written in the Scripture (Is. xxxviii. 19), "The father to the children shall make known the truth of God." Yea, it was for this reason I lay so long at Sinai (Deut. iv. 10, 11), to see the fire, and the cloud, and the darkness, that I might fear the Lord all the days of my life upon earth, and tell of his wondrous works to my children (Ps. lxxviii. 3–5).

Moses (Num. xxxiii. 1, 2) writ of the journeyings of the children of Israel, from Egypt to the land of Canaan; and commanded also, that they did remember their forty years' travel in the wilderness. "Thou shalt remember all the way which the Lord thy God led thee these forty years in the wilderness, to humble thee, *and* to prove thee, to know what *was* in thine heart, whether thou wouldest keep his commandments, or no" (Deut. viii. 2). Wherefore this I have endeavoured to do; and not only so, but to publish it also; that, if God will, others may be put in remembrance of what he hath done for their souls, by reading his work upon me.

It is profitable for Christians to be often calling to mind the very beginnings of grace with their souls. "It *is* a night to be much observed unto the Lord for bringing them out from the land of Egypt: this *is* that night of the Lord to be observed of all the children of Israel in their generations" (Exod. xii. 42). "O my God," saith David (Ps. xlii. 6), "my soul is cast down within me; therefore will I remember thee from the land of Jordan, and of the Hermonites, from the hill Mizar." He remembered also the lion and the bear, when he went to fight with the giant of Gath (1 Sam. xvii. 36, 37).

It was Paul's accustomed manner (Acts xxii.), and that when tried for his life (Acts xxiv), ever to open, before his judges, the manner of his conversion: he would think of that day, and that hour, in the which he first did meet with grace; for he found it support unto him. When God had brought the children of Israel through the Red Sea, far into the wilderness, yet they must turn quite about thither again, to remember the drowning of their enemies there (Num. xiv. 25). For though they sang his praise before, yet "they soon forgat his works" (Ps. cvi. 11–13).

In this discourse of mine you may see much; much, I say,

of the grace of God towards me. I thank God I can count it much, for it was above my sins and Satan's temptations too. I can remember my fears, and doubts, and sad months with comfort; they are as the head of Goliath in my hand. There was nothing to David like Goliath's sword, even that sword that should have been sheathed in his bowels; for the very sight and remembrance of that did preach forth God's deliverance to him. Oh, the remembrance of my great sins, of my great temptations, and of my great fears of perishing for ever! They bring afresh into my mind the remembrance of my great help, my great support from heaven, and the great grace that God extended to such a wretch as I.

My dear children, call to mind the former days, "and the years of ancient times: remember also your songs in the night; and commune with your own heart" (Ps. lxxvii. 5–12). Yea, look diligently, and leave no corner therein unsearched, for there is treasure hid, even the treasure of your first and second experience of the grace of God toward you. Remember, I say, the word that first laid hold upon you; remember your terrors of conscience, and fear of death and hell; remember also your tears and prayers to God; yea, how you sighed under every hedge for mercy. Have you never a hill Mizar to remember? Have you forgot the close, the milk house, the stable, the barn, and the like, where God did visit your soul? Remember also the Word—the Word, I say, upon which the Lord hath caused you to hope. If you have sinned against light; if you are tempted to blaspheme; if you are down in despair; if you think God fights against you; or if heaven is hid from your eyes, remember it was thus with your father, but out of them all the Lord delivered me.

I could have enlarged much in this my discourse, of my temptations and troubles for sin; as also of the merciful kindness and working of God with my soul. I could also have stepped into a style much higher than this in which I have here discoursed, and could have adorned all things more than here I have seemed to do, but I dare not. God did not play in convincing of me, the devil did not play in tempting of me, neither did I play when I sunk as into a bottomless pit, when the pangs of hell caught hold upon me; wherefore I may not play in my relating of them, but be plain and simple, and lay down the thing as it was. He that liketh it, let him receive it; and he that does not, let him produce a better. Farewell.

My dear children, the milk and honey is beyond this wilderness. God be merciful to you, and grant that you be not slothful to go in to possess the land.

JOHN BUNYAN.

GRACE ABOUNDING TO THE CHIEF OF SINNERS;

OR, A BRIEF RELATION OF THE EXCEEDING MERCY OF GOD IN CHRIST, TO HIS POOR SERVANT JOHN BUNYAN

1. In this my relation of the merciful working of God upon my soul, it will not be amiss, if, in the first place, I do, in a few words, give you a hint of my pedigree, and manner of bringing up; that thereby the goodness and bounty of God towards me, may be the more advanced and magnified before the sons of men.

2. For my descent then, it was, as is well known by many, of a low and inconsiderable generation; my father's house being of that rank that is meanest and most despised of all the families in the land. Wherefore I have not here, as others, to boast of noble blood, or of a high-born state, according to the flesh; though, all things considered, I magnify the heavenly Majesty, for that by this door he brought me into this world, to partake of the grace and life that is in Christ by the gospel.

3. But yet, notwithstanding the meanness and inconsiderableness of my parents, it pleased God to put it into their hearts to put me to school, to learn both to read and write; the which I also attained, according to the rate of other poor men's children; though, to my shame I confess, I did soon lose that little I learned, and that even almost utterly, and that long before the Lord did work his gracious work of conversion upon my soul.

4. As for my own natural life, for the time that I was without God in the world, it was indeed according to the course of this world, and "the spirit that now worketh in

the children of disobedience" (Eph. ii. 2, 3). It was my
delight to be "taken captive by the devil at his will"
(2 Tim. ii. 26). Being filled with all unrighteousness: the
which did also so strongly work and put forth itself, both
in my heart and life, and that from a child, that I had but
few equals, especially considering my years, which were
tender, being few, both for cursing, swearing, lying, and
blaspheming the holy name of God.

5. Yea, so settled and rooted was I in these things, that
they became as a second nature to me; the which, as I also
have with soberness considered since, did so offend the Lord,
that even in my childhood he did scare and affright me with
fearful dreams, and did terrify me with dreadful visions;
for often, after I had spent this and the other day in sin,
I have in my bed been greatly afflicted, while asleep, with
the apprehensions of devils and wicked spirits, who still,
as I then thought, laboured to draw me away with them,
of which I could never be rid.

6. Also I should, at these years, be greatly afflicted and
troubled with the thoughts of the day of judgment, and that
both night and day, and should tremble at the thoughts of
the fearful torments of hell fire; still fearing that it would
be my lot to be found at last amongst those devils and
hellish fiends, who are there bound down with the chains
and bonds of eternal darkness, "unto the judgment of the
great day."

7. These things, I say, when I was but a child but nine
or ten years old, did so distress my soul, that when in the
midst of my many sports and childish vanities, amidst my
vain companions, I was often much cast down and afflicted
in my mind therewith, yet could I not let go my sins. Yea,
I was also then so overcome with despair of life and heaven,
that I should often wish either that there had been no hell,
or that I had been a devil—supposing they were only tor-
mentors; that if it must needs be that I went thither, I might
be rather a tormentor, than be tormented myself.

8. A while after, these terrible dreams did leave me, which
also I soon forgot; for my pleasures did quickly cut off the
remembrance of them, as if they had never been: wherefore,
with more greediness, according to the strength of nature,
I did still let loose the reins to my lusts, and delighted in all

transgression against the law of God: so that, until I came to the state of marriage, I was the very ringleader of all the youth that kept me company, into all manner of vice and ungodliness.

9. Yea, such prevalency had the lusts and fruits of the flesh in this poor soul of mine, that had not a miracle of precious grace prevented, I had not only perished by the stroke of eternal justice, but had also laid myself open, even to the stroke of those laws, which bring some to disgrace and open shame before the face of the world.

10. In these days, the thoughts of religion were very grievous to me; I could neither endure it myself, nor that any other should; so that, when I have seen some read in those books that concerned Christian piety, it would be as it were a prison to me. Then I said unto God, "Depart from me, for I desire not the knowledge of thy ways" (Job xxi. 14). I was now void of all good consideration, heaven and hell were both out of sight and mind; and as for saving and damning, they were least in my thoughts. O Lord, thou knowest my life, and my ways were not hid from thee.

11. Yet this I well remember, that though I could myself sin with the greatest delight and ease, and also take pleasure in the vileness of my companions; yet, even then, if I have at any time seen wicked things, by those who professed goodness, it would make my spirit tremble. As once, above all the rest, when I was in my height of vanity, yet hearing one to swear that was reckoned for a religious man, it had so great a stroke upon my spirit, that it made my heart to ache.

12. But God did not utterly leave me, but followed me still, not now with convictions, but judgments; yet such as were mixed with mercy. For once I fell into a creek of the sea, and hardly escaped drowning. Another time I fell out of a boat into Bedford river, but mercy yet preserved me alive. Besides, another time, being in the field with one of my companions, it chanced that an adder passed over the highway; so I, having a stick in my hand, struck her over the back; and having stunned her, I forced open her mouth with my stick, and plucked her sting out with my fingers; by which act, had not God been merciful unto me, I might, by my desperateness, have brought myself to mine end.

13. This also have I taken notice of with thanksgiving; when I was a soldier, I, with others, were drawn out to go to such a place to besiege it; but when I was just ready to go, one of the company desired to go in my room; to which, when I had consented, he took my place; and coming to the siege, as he stood sentinel, he was shot into the head with a musket bullet, and died.

14. Here, as I said, were judgments and mercy, but neither of them did awaken my soul to righteousness; wherefore I sinned still, and grew more and more rebellious against God, and careless of mine own salvation.

15. Presently after this, I changed my condition into a married state, and my mercy was to light upon a wife whose father was counted godly. This woman and I, though we came together as poor as poor might be, not having so much household stuff as a dish or spoon betwixt us both, yet this she had for her part, *The Plain Man's Pathway to Heaven*, and *The Practice of Piety*, which her father had left her when he died. In these two books I should sometimes read with her, wherein I also found some things that were somewhat pleasing to me; but all this while I met with no conviction. She also would be often telling of me, what a godly man her father was, and how he would reprove and correct vice, both in his house, and amongst his neighbours; what a strict and holy life he lived in his day, both in word and deed.

16. Wherefore these books with this relation, though they did not reach my heart, to awaken it about my sad and sinful state, yet they did beget within me some desires to religion: so that, because I knew no better, I fell in very eagerly with the religion of the times; to wit, to go to church twice a day, and that too with the foremost; and there should very devoutly, both say and sing as others did, yet retaining my wicked life; but withal, I was so overrun with a spirit of superstition, that I adored, and that with great devotion, even all things, both the high place, priest, clerk, vestment, service, and what else belonging to the church; counting all things holy that were therein contained, and especially the priest and clerk most happy, and without doubt, greatly blessed, because they were the servants, as I then thought, of God, and were principal in the holy temple, to do his work therein.

17. This conceit grew so strong in little time upon my spirit, that had I but seen a priest, though never so sordid and debauched in his life, I should find my spirit fall under him, reverence him, and knit unto him; yea, I thought for the love I did bear unto them, supposing they were the ministers of God, I could have lain down at their feet, and have been trampled upon by them; their name, their garb, and work, did so intoxicate and bewitch me.

18. After I had been thus for some considerable time, another thought came into my mind; and that was, whether we were of the Israelites, or no? For finding in the Scriptures that they were once the peculiar people of God, thought I, if I were one of this race, my soul must needs be happy. Now again, I found within me a great longing to be resolved about this question, but could not tell how I should. At last I asked my father of it; who told me, No, we were not. Wherefore then I fell in my spirit as to the hopes of that, and so remained.

19. But all this while, I was not sensible of the danger and evil of sin; I was kept from considering that sin would damn me, what religion soever I followed, unless I was found in Christ. Nay, I never thought of him, nor whether there was one, or no. Thus man, while blind, doth wander, but wearieth himself with vanity, for he knoweth not the way to the city of God (Eccles. x. 15).

20. But one day, amongst all the sermons our parson made, his subject was, to treat of the Sabbath-day, and of the evil of breaking that, either with labour, sports, or otherwise. Now I was, notwithstanding my religion, one that took much delight in all manner of vice, and especially that was the day that I did solace myself therewith, wherefore I fell in my conscience under his sermon, thinking and believing that he made that sermon on purpose to show me my evil doing; and at that time I felt what guilt was, though never before, that I can remember; but then I was, for the present, greatly loaden therewith, and so went home when the sermon was ended, with a great burden upon my spirit.

21. This, for that instant, did benumb the sinews of my best delights, and did imbitter my former pleasures to me; but behold, it lasted not, for before I had well dined, the

trouble began to go off my mind, and my heart returned to its old course: but oh! how glad was I, that this trouble was gone from me, and that the fire was put out, that I might sin again without control! Wherefore, when I had satisfied nature with my food, I shook the sermon out of my mind, and to my old custom of sports and gaming I returned with great delight.

22. But the same day, as I was in the midst of a game at cat, and having struck it one blow from the hole, just as I was about to strike it the second time, a voice did suddenly dart from heaven into my soul, which said, Wilt thou leave thy sins and go to heaven, or have thy sins and go to hell? At this I was put to an exceeding maze; wherefore, leaving my cat upon the ground, I looked up to heaven, and was, as if I had, with the eyes of my understanding, seen the Lord Jesus looking down upon me, as being very hotly displeased with me, and as if he did severely threaten me with some grievous punishment for these and other my ungodly practices.

23. I had no sooner thus conceived in my mind, but suddenly this conclusion was fastened on my spirit, for the former hint did set my sins again before my face, that I had been a great and grievous sinner, and that it was now too late for me to look after heaven; for Christ would not forgive me, nor pardon my transgressions. Then I fell to musing upon this also; and while I was thinking on it, and fearing lest it should be so, I felt my heart sink in despair, concluding it was too late; and therefore I resolved in my mind I would go on in sin: for, thought I, if the case be thus, my state is surely miserable; miserable if I leave my sins, and but miserable if I follow them; I can but be damned, and if I must be so, I had as good be damned for many sins, as to be damned for few.

24. Thus I stood in the midst of my play, before all that then were present; but yet I told them nothing: but I say, I having made this conclusion, I returned desperately to my sport again; and I well remember, that presently this kind of despair did so possess my soul, that I was persuaded I could never attain to other comfort than what I should get in sin; for heaven was gone already, so that on that I must not think; wherefore I found within me a great

desire to take my fill of sin, still studying what sin was yet
to be committed, that I might taste the sweetness of it;
and I made as much haste as I could to fill my belly
with its delicates, lest I should die before I had my
desire; for that I feared greatly. In these things, I protest
before God, I lie not, neither do I feign this sort of speech;
these were really, strongly, and with all my heart, my
desires; the good Lord, whose mercy is unsearchable, forgive
me my transgressions.

25. And I am very confident, that this temptation of the
devil is more usual amongst poor creatures than many are
aware of, even to overrun their spirits with a scurvy and
seared frame of heart, and benumbing of conscience; which
frame, he stilly and slily supplieth with such despair, that
though not much guilt attendeth the soul, yet they continually have a secret conclusion within them, that there is
no hopes for them; for they have loved sins, "therefore after
them they will go" (Jer. ii. 25; xviii. 12).

26. Now therefore I went on in sin with great greediness
of mind, still grudging that I could not be so satisfied with
it as I would. This did continue with me about a month, or
more; but one day, as I was standing at a neighbour's shop-
window, and there cursing and swearing, and playing the
madman, after my wonted manner, there sat within the
woman of the house, and heard me, who, though she was a
very loose and ungodly wretch, yet protested that I swore
and cursed at that most fearful rate, that she was made to
tremble to hear me; and told me further, That I was the
ungodliest fellow for swearing that ever she heard in all her
life; and that I, by thus doing, was able to spoil all the youth
in a whole town, if they came but in my company.

27. At this reproof I was silenced, and put to secret shame,
and that too, as I thought, before the God of heaven; wherefore, while I stood there, and hanging down my head, I
wished with all my heart that I might be a little child again,
that my father might learn me to speak without this wicked
way of swearing; for, thought I, I am so accustomed to it,
that it is in vain for me to think of a reformation, for I
thought it could never be.

28. But how it came to pass, I know not; I did from this
time forward so leave my swearing, that it was a great

wonder to myself to observe it; and whereas before, I knew not how to speak unless I put an oath before, and another behind, to make my words have authority; now, I could, without it, speak better, and with more pleasantness, than ever I could before. All this while I knew not Jesus Christ, neither did I leave my sports and plays.

29. But quickly after this, I fell in company with one poor man that made profession of religion; who, as I then thought, did talk pleasantly of the Scriptures, and of the matters of religion; wherefore, falling into some love and liking to what he said, I betook me to my Bible, and began to take great pleasure in reading, but especially with the historical part thereof; for, as for Paul's epistles, and Scriptures of that nature, I could not away with them, being as yet but ignorant, either of the corruptions of my nature, or of the want and worth of Jesus Christ to save me.

30. Wherefore I fell to some outward reformation, both in my words and life, and did set the commandments before me for my way to heaven; which commandments I also did strive to keep, and, as I thought, did keep them pretty well sometimes, and then I should have comfort; yet now and then should break one, and so afflict my conscience; but then I should repent, and say I was sorry for it, and promise God to do better next time, and there get help again, for then I thought I pleased God as well as any man in England.

31. Thus I continued about a year; all which time our neighbours did take me to be a very godly man, a new and religious man, and did marvel much to see such a great and famous alteration in my life and manners; and, indeed, so it was, though yet I knew not Christ, nor grace, nor faith, nor hope; and, truly, as I have well seen since, had I then died, my state had been most fearful; well, this, I say, continued about a twelvemonth or more.

32. But, I say, my neighbours were amazed at this my great conversion, from prodigious profaneness, to something like a moral life; and, truly, so they well might; for this my conversion was as great, as for Tom of Bedlam to become a sober man. Now, therefore, they began to praise, to commend, and to speak well of me, both to my face, and behind my back. Now, I was, as they said, become godly; now, I was become a right honest man. But, oh! when I understood

that these were their words and opinions of me, it pleased me mighty well. For though, as yet, I was nothing but a poor painted hypocrite, yet I loved to be talked of as one that was truly godly. I was proud of my godliness, and, indeed, I did all I did, either to be seen of, or to be well spoken of, by man. And thus I continued for about a twelvemonth or more.

33. Now, you must know, that before this I had taken much delight in ringing, but my conscience beginning to be tender, I thought such practice was but vain, and therefore forced myself to leave it, yet my mind hankered; wherefore I should go to the steeple house, and look on it, though I durst not ring. But I thought this did not become religion neither, yet I forced myself, and would look on still; but quickly after, I began to think, How, if one of the bells should fall? Then I chose to stand under a main beam, that lay overthwart the steeple, from side to side, thinking there I might stand sure, but then I should think again, should the bell fall with a swing, it might first hit the wall, and then rebounding upon me, might kill me for all this beam. This made me stand in the steeple door; and now, thought I, I am safe enough; for, if a bell should then fall, I can slip out behind these thick walls, and so be preserved notwithstanding.

34. So, after this, I would yet go to see them ring, but would not go farther than the steeple door; but then it came into my head, How, if the steeple itself should fall? And this thought, it may fall for aught I know, when I stood and looked on, did continually so shake my mind, that I durst not stand at the steeple door any longer, but was forced to flee, for fear the steeple should fall upon my head.

35. Another thing was my dancing; I was a full year before I could quite leave that; but all this while, when I thought I kept this or that commandment, or did, by word or deed, anything that I thought was good, I had great peace in my conscience; and should think with myself, God cannot choose but be now pleased with me; yea, to relate it in mine own way, I thought no man in England could please God better than I.

36. But poor wretch as I was, I was all this while ignorant of Jesus Christ, and going about to establish my own

righteousness; and had perished therein, had not God, in mercy, showed me more of my state of nature.

37. But upon a day, the good providence of God did cast me to Bedford, to work on my calling; and in one of the streets of that town, I came where there were three or four poor women sitting at a door in the sun, and talking about the things of God; and being now willing to hear them discourse, I drew near to hear what they said, for I was now a brisk talker also myself in the matters of religion, but now I may say, I heard, but I understood not; for they were far above, out of my reach; for their talk was about a new birth, the work of God on their hearts, also how they were convinced of their miserable state by nature; they talked how God had visited their souls with his love in the Lord Jesus, and with what words and promises they had been refreshed, comforted, and supported against the temptations of the devil. Moreover, they reasoned of the suggestions and temptations of Satan in particular; and told to each other by which they had been afflicted, and how they were borne up under his assaults. They also discoursed of their own wretchedness of heart, of their unbelief; and did contemn, slight, and abhor their own righteousness, as filthy and insufficient to do them any good.

38. And methought they spake as if joy did make them speak; they spake with such pleasantness of Scripture language, and with such appearance of grace in all they said, that they were to me as if they had found a new world, as if they were people that dwelt alone, and were not to be reckoned among their neighbours (Num. xxiii. 9).

39. At this I felt my own heart began to shake, as mistrusting my condition to be naught; for I saw that in all my thoughts about religion and salvation, the new birth did never enter into my mind, neither knew I the comfort of the Word and promise, nor the deceitfulness and treachery of my own wicked heart. As for secret thoughts, I took no notice of them; neither did I understand what Satan's temptations were, nor how they were to be withstood and resisted, etc.

40. Thus, therefore, when I had heard and considered what they said, I left them, and went about my employment again, but their talk and discourse went with me; also my

heart would tarry with them, for I was greatly affected with their words, both because by them I was convinced that I wanted the true tokens of a truly godly man, and also because by them I was convinced of the happy and blessed condition of him that was such a one.

41. Therefore I should often make it my business to be going again and again into the company of these poor people, for I could not stay away; and the more I went amongst them, the more I did question my condition; and as I still do remember, presently I found two things within me, at which I did sometimes marvel, especially considering what a blind, ignorant, sordid, and ungodly wretch but just before I was; the one was a very great softness and tenderness of heart, which caused me to fall under the conviction of what by Scripture they asserted; and the other was a great bending in my mind to a continual meditating on it, and on all other good things which at any time I heard or read of.

42. By these things my mind was now so turned, that it lay like a horse leech at the vein, still crying out, Give, give (Prov. xxx. 15); yea, it was so fixed on eternity, and on the things about the kingdom of heaven, that is, so far as I knew, though as yet, God knows, I knew but little; that neither pleasures, nor profits, nor persuasions, nor threats, could loosen it, or make it let go his hold; and though I may speak it with shame, yet it is in very deed a certain truth, it would then have been as difficult for me to have taken my mind from heaven to earth, as I have found it often since to get it again from earth to heaven.

43. One thing I may not omit: There was a young man in our town, to whom my heart before was knit more than to any other, but he being a most wicked creature for cursing, and swearing, and whoring, I now shook him off, and forsook his company; but about a quarter of a year after I had left him, I met him in a certain lane, and asked him how he did; he, after his old swearing and mad way, answered, He was well. But, Harry, said I, why do you swear and curse thus? What will become of you, if you die in this condition? He answered me in a great chafe, What would the devil do for company, if it were not for such as I am?

44. About this time I met with some Ranters' books,

that were put forth by some of our countrymen, which books were also highly in esteem by several old professors; some of these I read, but was not able to make a judgment about them; wherefore as I read in them, and thought upon them, feeling myself unable to judge, I should betake myself to hearty prayer in this manner: O Lord, I am a fool, and not able to know the truth from error: Lord, leave me not to my own blindness, either to approve of, or condemn this doctrine; if it be of God, let me not despise it; if it be of the devil, let me not embrace it. Lord, I lay my soul, in this matter, only at thy foot; let me not be deceived, I humbly beseech thee. I had one religious intimate companion all this while, and that was the poor man that I spoke of before; but about this time he also turned a most devilish Ranter, and gave himself up to all manner of filthiness, especially uncleanness; he would also deny that there was a God, angel, or spirit; and would laugh at all exhortations to sobriety. When I laboured to rebuke his wickedness, he would laugh the more, and pretend that he had gone through all religions, and could never light on the right till now. He told me also, that in a little time I should see all professors turn to the ways of the Ranters. Wherefore, abominating those cursed principles, I left his company forthwith, and became to him as great a stranger, as I had been before a familiar.

45. Neither was this man only a temptation to me; but my calling lying in the country, I happened to light into several people's company, who, though strict in religion formerly, yet were also swept away by these Ranters. These would also talk with me of their ways, and condemn me as legal and dark; pretending that they only had attained to perfection that could do what they would, and not sin. Oh! these temptations were suitable to my flesh, I being but a young man, and my nature in its prime; but God, who had, as I hope, designed me for better things, kept me in the fear of his name, and did not suffer me to accept of such principles. And blessed be God, who put it into my heart to cry to him to be kept and directed, still distrusting mine own wisdom; for I have since seen even the effect of that prayer, in his preserving me not only from ranting errors, but from those also that have sprung up since. The Bible was precious to me in those days.

46. And now, methought, I began to look into the Bible with new eyes, and read as I never did before; and especially the epistles of the apostle Paul were sweet and pleasant to me; and, indeed, I was then never out of the Bible, either by reading or meditation; still crying out to God, that I might know the truth, and way to heaven and glory.

47. And as I went on and read, I lighted on that passage, "To one is given by the Spirit the word of wisdom; to another the word of knowledge by the same Spirit; *and* to another faith," etc. (1 Cor. xii. 8, 9). And though, as I have since seen, that by this Scripture the Holy Ghost intends, in special, things extraordinary, yet on me it did then fasten with conviction, that I did want things ordinary, even that understanding and wisdom that other Christians had. On this word I mused, and could not tell what to do, especially this word faith put me to it, for I could not help it, but sometimes must question, whether I had any faith or no; for I feared that it shut me out of all the blessings that other good people had given them of God; but I was loath to conclude I had no faith in my soul; for if I do so, thought I, then I shall count myself a very castaway indeed.

48. No, said I with myself, though I am convinced that I am an ignorant sot, and that I want those blessed gifts of knowledge and understanding that other good people have; yet, at a venture, I will conclude I am not altogether faithless, though I know not what faith is. For it was showed me, and that too, as I have since seen, by Satan, that those who conclude themselves in a faithless state, have neither rest nor quiet in their souls; and I was loath to fall quite into despair.

49. Wherefore, by this suggestion, I was for a while made afraid to see my want of faith; but God would not suffer me thus to undo and destroy my soul, but did continually, against this my blind and sad conclusion, create still within me such suppositions, insomuch that I might in this deceive myself, that I could not rest content, until I did now come to some certain knowledge, whether I had faith or no; this always running in my mind, But how if you want faith indeed? But how can you tell you have faith? And, besides, I saw for certain, if I had not, I was sure to perish for ever.

50. So that though I endeavoured at the first to look

over the business of faith, yet in a little time, I better considering the matter, was willing to put myself upon the trial, whether I had faith or no. But, alas, poor wretch, so ignorant and brutish was I, that I knew to this day no more how to do it, than I know how to begin and accomplish that rare and curious piece of art which I never yet saw nor considered.

51. Wherefore, while I was thus considering, and being put to my plunge about it, for you must know, that as yet I had in this matter broken my mind to no man, only did hear and consider, the tempter came in with his delusion, That there was no way for me to know I had faith, but by trying to work some miracle; urging those Scriptures that seem to look that way, for the enforcing and strengthening his temptation. Nay, one day as I was betwixt Elstow and Bedford, the temptation was hot upon me to try if I had faith, by doing of some miracle: which miracle at that time was this, I must say to the puddles that were in the horse pads, Be dry; and to the dry places, Be you the puddles. And truly, one time I was a-going to say so indeed; but just as I was about to speak, this thought came into my mind, But go under yonder hedge and pray first, that God would make you able. But when I had concluded to pray, this came hot upon me, That if I prayed, and came again and tried to do it, and yet did nothing notwithstanding, then be sure I had no faith, but was a castaway and lost. Nay, thought I, if it be so, I will never try yet, but will stay a little longer.

52. So I continued at a great loss; for I thought, if they only had faith, which could do so wonderful things, then I concluded, that, for the present, I neither had it, nor yet, for time to come, were ever like to have it. Thus I was tossed betwixt the devil and my own ignorance, and so perplexed, especially at some times, that I could not tell what to do.

53. About this time, the state and happiness of these poor people at Bedford was thus, in a dream or vision, represented to me. I saw, as if they were set on the sunny side of some high mountain, there refreshing themselves with the pleasant beams of the sun, while I was shivering and shrinking in the cold, afflicted with frost, snow, and dark clouds. Methought, also, betwixt me and them, I saw a wall that did compass

about this mountain; now, through this wall my soul did greatly desire to pass; concluding, that if I could, I would go even into the very midst of them, and there also comfort myself with the heat of their sun.

54. About this wall I thought myself, to go again and again, still prying as I went, to see if I could find some way or passage, by which I might enter therein; but none could I find for some time. At the last, I saw, as it were, a narrow gap, like a little doorway in the wall, through which I attempted to pass; but the passage being very strait and narrow, I made many efforts to get in, but all in vain, even until I was well-nigh quite beat out, by striving to get in; at last, with great striving, methought I at first did get in my head, and after that, by a sidling striving, my shoulders, and my whole body; then was I exceeding glad, and went and sat down in the midst of them, and so was comforted with the light and heat of their sun.

55. Now, this mountain and wall, etc., was thus made out to me—the mountain signified the church of the living God; the sun that shone thereon, the comfortable shining of his merciful face on them that were therein; the wall, I thought, was the Word, that did make separation between the Christians and the world; and the gap which was in this wall, I thought, was Jesus Christ, who is the way to God the Father (John xiv. 6, Matt. vii. 14). But forasmuch as the passage was wonderful narrow, even so narrow, that I could not, but with great difficulty, enter in thereat, it showed me that none could enter into life, but those that were in downright earnest, and unless also they left this wicked world behind them; for here was only room for body and soul, but not for body and soul, and sin.

56. This resemblance abode upon my spirit many days; all which time I saw myself in a forlorn and sad condition, but yet was provoked to a vehement hunger and desire to be one of that number that did sit in the sunshine. Now also I should pray wherever I was, whether at home or abroad, in house or field, and should also often, with lifting up of heart, sing that of the 51st Psalm, *O Lord, consider my distress*; for as yet I knew not where I was.

57. Neither as yet could I attain to any comfortable persuasion that I had faith in Christ; but instead of having

satisfaction, here I began to find my soul to be assaulted with fresh doubts about my future happiness; especially with such as these, Whether I was elected? But how, if the day of grace should now be past and gone?

58. By these two temptations I was very much afflicted and disquieted; sometimes by one, and sometimes by the other of them. And first, to speak of that about my questioning my election, I found at this time, that though I was in a flame to find the way to heaven and glory, and though nothing could beat me off from this, yet this question did so offend and discourage me, that I was, especially at some times, as if the very strength of my body also had been taken away by the force and power thereof. This scripture did also seem to me to trample upon all my desires, "*It is* not of him that willeth, nor of him that runneth, but of God that sheweth mercy" (Rom. ix. 16).

59. With this scripture I could not tell what to do; for I evidently saw, that unless the great God, of his infinite grace and bounty, had voluntarily chosen me to be a vessel of mercy, though I should desire, and long and labour until my heart did break, no good could come of it. Therefore, this would still stick with me, How can you tell that you are elected? And what if you should not? How then?

60. O Lord, thought I, what if I should not, indeed? It may be you are not, said the tempter; it may be so, indeed, thought I. Why, then, said Satan, you had as good leave off, and strive no further; for if, indeed, you should not be elected and chosen of God, there is no talk of your being saved; "For *it is* neither of him that willeth, nor of him that runneth, but of God that sheweth mercy."

61. By these things I was driven to my wits' end, not knowing what to say, or how to answer these temptations. Indeed, I little thought that Satan had thus assaulted me, but that rather it was my own prudence, thus to start the question; for, that the elect only attained eternal life, that I, without scruple, did heartily close withal; but that myself was one of them, there lay all the question.

62. Thus, therefore, for several days, I was greatly assaulted and perplexed, and was often, when I have been walking, ready to sink where I went, with faintness in my mind; but one day, after I had been so many weeks oppressed

and cast down therewith, as I was now quite giving up the ghost of all my hopes of ever attaining life, that sentence fell with weight upon my spirit, "Look at the generations of old and see; did ever any trust in the Lord, and was confounded?"

63. At which I was greatly lightened and encouraged in my soul; for thus, at that very instant, it was expounded to me, Begin at the beginning of Genesis, and read to the end of the Revelations, and see if you can find that there was ever any that trusted in the Lord, and was confounded. So, coming home, I presently went to my Bible to see if I could find that saying, not doubting but to find it presently; for it was so fresh, and with such strength and comfort on my spirit, that I was as if it talked with me.

64. Well, I looked, but I found it not; only it abode upon me; then I did ask first this good man, and then another, if they knew where it was, but they knew no such place. At this I wondered, that such a sentence should so suddenly, and with such comfort and strength, seize and abide upon my heart, and yet that none could find it, for I doubted not but it was in holy Scripture.

65. Thus I continued above a year, and could not find the place; but at last, casting my eye into the Apocrypha books, I found it in Ecclesiasticus ii. 10. This, at the first, did somewhat daunt me; but because, by this time, I had got more experience of the love and kindness of God, it troubled me the less; especially when I considered, that though it was not in those texts that we call holy and canonical, yet forasmuch as this sentence was the sum and substance of many of the promises, it was my duty to take the comfort of it; and I bless God for that word, for it was of God to me: that word doth still, at times, shine before my face.

66. After this, that other doubt did come with strength upon me, But how if the day of grace should be past and gone? How if you have overstood the time of mercy? Now, I remember that one day, as I was walking into the country, I was much in the thoughts of this, But how if the day of grace be past? And to aggravate my trouble, the tempter presented to my mind those good people of Bedford, and suggested thus unto me, That these being converted already,

they were all that God would save in those parts; and that I came too late, for these had got the blessing before I came.

67. Now was I in great distress, thinking in very deed that this might well be so; wherefore I went up and down bemoaning my sad condition, counting myself far worse than a thousand fools, for standing off thus long, and spending so many years in sin as I had done; still crying out, Oh, that I had turned sooner! Oh, that I had turned seven years ago! It made me also angry with myself, to think that I should have no more wit, but to trifle away my time till my soul and heaven were lost.

68. But when I had been long vexed with this fear, and was scarce able to take one step more, just about the same place where I received my other encouragement, these words broke in upon my mind, "Compel them to come in, that my house may be filled"; "and yet there is room" (Luke xiv. 22, 23). These words, but especially them, "And yet there is room," were sweet words to me; for, truly, I thought that by them I saw there was place enough in heaven for me; and, moreover, that when the Lord Jesus did speak these words, he then did think of me; and that he knowing that the time would come that I should be afflicted with fear that there was no place left for me in his bosom, did before speak this word, and leave it upon record, that I might find help thereby against this vile temptation. This, I then verily believed.

69. In the light and encouragement of this word, I went a pretty while; and the comfort was the more, when I thought that the Lord Jesus should think on me so long ago, and that he should speak them words on purpose for my sake; for I did then think, verily, that he did on purpose speak them, to encourage me withal.

70. But I was not without my temptations to go back again; temptations, I say, both from Satan, mine own heart, and carnal acquaintance; but I thank God these were outweighed by that sound sense of death and of the day of judgment, which abode, as it were, continually in my view; I should often also think on Nebuchadnezzar, of whom it is said, He had given him all the kingdoms of the earth (Dan. v. 19). Yet, thought I, if this great man had all his

portion in this world, one hour in hell fire would make him forget all. Which consideration was a great help to me.

71. I was almost made, about this time, to see something concerning the beasts that Moses counted clean and unclean. I thought those beasts were types of men; the clean, types of them that were the people of God; but the unclean, types of such as were the children of the wicked one. Now, I read that the clean beasts chewed the cud; that is, thought I, they show us we must feed upon the Word of God. They also parted the hoof; I thought that signified we must part, if we would be saved, with the ways of ungodly men. And also, in further reading about them I found that though we did chew the cud as the hare, yet if we walked with claws like a dog, or if we did part the hoof like the swine, yet if we did not chew the cud as the sheep, we were still, for all that, but unclean; for I thought the hare to be a type of those that talk of the Word, yet walk in the ways of sin; and that the swine was like him that parteth with his outward pollutions, but still wanteth the Word of faith, without which there could be no way of salvation, let a man be never so devout (Deut. xiv.). After this I found, by reading the Word, that those that must be glorified with Christ in another world must be called by him here; called to the partaking of a share in his Word and righteousness, and to the comforts and first fruits of his Spirit, and to a peculiar interest in all those heavenly things which do indeed fore fit the soul for that rest and house of glory which is in heaven above.

72. Here, again, I was at a very great stand, not knowing what to do, fearing I was not called; for, thought I, if I be not called, what then can do me good? None but those who are effectually called, inherit the kingdom of heaven. But oh! how I now loved those words that spake of a Christian's calling! as when the Lord said to one, "Follow me," and to another, "Come after me." And oh! thought I, that he would say so to me too, how gladly would I run after him!

73. I cannot now express with what longings and breakings in my soul I cried to Christ to call me. Thus I continued for a time, all on a flame to be converted to Jesus Christ; and did also see at that day, such glory in a converted state, that I could not be contented without a share therein.

Gold! could it have been gotten for gold, what could I have given for it! had I had a whole world it had all gone ten thousand times over for this, that my soul might have been in a converted state.

74. How lovely now was everyone in my eyes that I thought to be converted men and women! they shone, they walked like a people that carried the broad seal of heaven about them. Oh! I saw the lot was fallen to them in pleasant places, and they had a goodly heritage (Ps. xvi. 6). But that which made me sick was that of Christ, in Mark, He went up into a mountain and called to him whom he would, and they came unto him (Mark iii. 13).

75. This scripture made me faint and fear, yet it kindled fire in my soul. That which made me fear was this, lest Christ should have no liking to me, for he called "whom he would." But oh! the glory that I saw in that condition did still so engage my heart that I could seldom read of any that Christ did call but I presently wished, Would I had been in their clothes; would I had been born Peter; would I had been born John; or would I had been by and had heard him when he called them, how would I have cried, O Lord, call me also. But oh! I feared he would not call me.

76. And truly the Lord let me go thus many months together and showed me nothing; either that I was already, or should be called hereafter. But at last, after much time spent, and many groans to God, that I might be made partaker of the holy and heavenly calling, that Word came in upon me: "I will cleanse their blood *that* I have not cleansed: for the Lord dwelleth in Zion" (Joel iii. 21). These words I thought were sent to encourage me to wait still upon God, and signified unto me, that if I were not already, yet time might come I might be in truth converted unto Christ.

77. About this time I began to break my mind to those poor people in Bedford, and to tell them my condition, which, when they had heard, they told Mr. Gifford of me, who himself also took occasion to talk with me, and was willing to be well persuaded of me, though I think but from little grounds: but he invited me to his house, where I should hear him confer with others, about the dealings of God with the soul; from all which I still received more conviction, and from that time began to see something of the vanity and

inward wretchedness of my wicked heart, for as yet I knew no great matter therein; but now it began to be discovered unto me, and also to work at that rate for wickedness as it never did before. Now I evidently found that lusts and corruptions would strongly put forth themselves within me, in wicked thoughts and desires, which I did not regard before; my desires also for heaven and life began to fail. I found also, that whereas before my soul was full of longing after God, now my heart began to hanker after every foolish vanity; yea, my heart would not be moved to mind that that was good; it began to be careless, both of my soul and heaven; it would now continually hang back, both to, and in every duty; and was as a clog on the leg of a bird to hinder her from flying.

78. Nay, thought I, now I grow worse and worse; now am I farther from conversion than ever I was before. Wherefore I began to sink greatly in my soul, and began to entertain such discouragement in my heart as laid me low as hell. If now I should have burned at a stake, I could not believe that Christ had love for me; alas, I could neither hear him, nor see him, nor feel him, nor savour any of his things; I was driven as with a tempest, my heart would be unclean, the Canaanites would dwell in the land.

79. Sometimes I would tell my condition to the people of God, which, when they heard, they would pity me, and would tell me of the promises; but they had as good have told me that I must reach the sun with my finger as have bidden me receive or rely upon the promise; and as soon as I should have done it, all my sense and feeling was against me; and I saw I had a heart that would sin, and that lay under a law that would condemn.

80. These things have often made me think of that child which the father brought to Christ, who, while he was yet a-coming to him, was thrown down by the devil, and also so rent and torn by him that he lay and wallowed, foaming (Luke ix. 42, Mark ix. 20).

81. Further, in these days I should find my heart to shut itself up against the Lord, and against his holy Word. I have found my unbelief to set, as it were, the shoulder to the door to keep him out, and that too even then, when I have with many a bitter sigh cried, Good Lord, break it open; Lord,

break these gates of brass, and cut these bars of iron asunder (Ps. cvii. 16). Yet that word would sometimes create in my heart a peaceable pause, "I girded thee, though thou hast not known me" (Is. xlv. 5).

82. But all this while as to the act of sinning, I never was more tender than now; I durst not take a pin or a stick, though but so big as a straw, for my conscience now was sore, and would smart at every touch; I could not now tell how to speak my words, for fear I should misplace them. Oh, how gingerly did I then go in all I did or said! I found myself as on a miry bog that shook if I did but stir; and was there left both of God and Christ, and the Spirit, and all good things.

83. But, I observe, though I was such a great sinner before conversion, yet God never much charged the guilt of the sins of my ignorance upon me; only he showed me I was lost if I had not Christ, because I had been a sinner; I saw that I wanted a perfect righteousness to present me without fault before God, and this righteousness was nowhere to be found, but in the person of Jesus Christ.

84. But my original and inward pollution, that, that was my plague and my affliction; that, I say, at a dreadful rate, always putting forth itself within me; that I had the guilt of, to amazement; by reason of that, I was more loathsome in my own eyes than was a toad; and I thought I was so in God's eyes too; sin and corruption, I said, would as naturally bubble out of my heart, as water would bubble out of a fountain. I thought now that everyone had a better heart than I had; I could have changed heart with anybody; I thought none but the devil himself could equalise me for inward wickedness and pollution of mind. I fell, therefore, at the sight of my own vileness, deeply into despair; for I concluded that this condition that I was in could not stand with a state of grace. Sure, thought I, I am forsaken of God; sure I am given up to the devil, and to a reprobate mind; and thus I continued a long while, even for some years together.

85. While I was thus afflicted with the fears of my own damnation, there were two things would make me wonder; the one was, when I saw old people hunting after the things of this life, as if they should live here always; the other was, when I found professors much distressed and cast down,

when they met with outward losses; as of husband, wife, child, etc. Lord, thought I, what ado is here about such little things as these! What seeking after carnal things by some, and what grief in others for the loss of them! If they so much labour after, and spend so many tears for the things of this present life, how am I to be bemoaned, pitied, and prayed for! My soul is dying, my soul is damning. Were my soul but in a good condition, and were I but sure of it, oh! how rich should I esteem myself, though blessed but with bread and water; I should count those but small afflictions, and should bear them as little burdens. "A wounded spirit who can bear?"

86. And though I was thus troubled, and tossed, and afflicted, with the sight and sense and terror of my own wickedness, yet I was afraid to let this sight and sense go quite off my mind; for I found, that unless guilt of conscience was taken off the right way, that is, by the blood of Christ, a man grew rather worse for the loss of his trouble of mind, than better. Wherefore, if my guilt lay hard upon me, then I should cry that the blood of Christ might take it off; and if it was going off without it (for the sense of sin would be sometimes as if it would die, and go quite away), then I would also strive to fetch it upon my heart again, by bringing the punishment for sin in hell fire upon my spirits; and should cry, Lord, let it not go off my heart, but the right way, but by the blood of Christ, and by the application of thy mercy, through him, to my soul; for that scripture lay much upon me, "without shedding of blood is no remission" (Heb. ix. 22). And that which made me the more afraid of this was, because I had seen some who, though when they were under wounds of conscience, then they would cry and pray; but they seeking rather present ease from their trouble, than pardon for their sin, cared not how they lost their guilt, so they got it out of their mind; and, therefore, having got it off the wrong way, it was not sanctified unto them; but they grew harder and blinder, and more wicked after their trouble. This made me afraid, and made me cry to God the more, that it might not be so with me.

87. And now was I sorry that God had made me a man, for I feared I was a reprobate; I counted man as unconverted, the most doleful of all the creatures. Thus being

afflicted and tossed about my sad condition, I counted myself alone, and above the most of men unblessed.

88. Yea, I thought it impossible that ever I should attain to so much goodness of heart, as to thank God that he had made me a man. Man indeed is the most noble by creation, of all creatures in the visible world; but by sin he has made himself the most ignoble. The beasts, birds, fishes, etc., I blessed their condition, for they had not a sinful nature, they were not obnoxious to the wrath of God; they were not to go to hell fire after death; I could therefore have rejoiced, had my condition been as any of theirs.

89. In this condition I went a great while; but when comforting time was come, I heard one preach a sermon upon those words in the Song (iv. 1), "Behold, thou *art* fair, my love; behold, thou *art* fair." But at that time he made these two words, "My love," his chief and subject matter; from which, after he had a little opened the text, he observed these several conclusions: 1. That the church, and so every saved soul, is Christ's love, when loveless. 2. Christ's love without a cause. 3. Christ's love when hated of the world. 4. Christ's love when under temptation, and under desertion. 5. Christ's love from first to last.

90. But I got nothing by what he said at present, only when he came to the application of the fourth particular, this was the word he said: If it be so, that the saved soul is Christ's love when under temptation and desertion; then, poor tempted soul, when thou art assaulted and afflicted with temptation, and the hidings of God's face, yet think on these two words, "My love," still.

91. So as I was a-going home, these words came again into my thoughts; and I well remember, as they came in, I said thus in my heart, What shall I get by thinking on these two words? This thought had no sooner passed through my heart, but the words began thus to kindle in my spirit, "Thou art my love, thou art my love," twenty times together; and still as they ran thus in my mind, they waxed stronger and warmer, and began to make me look up; but being as yet between hope and fear, I still replied in my heart, But is it true, but is it true? At which, that sentence fell in upon me, He "wist not that it was true which was done by the angel" (Acts xii. 9).

92. Then I began to give place to the word, which, with power, did over and over make this joyful sound within my soul, Thou art my love, thou art my love; and nothing shall separate thee from my love; and with that, Rom. viii. 39 came into my mind. Now was my heart filled full of comfort and hope, and now I could believe that my sins should be forgiven me; yea, I was now so taken with the love and mercy of God, that I remember I could not tell how to contain till I got home; I thought I could have spoken of his love, and of his mercy to me, even to the very crows that sat upon the ploughed lands before me, had they been capable to have understood me; wherefore I said in my soul, with much gladness, Well, I would I had a pen and ink here, I would write this down before I go any farther, for surely I will not forget this forty years hence; but alas! within less than forty days, I began to question all again; which made me begin to question all still.

93. Yet still at times, I was helped to believe that it was a true manifestation of grace unto my soul, though I had lost much of the life and savour of it. Now about a week or fortnight after this, I was much followed by this scripture, "Simon, Simon, behold, Satan hath desired *to have* you" (Luke xxii. 31). And sometimes it would sound so loud within me, yea, and as it were call so strongly after me, that once above all the rest, I turned my head over my shoulder, thinking verily that some man had, behind me, called to me; being at a great distance, methought he called so loud; it came, as I have thought since, to have stirred me up to prayer, and to watchfulness; it came to acquaint me that a cloud and a storm was coming down upon me, but I understood it not.

94. Also, as I remember, that time that it called to me so loud, was the last time that it sounded in mine ear; but methinks I hear still with what a loud voice these words, Simon, Simon, sounded in mine ears. I thought verily, as I have told you, that somebody had called after me, that was half a mile behind me; and although that was not my name, yet it made me suddenly look behind me, believing that he that called so loud meant me.

95. But so foolish was I, and ignorant, that I knew not the reason of this sound; which, as I did both see and feel

soon after, was sent from heaven as an alarm, to awaken
me to provide for what was coming; only it would make me
muse and wonder in my mind, to think what should be the
reason that this scripture, and that at this rate, so often
and so loud, should still be sounding and rattling in mine
ears; but, as I said before, I soon after perceived the end
of God therein.

96. For about the space of a month after, a very great
storm came down upon me, which handled me twenty times
worse than all I had met with before; it came stealing upon
me, now by one piece, then by another; first, all my comfort
was taken from me, then darkness seized upon me, after
which whole floods of blasphemies, both against God,
Christ, and the Scriptures, were poured upon my spirit, to
my great confusion and astonishment. These blasphemous
thoughts were such as also stirred up questions in me,
against the very being of God, and of his only beloved
Son; as, whether there were, in truth, a God, or Christ, or
no? And whether the holy Scriptures were not rather a fable,
and cunning story, than the holy and pure Word of God?

97. The tempter would also much assault me with this,
How can you tell but that the Turks had as good Scriptures
to prove their Mahomet the Saviour, as we have to prove
our Jesus is? And, could I think, that so many ten thousands,
in so many countries and kingdoms, should be without the
knowledge of the right way to heaven; if there were indeed
a heaven, and that we only, who live in a corner of the earth,
should alone be blessed therewith? Everyone doth think his
own religion rightest, both Jews and Moors, and Pagans!
and how if all our faith, and Christ, and Scriptures, should
be but a think-so too?

98. Sometimes I have endeavoured to argue against these
suggestions, and to set some of the sentences of blessed Paul
against them; but, alas! I quickly felt, when I thus did,
such arguings as these would return again upon me, Though
we made so great a matter of Paul, and of his words, yet
how could I tell, but that in very deed, he being a subtle
and cunning man, might give himself up to deceive with
strong delusions; and also take both that pains and travail,
to undo and destroy his fellows?

99. These suggestions, with many other which at this

time I may not, nor dare not utter, neither by word nor pen, did make such a seizure upon my spirit, and did so over-weigh my heart, both with their number, continuance, and fiery force, that I felt as if there were nothing else but these from morning to night within me; and as though, indeed, there could be room for nothing else; and also concluded that God had, in very wrath to my soul, given me up unto them, to be carried away with them, as with a mighty whirlwind.

100. Only by the distaste that they gave unto my spirit, I felt there was something in me that refused to embrace them. But this consideration I then only had, when God gave me leave to swallow my spittle, otherwise the noise, and strength, and force of these temptations, would drown and overflow; and as it were, bury all such thoughts or the remembrance of any such thing. While I was in this temptation, I should often find my mind suddenly put upon it, to curse and swear, or to speak some grievous thing against God, or Christ his Son, and of the Scriptures.

101. Now I thought, surely I am possessed of the devil; at other times again, I thought I should be bereft of my wits; for instead of lauding and magnifying God the Lord with others, if I have but heard him spoken of, presently some most horrible blasphemous thought or other would bolt out of my heart against him; so that whether I did think that God was, or again did think there were no such thing, no love, nor peace, nor gracious disposition could I feel within me.

102. These things did sink me into very deep despair; for I concluded, that such things could not possibly be found amongst them that loved God. I often, when these temptations have been with force upon me, did compare myself in the case of such a child, whom some gipsy hath by force took up under her apron, and is carrying from friend and country; kick sometimes I did, and also scream and cry; but yet I was as bound in the wings of the temptation, and the wind would carry me away. I thought also of Saul, and of the evil spirit that did possess him; and did greatly fear that my condition was the same with that of his (1 Sam. xvi. 14).

103. In these days, when I have heard others talk of what

was the sin against the Holy Ghost, then would the tempter so provoke me to desire to sin that sin, that I was as if I could not, must not, neither should be quiet until I had committed that; now, no sin would serve but that; if it were to be committed by speaking of such a word, then I have been as if my mouth would have spoken that word, whether I would or no; and in so strong a measure was this temptation upon me, that often I have been ready to clap my hand under my chin, to hold my mouth from opening; and to that end also I have had thoughts at other times, to leap with my head downward, into some muck-hill hole or other, to keep my mouth from speaking.

104. Now I blessed the condition of the dog and toad, and counted the estate of everything that God had made far better than this dreadful state of mine, and such as my companions was; yea, gladly would I have been in the condition of dog or horse, for I knew they had no soul to perish under the everlasting weights of hell for sin, as mine was like to do. Nay, and though I saw this, felt this, and was broken to pieces with it, yet that which added to my sorrow was, that I could not find that with all my soul I did desire deliverance. That scripture did also tear and rend my soul, in the midst of these distractions, "The wicked *are* like the troubled sea, when it cannot rest, whose waters cast up mire and dirt. *There is* no peace, saith my God, to the wicked" (Is. lvii. 20, 21).

105. And now my heart was, at times, exceeding hard; if I would have given a thousand pounds for a tear, I could not shed one; no, nor sometimes scarce desire to shed one. I was much dejected to think that this should be my lot. I saw some could mourn and lament their sin; and others, again, could rejoice, and bless God for Christ; and others, again, could quietly talk of, and with gladness remember, the Word of God; while I only was in the storm or tempest. This much sunk me; I thought my condition was alone. I should, therefore, much bewail my hard hap; but get out of, or get rid of, these things, I could not.

106. While this temptation lasted, which was about a year, I could attend upon none of the ordinances of God but with sore and great affliction. Yea, then was I most distressed with blasphemies; if I have been hearing the

Word, then uncleanness, blasphemies, and despair would hold me as captive there; if I have been reading, then, sometimes, I had sudden thoughts to question all I read; sometimes, again, my mind would be so strangely snatched away, and possessed with other things, that I have neither known, nor regarded, nor remembered so much as the sentence that but now I have read.

107. In prayer, also, I have been greatly troubled at this time; sometimes I have thought I should see the devil, nay, thought I have felt him, behind me, pull my clothes; he would be, also, continually at me in the time of prayer to have done; break off, make haste, you have prayed enough, and stay no longer, still drawing my mind away. Sometimes, also, he would cast in such wicked thoughts as these: that I must pray to him, or for him. I have thought sometimes of that—Fall down, or, "if thou wilt fall down and worship me" (Matt. iv. 9).

108. Also, when, because I have had wandering thoughts in the time of this duty, I have laboured to compose my mind and fix it upon God, then, with great force, hath the tempter laboured to distract me, and confound me, and to turn away my mind, by presenting to my heart and fancy the form of a bush, a bull, a besom, or the like, as if I should pray to those; to these he would, also, at some times especially, so hold my mind that I was as if I could think of nothing else, or pray to nothing else but to these, or such as they.

109. Yet, at times I should have some strong and heart-affecting apprehensions of God, and the reality of the truth of his gospel; but, oh! how would my heart, at such times, put forth itself with inexpressible groanings. My whole soul was then in every word; I should cry with pangs after God that he would be merciful unto me; but then I should be daunted again with such conceits as these; I should think that God did mock at these, my prayers, saying, and that in the audience of the holy angels, This poor simple wretch doth hanker after me as if I had nothing to do with my mercy but to bestow it on such as he. Alas, poor fool! how art thou deceived! It is not for such as thee to have favour with the Highest.

110. Then hath the tempter come upon me, also, with such discouragements as these: You are very hot for mercy,

but I will cool you; this frame shall not last always; many
have been as hot as you for a spirit, but I have quenched
their zeal. And with this, such and such who were fallen
off would be set before mine eyes. Then I should be afraid
that I should do so too; but, thought I, I am glad this comes
into my mind. Well, I will watch, and take what heed I can.
Though you do, said Satan, I shall be too hard for you; I
will cool you insensibly, by degrees, by little and little.
What care I, saith he, though I be seven years in chilling
your heart if I can do it at last? Continual rocking will lull
a crying child asleep. I will ply it close, but I will have my
end accomplished. Though you be burning hot at present,
yet, if I can pull you from this fire, I shall have you cold
before it be long.

111. These things brought me into great straits; for as I
at present could not find myself fit for present death, so I
thought to live long would make me yet more unfit; for time
would make me forget all, and wear even the remembrance
of the evil of sin, the worth of heaven, and the need I had of
the blood of Christ to wash me, both out of mind and thought;
but I thank Christ Jesus these things did not at present
make me slack my crying, but rather did put me more upon
it, like her who met with the adulterer (Deut. xxii. 27); in
which days that was a good word to me after I had suffered
these things a while: "I am persuaded that neither . . .
height, nor depth, nor life," etc., "shall . . . separate us
from the love of God, which is in Christ Jesus" (Rom. viii. 38).
And now I hoped long life should not destroy me, nor make
me miss of heaven.

112. Yet I had some supports in this temptation, though
they were then all questioned by me; that in the third of
Jeremiah, at the first, was something to me, and so was the
consideration of the fifth verse of that chapter; that though
we have spoken and done as evil things as we could, yet
we should cry unto God, "My Father, thou art the guide of
my youth"; and should return unto him.

113. I had, also, once a sweet glance from that in 2 Cor.
v. 21: "For he hath made him to be sin for us, who knew no
sin; that we might be made the righteousness of God in
him." I remember, also, that one day as I was sitting in a
neighbour's house, and there very sad at the consideration

of my many blasphemies, and as I was saying in my mind, What ground have I to think that I, who have been so vile and abominable, should ever inherit eternal life? that word came suddenly upon me, "What shall we then say to these things? If God *be* for us, who *can be* against us?" (Rom. viii. 31). That, also, was an help unto me, "Because I live, ye shall live also" (John xiv. 19). But these were but hints, touches, and short visits, though very sweet when present; only they lasted not; but, like to Peter's sheet, of a sudden were caught up from me to heaven again (Acts x. 16).

114. But afterwards the Lord did more fully and graciously discover himself unto me; and, indeed, did quite, not only deliver me from the guilt that, by these things, was laid upon my conscience, but also from the very filth thereof; for the temptation was removed, and I was put into my right mind again, as other Christians were.

115. I remember that one day, as I was travelling into the country and musing on the wickedness and blasphemy of my heart, and considering of the enmity that was in me to God, that scripture came in my mind, He hath "made peace through the blood of his cross" (Col. i. 20). By which I was made to see, both again, and again, and again, that day, that God and my soul were friends by this blood; yea, I saw that the justice of God and my sinful soul could embrace and kiss each other through this blood. This was a good day to me; I hope I shall not forget it.

116. At another time, as I sat by the fire in my house, and musing on my wretchedness, the Lord made that also a precious word unto me, "Forasmuch, then, as the children are partakers of flesh and blood, he also himself likewise took part of the same; that through death he might destroy him that had the power of death, that is, the devil, and deliver them who, through fear of death, were all their lifetime subject to bondage" (Heb. ii. 14, 15). I thought that the glory of these words was then so weighty on me that I was, both once and twice, ready to swoon as I sat; yet not with grief and trouble, but with solid joy and peace.

117. At this time, also, I sat under the ministry of holy Mr. Gifford, whose doctrine, by God's grace, was much for my stability. This man made it much his business to deliver the people of God from all those faults and unsound rests

that, by nature, we are prone to take and make to our souls. He pressed us to take special heed that we took not up any truth upon trust—as from this, or that, or any other man or men—but to cry mightily to God that he would convince us of the reality thereof, and set us down therein, by his own Spirit, in the holy Word; for, said he, if you do otherwise when temptations come, if strongly, you, not having received them with evidence from heaven, will find you want that help and strength now to resist as once you thought you had.

118. This was as seasonable to my soul as the former and latter rain in their season; for I had found, and that by sad experience, the truth of these his words; for I had felt what no man can say, especially when tempted by the devil, that Jesus Christ is Lord but by the Holy Ghost. Wherefore I found my soul, through grace, very apt to drink in this doctrine, and to incline to pray to God that, in nothing that pertained to God's glory and my own eternal happiness, he would suffer me to be without the confirmation thereof from heaven; for now I saw clearly there was an exceeding difference betwixt the notions of flesh and blood, and the revelations of God in heaven; also, a great difference between that faith that is feigned, and according to man's wisdom, and of that which comes by a man's being born thereto of God (Matt. xvi. 15–17; 1 John v. 1).

119. But, oh! now, how was my soul led from truth to truth by God! even from the birth and cradle of the Son of God to his ascension and second coming from heaven to judge the world.

120. Truly, I then found, upon this account, the great God was very good unto me; for, to my remembrance, there was not anything that I then cried unto God to make known and reveal unto me but he was pleased to do it for me; I mean not one part of the gospel of the Lord Jesus, but I was orderly led into it. Methought I saw with great evidence, from the relation of the four evangelists, the wonderful work of God, in giving Jesus Christ to save us, from his conception and birth even to his second coming to judgment. Methought I was as if I had seen him born, as if I had seen him grow up, as if I had seen him walk through this world, from the cradle to his cross: to which, also, when he came,

I saw how gently he gave himself to be hanged and nailed on it for my sins and wicked doings. Also, as I was musing on this, his progress, that dropped on my spirit, He was ordained for the slaughter (1 Pet. i. 19, 20).

121. When I have considered also the truth of his resurrection, and have remembered that word, "Touch me not, Mary," etc., I have seen as if he leaped at the grave's mouth for joy that he was risen again, and had got the conquest over our dreadful foes (John xx. 17). I have also, in the spirit, seen him a man on the right hand of God the Father for me, and have seen the manner of his coming from heaven to judge the world with glory, and have been confirmed in these things by these scriptures following, Acts i. 9, 10; vii. 56; x. 42; Heb. vii. 24; viii. 3; Rev. i. 18; 1 Thess. iv. 17, 18.

122. Once I was much troubled to know whether the Lord Jesus was both man as well as God, and God as well as man; and truly, in those days, let men say what they would, unless I had it with evidence from heaven, all was as nothing to me, I counted not myself set down in any truth of God. Well, I was much troubled about this point, and could not tell how to be resolved; at last, that in the fifth of the Revelations came into my mind, "And I beheld, and lo, in the midst of the throne and of the four beasts, and in the midst of the elders, stood a Lamb." In the midst of the throne, thought I, there is his Godhead; in the midst of the elders, there is his manhood; but oh! methought this did glister! it was a goodly touch, and gave me sweet satisfaction. That other scripture also did help me much in this, "To us a child is born, unto us a son is given; and the government shall be upon his shoulder: and his name shall be called Wonderful, Counsellor, The mighty God, The everlasting Father, The Prince of Peace," etc. (Is. ix. 6).

123. Also, besides these teachings of God in his Word, the Lord made use of two things to confirm me in these things; the one was the errors of the Quakers, and the other was the guilt of sin; for as the Quakers did oppose his truth, so God did the more confirm me in it, by leading me into the scriptures that did wonderfully maintain it.

124. The errors that this people then maintained were: 1. That the holy Scriptures were not the Word of God. 2. That every man in the world had the spirit of Christ,

grace, faith, etc. 3. That Christ Jesus, as crucified, and dying 1600 years ago, did not satisfy divine justice for the sins of the people. 4. That Christ's flesh and blood was within the saints. 5. That the bodies of the good and bad that are buried in the churchyard shall not arise again. 6. That the resurrection is past with good men already. 7. That that man Jesus, that was crucified between two thieves on Mount Calvary, in the land of Canaan, by Jerusalem, was not ascended up above the starry heavens. 8. That he should not, even the same Jesus that died by the hands of the Jews, come again at the last day, and as man judge all nations, etc.

125. Many more vile and abominable things were in those days fomented by them, by which I was driven to a more narrow search of the Scriptures, and was, through their light and testimony, not only enlightened, but greatly confirmed and comforted in the truth; and, as I said, the guilt of sin did help me much, for still as that would come upon me, the blood of Christ did take it off again, and again, and again, and that too, sweetly, according to the Scriptures. O friends! cry to God to reveal Jesus Christ unto you; there is none teacheth like him.

126. It would be too long for me here to stay, to tell you in particular how God did set me down in all the things of Christ, and how he did, that he might so do, lead me into his words; yea, and also how he did open them unto me, make them shine before me, and cause them to dwell with me, talk with me, and comfort me over and over, both of his own being, and the being of his Son, and Spirit, and Word, and gospel.

127. Only this, as I said before I will say unto you again, that in general he was pleased to take this course with me; first, to suffer me to be afflicted with temptation concerning them, and then reveal them to me: as sometimes I should lie under great guilt for sin, even crushed to the ground therewith, and then the Lord would show me the death of Christ; yea, and so sprinkle my conscience with his blood, that I should find, and that before I was aware, that in that conscience where but just now did reign and rage the law, even there would rest and abide the peace and love of God through Christ.

128. Now had I an evidence, as I thought, of my salvation

from heaven, with many golden seals thereon, all hanging in my sight; now could I remember this manifestation and the other discovery of grace, with comfort; and should often long and desire that the last day were come, that I might for ever be inflamed with the sight, and joy, and communion with him whose head was crowned with thorns, whose face was spit on, and body broken, and soul made an offering for my sins: for whereas, before, I lay continually trembling at the mouth of hell, now methought I was got so far therefrom that I could not, when I looked back, scarce discern it; and, oh! thought I, that I were fourscore years old now, that I might die quickly, that my soul might be gone to rest.

129. But before I had got thus far out of these my temptations, I did greatly long to see some ancient godly man's experience, who had writ some hundreds of years before I was born; for those who had writ in our days, I thought, but I desire them now to pardon me, that they had writ only that which others felt, or else had, through the strength of their wits and parts, studied to answer such objections as they perceived others were perplexed with, without going down themselves into the deep. Well, after many such longings in my mind, the God in whose hands are all our days and ways, did cast into my hand, one day, a book of Martin Luther; it was his comment on the Galatians—it also was so old that it was ready to fall piece from piece if I did but turn it over. Now I was pleased much that such an old book had fallen into my hands; the which, when I had but a little way perused, I found my condition, in his experience, so largely and profoundly handled, as if his book had been written out of my heart. This made me marvel; for thus thought I, This man could not know anything of the state of Christians now, but must needs write and speak the experience of former days.

130. Besides, he doth most gravely, also, in that book, debate of the rise of these temptations, namely, blasphemy, desperation, and the like; showing that the law of Moses as well as the devil, death, and hell hath a very great hand therein, the which. at first, was very strange to me; but considering and watching, I found it so indeed. But of particulars here I intend nothing; only this, methinks, I

must let fall before all men, I do prefer this book of Martin Luther upon the Galatians, excepting the Holy Bible, before all the books that ever I have seen, as most fit for a wounded conscience.

131. And now I found, as I thought, that I loved Christ dearly; oh! methought my soul cleaved unto him, my affections cleaved unto him. I felt love to him as hot as fire; and now, as Job said, I thought I should die in my nest; but I did quickly find that my great love was but little, and that I, who had, as I thought, such burning love to Jesus Christ, could let him go again for a very trifle; God can tell how to abase us, and can hide pride from man. Quickly after this my love was tried to purpose.

132. For after the Lord had, in this manner, thus graciously delivered me from this great and sore temptation, and had set me down so sweetly in the faith of his holy gospel, and had given me such strong consolation and blessed evidence from heaven touching my interest in his love through Christ; the tempter came upon me again, and that with a more grievous and dreadful temptation than before.

133. And that was, To sell and part with this most blessed Christ, to exchange him for the things of this life, for anything. The temptation lay upon me for the space of a year, and did follow me so continually that I was not rid of it one day in a month, no, not sometimes one hour in many days together, unless when I was asleep.

134. And though, in my judgment, I was persuaded that those who were once effectually in Christ, as I hoped, through his grace, I had seen myself, could never lose him for ever —for "the land shall not be sold for ever, for the land *is* mine," saith God (Lev. xxv. 23)—yet it was a continual vexation to me to think that I should have so much as one such thought within me against a Christ, a Jesus, that had done for me as he had done; and yet then I had almost none others, but such blasphemous ones.

135. But it was neither my dislike of the thought, nor yet any desire and endeavour to resist it that in the least did shake or abate the continuation, or force and strength thereof; for it did always, in almost whatever I thought, intermix itself therewith in such sort that I could neither eat my food, stoop for a pin, chop a stick, or cast mine

eye to look on this or that, but still the temptation would
come, Sell Christ for this, or sell Christ for that; sell him,
sell him.

136. Sometimes it would run in my thoughts, not so little
as a hundred times together, Sell him, sell him, sell him;
against which I may say, for whole hours together, I have
been forced to stand as continually leaning and forcing my
spirit against it, lest haply, before I were aware, some
wicked thought might arise in my heart that might consent
thereto; and sometimes also the tempter would make me
believe I had consented to it, then should I be as tortured
upon a rack for whole days together.

137. This temptation did put me to such scares, lest I
should at sometimes, I say, consent thereto, and be overcome therewith, that by the very force of my mind, in
labouring to gainsay and resist this wickedness, my very
body also would be put into action or motion by way of
pushing or thrusting with my hands or elbows, still answering as fast as the destroyer said, Sell him; I will not, I will
not, I will not, I will not; no, not for thousands, thousands,
thousands of worlds. Thus reckoning lest I should in the
midst of these assaults, set too low a value of him, even
until I scarce well knew where I was, or how to be com-
posed again.

138. At these seasons he would not let me eat my food
at quiet; but, forsooth, when I was set at the table at my
meat, I must go hence to pray; I must leave my food now,
and just now, so counterfeit holy also would this devil be.
When I was thus tempted, I should say in myself, Now I am
at my meat, let me make an end. No, said he, you must do
it now, or you will displease God, and despise Christ. Wherefore I was much afflicted with these things; and because of
the sinfulness of my nature, imagining that these things
were impulses from God, I should deny to do it, as if I
denied God; and then should I be as guilty, because I did
not obey a temptation of the devil, as if I had broken the
law of God indeed.

139. But to be brief, one morning, as I did lie in my
bed, I was, as at other times, most fiercely assaulted with
this temptation, to sell and part with Christ; the wicked
suggestion still running in my mind, Sell him, sell him, sell

him, sell him, sell him, as fast as a man could speak; against which also, in my mind, as at other times, I answered, No, no, not for thousands, thousands, thousands, at least twenty times together. But at last, after much striving, even until I was almost out of breath, I felt this thought pass through my heart, Let him go, if he will! and I thought also, that I felt my heart freely consent thereto. Oh, the diligence of Satan! Oh, the desperateness of man's heart!

140. Now was the battle won, and down fell I, as a bird that is shot from the top of a tree, into great guilt, and fearful despair. Thus getting out of my bed, I went moping into the field; but God knows, with as heavy a heart as mortal man, I think, could bear; where, for the space of two hours, I was like a man bereft of life, and as now past all recovery, and bound over to eternal punishment.

141. And withal, that scripture did seize upon my soul, "Or profane person, as Esau, who for one morsel of meat, sold his birthright; for ye know, how that afterward, when he would have inherited the blessing, he was rejected; for he found no place of repentance, though he sought it carefully with tears" (Heb. xii. 16, 17).

142. Now was I as one bound, I felt myself shut up unto the judgment to come; nothing now for two years together would abide with me, but damnation, and an expectation of damnation; I say, nothing now would abide with me but this, save some few moments for relief, as in the sequel you will see.

143. These words were to my soul like fetters of brass to my legs, in the continual sound of which I went for several months together. But about ten or eleven o'clock one day, as I was walking under a hedge, full of sorrow and guilt, God knows, and bemoaning myself for this hard hap, that such a thought should arise within me; suddenly this sentence bolted in upon me, The blood of Christ remits all guilt. At this I made a stand in my spirit; with that, this word took hold upon me, "The blood of Jesus Christ, his Son, cleanseth us from all sin" (1 John i. 7.)

144. Now I began to conceive peace in my soul, and methought I saw as if the tempter did leer and steal away from me, as being ashamed of what he had done. At the same time also I had my sin, and the blood of Christ thus

represented to me, that my sin, when compared to the blood of Christ, was no more to it, than this little clot or stone before me, is to this vast and wide field that here I see. This gave me good encouragement for the space of two or three hours; in which time also, methought I saw, by faith, the Son of God, as suffering for my sins; but because it tarried not, I therefore sunk in my spirit, under exceeding guilt again.

145. But chiefly by the afore-mentioned scripture, concerning Esau's selling of his birthright; for that scripture would lie all day long, all the week long, yea, all the year long in my mind, and hold me down, so that I could by no means lift up myself; for when I would strive to turn me to this scripture, or that, for relief, still that sentence would be sounding in me, "For ye know, how that afterward, when he would have inherited the blessing . . . he found no place of repentance, though he sought it carefully with tears."

146. Sometimes, also, I should have a touch from that in Luke xxii. 32, "I have prayed for thee, that thy faith fail not"; but it would not abide upon me; neither could I indeed, when I considered my state, find ground to conceive in the least, that there should be the root of that grace within me, having sinned as I had done. Now was I torn and rent in heavy case, for many days together.

147. Then began I with sad and careful heart, to consider of the nature and largeness of my sin, and to search in the Word of God, if I could in any place espy a word of promise, or any encouraging sentence by which I might take relief. Wherefore I began to consider that third of Mark, All manner of sins and blasphemies shall be forgiven unto the sons of men, wherewith soever they shall blaspheme. Which place, methought, at a blush, did contain a large and glorious promise, for the pardon of high offences; but considering the place more fully, I thought it was rather to be understood as relating more chiefly to those who had, while in a natural estate, committed such things as there are mentioned; but not to me, who had not only received light and mercy, but that had, both after, and also contrary to that, so slighted Christ as I had done.

148. I feared therefore that this wicked sin of mine might

be that sin unpardonable, of which he there thus speaketh, "But he that shall blaspheme against the Holy Ghost hath never forgiveness, but is in danger of eternal damnation" (Mark iii. 29). And I did the rather give credit to this, because of that sentence in the Hebrews, "For ye know, how that afterward, when he would have inherited the blessing, he was rejected; for he found no place of repentance, though he sought it carefully with tears." And this stuck always with me.

149. And now was I both a burden and a terror to myself, nor did I ever so know, as now, what it was to be weary of my life, and yet afraid to die. Oh, how gladly now would I have been anybody but myself! Anything but a man! and in any condition but mine own! for there was nothing did pass more frequently over my mind, than that it was impossible for me to be forgiven my transgression, and to be saved from wrath to come.

150. And now began I to labour to call again time that was past; wishing a thousand times twice told, that the day was yet to come, when I should be tempted to such a sin; concluding with great indignation, both against my heart, and all assaults, how I would rather have been torn in pieces, than found a consenter thereto. But, alas! these thoughts, and wishings, and resolvings, were now too late to help me; the thought had passed my heart, God hath let me go, and I am fallen. Oh! thought I, "that it was with me as in months past, as in the days *when* God preserved me!" (Job xxix. 2).

151. Then again, being loath and unwilling to perish, I began to compare my sin with others, to see if I could find that any of those that were saved had done as I had done. So I considered David's adultery and murder, and found them most heinous crimes; and those too committed after light and grace received; but yet by considering, I perceived that his transgressions were only such as were against the law of Moses; from which the Lord Christ could, with the consent of his Word, deliver him: but mine was against the gospel; yea, against the Mediator thereof; I had sold my Saviour.

152. Now again should I be as if racked upon the wheel, when I considered, that, besides the guilt that possessed me,

I should be so void of grace, so bewitched. What, thought I, must it be no sin but this? Must it needs be the *great transgression* (Ps. xix. 13)? Must *that* wicked one touch my soul (1 John v. 18)? Oh, what stings did I find in all these sentences!

153. What, thought I, is there but one sin that is unpardonable? But one sin that layeth the soul without the reach of God's mercy; and must I be guilty of that? Must it needs be that? Is there but one sin among so many millions of sins, for which there is no forgiveness; and must I commit this? Oh, unhappy sin! Oh, unhappy man! These things would so break and confound my spirit, that I could not tell what to do; I thought, at times, they would have broke my wits; and still, to aggravate my misery, that would run in my mind, "Ye know how that afterward, when he would have inherited the blessing, he was rejected." Oh! none knows the terrors of those days but myself.

154. After this I came to consider of Peter's sin, which he committed in denying his master; and indeed, this came nighest to mine, of any that I could find; for he had denied his Saviour, as I, and that after light and mercy received; yea, and that too, after warning given him. I also considered, that he did it both once and twice; and that, after time to consider betwixt. But though I put all these circumstances together, that, if possible, I might find help, yet I considered again, that his was but a denial of his master, but mine was a selling of my Saviour. Wherefore I thought with myself, that I came nearer to Judas, than either to David or Peter.

155. Here again my torment would flame out and afflict me; yea, it would grind me, as it were, to powder, to discern the preservation of God towards others, while I fell into the snare; for in my thus considering of other men's sins, and comparing of them with my own, I could evidently see how God preserved them, notwithstanding their wickedness, and would not let them, as he had let me, to become a son of perdition.

156. But oh, how did my soul, at this time, prize the preservation that God did set about his people! Ah, how safely did I see them walk, whom God had hedged in! They were within his care, protection, and special providence;

though they were full as bad as I by nature; yet because
he loved them, he would not suffer them to fall without the
range of mercy; but as for me, I was gone, I had done it;
he would not preserve me, nor keep me; but suffered me,
because I was a reprobate, to fall as I had done. Now, did
those blessed places, that spake of God's keeping his people,
shine like the sun before me, though not to comfort me,
but to show me the blessed state and heritage of those whom
the Lord had blessed.

157. Now I saw, that as God had his hand in all providences and dispensations that overtook his elect, so he had
his hand in all the temptations that they had to sin against
him, not to animate them unto wickedness, but to choose
their temptations and troubles for them; and also to leave
them, for a time, to such sins only as might not destroy,
but humble them; as might not put them beyond, but lay
them in the way of the renewing of his mercy. But oh, what
love, what care, what kindness and mercy did I now see,
mixing itself with the most severe and dreadful of all God's
ways to his people! He would let David, Hezekiah, Solomon,
Peter, and others fall, but he would not let them fall into
sin unpardonable, nor into hell for sin. Oh! thought I, these
be the men that God hath loved; these be the men that
God, though he chastiseth them, keeps them in safety by
him, and them whom he makes to abide under the shadow
of the Almighty. But all these thoughts added sorrow, grief,
and horror to me, as whatever I now thought on, it was
killing to me. If I thought how God kept his own, that was
killing to me. If I thought of how I was falling myself, that
was killing to me. As all things wrought together for the
best, and to do good to them that were the called, according
to his purpose; so I thought that all things wrought for my
damage, and for my eternal overthrow.

158. Then, again, I began to compare my sin with the
sin of Judas, that, if possible, I might find that mine differed
from that which, in truth, is unpardonable. And, oh! thought
I, if it should differ from it, though but the breadth of an
hair, what a happy condition is my soul in! And, by considering, I found that Judas did his intentionally, but mine
was against my prayer and strivings; besides, his was committed with much deliberation, but mine in a fearful hurry,

on a sudden; all this while I was tossed to and fro, like the locusts, and driven from trouble to sorrow; hearing always the sound of Esau's fall in mine ears, and of the dreadful consequences thereof.

159. Yet this consideration about Judas, his sin, was, for a while, some little relief unto me; for I saw I had not, as to the circumstances, transgressed so foully as he. But this was quickly gone again, for, I thought with myself, there might be more ways than one to commit the unpardonable sin; also I thought that there might be degrees of that, as well as of other transgressions; wherefore, for aught I yet could perceive, this iniquity of mine might be such, as might never be passed by.

160. I was often now ashamed, that I should be like such an ugly man as Judas; I thought, also, how loathsome I should be unto all the saints at the day of judgment; insomuch, that now I could scarce see a good man, that I believed had a good conscience, but I should feel my heart tremble at him, while I was in his presence. Oh! now I saw a glory in walking with God, and what a mercy it was to have a good conscience before him.

161. I was much about this time tempted to content myself, by receiving some false opinion; as that there should be no such thing as a day of judgment, that we should not rise again, and that sin was no such grievous thing; the tempter suggesting thus, For if these things should indeed be true, yet to believe otherwise, would yield you ease for the present. If you must perish, never torment yourself so much beforehand; drive the thoughts of damning out of your mind, by possessing your mind with some such conclusions that Atheists and Ranters do use to help themselves withal.

162. But, oh! when such thoughts have led through my heart, how, as it were, within a step, hath death and judgment been in my view! methought the judge stood at the door, I was as if it was come already; so that such things could have no entertainment. But, methinks, I see by this, that Satan will use any means to keep the soul from Christ; he loveth not an awakened frame of spirit; security, blindness, darkness, and error is the very kingdom and habitation of the wicked one.

163. I found it hard work now to pray to God, because

despair was swallowing me up; I thought I was, as with a tempest, driven away from God, for always when I cried to God for mercy, this would come in, It is too late, I am lost, God hath let me fall; not to my correction, but condemnation; my sin is unpardonable; and I know, concerning Esau, how that, after he had sold his birthright, he would have received the blessing, but was rejected. About this time, I did light on that dreadful story of that miserable mortal, Francis Spira; a book that was to my troubled spirit as salt, when rubbed into a fresh wound; every sentence in that book, every groan of that man, with all the rest of his actions in his dolours, as his tears, his prayers, his gnashing of teeth, his wringing of hands, his twining and twisting, languishing and pining away under that mighty hand of God that was upon him, was as knives and daggers in my soul; especially that sentence of his was frightful to me, Man knows the beginning of sin, but who bounds the issues thereof? Then would the former sentence, as the conclusion of all, fall like a hot thunderbolt again upon my conscience; "for you know how that afterward, when he would have inherited the blessing, he was rejected; for he found no place of repentance, though he sought it carefully with tears."

164. Then was I struck into a very great trembling, insomuch that at sometimes I could, for whole days together, feel my very body, as well as my mind, to shake and totter under the sense of the dreadful judgment of God, that should fall on those that have sinned that most fearful and unpardonable sin. I felt also such a clogging and heat at my stomach, by reason of this my terror, that I was, especially at some times, as if my breast bone would have split in sunder; then I thought of that concerning Judas, who, by his falling headlong, burst asunder, and all his bowels gushed out (Acts i. 18).

165. I feared also that this was the mark that the Lord did set on Cain, even continual fear and trembling, under the heavy load of guilt that he had charged on him for the blood of his brother Abel. Thus did I wind, and twine, and shrink, under the burden that was upon me; which burden also did so oppress me, that I could neither stand, nor go, nor lie, either at rest or quiet.

166. Yet that saying would sometimes come to my mind,

He hath received gifts for the rebellious (Ps. lxviii. 18). "The rebellious," thought I; why, surely they are such as once were under subjection to their prince, even those who, after they have sworn subjection to his government, have taken up arms against him; and this, thought I, is my very condition; once I loved him, feared him, served him; but now I am a rebel; I have sold him, I have said, Let him go if he will; but yet he has gifts for rebels, and then why not for me?

167. This sometimes I thought on, and should labour to take hold thereof, that some, though small, refreshment might have been conceived by me; but in this also I missed of my desire, I was driven with force beyond it, I was like a man that is going to the place of execution, even by that place where he would fain creep in and hide himself, but may not.

168. Again, after I had thus considered the sins of the *saints* in particular, and found mine went beyond them, then I began to think thus with myself: Set the case I should put all theirs together, and mine alone against them, might I not then find some encouragement? For if mine, though bigger than any one, yet should but be equal to all, then there is hopes; for that blood that hath virtue enough in it to wash away all theirs, hath also virtue enough in it to do away mine, though this one be full as big, if no bigger, than all theirs. Here, again, I should consider the sin of David, of Solomon, of Manasseh, of Peter, and the rest of the great offenders; and should also labour, what I might with fairness, to aggravate and heighten their sins by several circumstances: but, alas! it was all in vain.

169. I should think with myself that David shed blood to cover his adultery, and that by the sword of the children of Ammon; a work that could not be done but by continuance and deliberate contrivance, which was a great aggravation to his sin. But then this would turn upon me: Ah! but these were but sins against the law, from which there was a Jesus sent to save them; but yours is a sin against the Saviour, and who shall save you from that?

170. Then I thought on Solomon, and how he sinned in loving strange women, in falling away to their idols, in building them temples, in doing this after light, in his old

age, after great mercy received; but the same conclusion that cut me off in the former consideration, cut me off as to this; namely, that all those were but sins against the law, for which God had provided a remedy; but I had sold my Saviour, and there now remained no more sacrifice for sin.

171. I would then add to those men's sins, the sins of Manasseh, how that he built altars for idols in the house of the Lord; he also observed times, used enchantment, had to do with wizards, was a wizard, had his familiar spirits, burned his children in the fire in sacrifice to devils, and made the streets of Jerusalem run down with the blood of innocents. These, thought I, are great sins, sins of a bloody colour; yea, it would turn again upon me: They are none of them of the nature of yours; you have parted with Jesus, you have sold your Saviour.

172. This one consideration would always kill my heart, My sin was point-blank against my Saviour; and that too, at that height, that I had in my heart said of him, Let him go if he will. Oh! methought, this sin was bigger than the sins of a country, of a kingdom, or of the whole world, no one pardonable, nor all of them together, was able to equal mine; mine outwent them every one.

173. Now I should find my mind to flee from God, as from the face of a dreadful judge; yet this was my torment, I could not escape his hand: "It is a fearful thing to fall into the hands of the living God" (Heb. x. 31). But blessed be his grace, that scripture, in these flying sins, would call as running after me, "I have blotted out, as a thick cloud, thy transgressions; and, as a cloud, thy sins: return unto me, for I have redeemed thee" (Is. xliv. 22). This, I say, would come in upon my mind, when I was fleeing from the face of God; for I did flee from his face, that is, my mind and spirit fled before him; by reason of his highness, I could not endure; then would the text cry, "Return unto me"; it would cry aloud with a very great voice, "Return unto me, for I have redeemed thee." Indeed, this would make me make a little stop, and, as it were, look over my shoulder behind me, to see if I could discern that the God of grace did follow me with a pardon in his hand, but I could no sooner do that, but all would be clouded and darkened again by that sentence, "For you know how that afterward, when he would

have inherited the blessing, he found no place of repentance, though he sought it carefully with tears." Wherefore I could not return, but fled, though at sometimes it cried, "Return, return," as if it did holloa after me. But I feared to close in therewith, lest it should not come from God; for that other, as I said, was still sounding in my conscience, "For you know how that afterward, when he would have inherited the blessing, he was rejected," etc.

174. Once as I was walking to and fro in a good man's shop, bemoaning of myself in my sad and doleful state, afflicting myself with self-abhorrence for this wicked and ungodly thought; lamenting, also, this hard hap of mine, for that I should commit so great a sin, greatly fearing I should not be pardoned; praying, also, in my heart, that if this sin of mine did differ from that against the Holy Ghost, the Lord would show it me. And being now ready to sink with fear, suddenly there was, as if there had rushed in at the window, the noise of wind upon me, but very pleasant, and as if I heard a voice speaking, Didst ever refuse to be justified by the blood of Christ? And, withal my whole life and profession past was, in a moment, opened to me, wherein I was made to see that designedly I had not; so my heart answered groaningly, No. Then fell, with power, that word of God upon me, "See that ye refuse not him that speaketh" (Heb. xii. 25). This made a strange seizure upon my spirit; it brought light with it, and commanded a silence in my heart of all those tumultuous thoughts that before did use, like masterless hell-hounds, to roar and bellow, and make a hideous noise within me. It showed me, also, that Jesus Christ had yet a word of grace and mercy for me, that he had not, as I had feared, quite forsaken and cast off my soul; yea, this was a kind of a chide for my proneness to desperation; a kind of a threatening me if I did not, notwithstanding my sins and the heinousness of them, venture my salvation upon the Son of God. But as to my determining about this strange dispensation, what it was I knew not; or from whence it came I know not. I have not yet, in twenty years' time, been able to make a judgment of it; I thought then what here I shall be loath to speak. But verily, that sudden rushing wind was as if an angel had come upon me; but both it and the salvation I will leave until the day of

judgment; only this I say, it commanded a great calm in my soul, it persuaded me there might be hope; it showed me, as I thought, what the sin unpardonable was, and that my soul had yet the blessed privilege to flee to Jesus Christ for mercy. But, I say, concerning this dispensation, I know not what yet to say unto it; which was, also, in truth, the cause that, at first, I did not speak of it in the book; I do now, also, leave it to be thought on by men of sound judgment. I lay not the stress of my salvation thereupon, but upon the Lord Jesus, in the promise; yet, seeing I am here unfolding of my secret things, I thought it might not be altogether inexpedient to let this also show itself, though I cannot now relate the matter as there I did experience it. This lasted, in the savour of it, for about three or four days, and then I began to mistrust and to despair again.

175. Wherefore, still my life hung in doubt before me, not knowing which way I should tip; only this I found my soul desire, even to cast itself at the foot of grace, by prayer and supplication. But, oh! it was hard for me now to bear the face to pray to this Christ for mercy, against whom I had thus most vilely sinned; it was hard work, I say, to offer to look him in the face against whom I had so vilely sinned; and, indeed, I have found it as difficult to come to God by prayer, after backsliding from him, as to do any other thing. Oh, the shame that did now attend me! especially when I thought I am now a-going to pray to him for mercy that I had so lightly esteemed but a while before! I was ashamed, yea, even confounded, because this villany had been committed by me; but I saw there was but one way with me, I must go to him and humble myself unto him, and beg that he, of his wonderful mercy, would show pity to me, and have mercy upon my wretched sinful soul.

176. Which, when the tempter perceived, he strongly suggested to me, That I ought not to pray to God; for prayer was not for any in my case, neither could it do me good, because I had rejected the Mediator, by whom all prayer came with acceptance to God the Father, and without whom no prayer could come into his presence. Wherefore, now to pray is but to add sin to sin; yea, now to pray, seeing God has cast you off, is the next way to anger and offend him more than you ever did before.

177. For God, saith he, hath been weary of you for these several years already, because you are none of his; your bawlings in his ears hath been no pleasant voice to him; and, therefore, he let you sin this sin, that you might be quite cut off; and will you pray still? This the devil urged, and set forth that, in Numbers, when Moses said to the children of Israel, That because they would not go up to possess the land when God would have them, therefore, for ever after, God did bar them out from thence, though they prayed they might, with tears (Num. xiv. 36, 37, etc.).

178. As it is said in another place (Exod. xxi. 14), the man that sins presumptuously shall be taken from God's altar, that he may die; even as Joab was by King Solomon, when he thought to find shelter there (1 Kings ii. 28, etc.). These places did pinch me very sore; yet, my case being desperate, I thought with myself I can but die; and if it must be so, it shall once be said, that such an one died at the foot of Christ in prayer. This I did, but with great difficulty, God doth know; and that because, together with this, still that saying about Esau would be set at my heart, even like a flaming sword, to keep the way of the tree of life, lest I should taste thereof and live. Oh! who knows how hard a thing I found it to come to God in prayer.

179. I did also desire the prayers of the people of God for me, but I feared that God would give them no heart to do it; yea, I trembled in my soul to think that some or other of them would shortly tell me, that God had said those words to them that he once did say to the prophet concerning the children of Israel, "Pray not thou for this people," for I have rejected them (Jer. xi. 14). So, pray not for him, for I have rejected him. Yea, I thought that he had whispered this to some of them already, only they durst not tell me so, neither durst I ask them of it, for fear, if it should be so, it would make me quite beside myself. Man knows the beginning of sin, said Spira, but who bounds the issues thereof?

180. About this time I took an opportunity to break my mind to an ancient Christian, and told him all my case; I told him, also, that I was afraid that I had sinned the sin against the Holy Ghost; and he told me he thought so too. Here, therefore, I had but cold comfort; but, talking

a little more with him, I found him, though a good man, a stranger to much combat with the devil. Wherefore, I went to God again, as well as I could, for mercy still.

181. Now, also, did the tempter begin to mock me in my misery, saying, that, seeing I had thus parted with the Lord Jesus, and provoked him to displeasure, who would have stood between my soul and the flame of devouring fire, there was now but one way, and that was, to pray that God the Father would be the Mediator betwixt his Son and me, that we might be reconciled again, and that I might have that blessed benefit in him that his blessed saints enjoyed.

182. Then did that scripture seize upon my soul, He is of one mind, and who can turn him? Oh! I saw it was as easy to persuade him to make a new world, a new covenant, or new Bible, besides that we have already, as to pray for such a thing. This was to persuade him that what he had done already was mere folly, and persuade with him to alter, yea, to disannul, the whole way of salvation; and then would that saying rend my soul asunder, "Neither is there salvation in any other: for there is none other name under heaven, given among men, whereby we must be saved" (Acts iv. 12).

183. Now, the most free, and full, and gracious words of the gospel were the greatest torment to me; yea, nothing so afflicted me as the thoughts of Jesus Christ, the remembrance of a Saviour; because I had cast him off, brought forth the villany of my sin, and my loss by it to mind; nothing did twinge my conscience like this. Every time that I thought of the Lord Jesus, of his grace, love, goodness, kindness, gentleness, meekness, death, blood, promises and blessed exhortations, comforts and consolations, it went to my soul like a sword; for still, unto these my considerations of the Lord Jesus, these thoughts would make place for themselves in my heart; aye, this is the Jesus, the loving Saviour, the Son of God, whom thou hast parted with, whom you slighted, despised, and abused. This is the only Saviour, the only Redeemer, the only one that could so love sinners as to wash them from their sins in his own most precious blood; but you have no part nor lot in this Jesus, you have put him from you, you have said in your heart, Let him go if he will. Now, therefore, you are severed from him; you

have severed yourself from him. Behold, then, his goodness, but yourself to be no partaker of it. Oh, thought I, what have I lost! What have I parted with! What have I disinherited my poor soul of! Oh! it is sad to be destroyed by the grace and mercy of God; to have the Lamb, the Saviour, turn lion and destroyer (Rev. vi.). I also trembled, as I have said, at the sight of the saints of God, especially at those that greatly loved him, and that made it their business to walk continually with him in this world; for they did, both in their words, their carriages, and all their expressions of tenderness and fear to sin against their precious Saviour, condemn, lay guilt upon, and also add continual affliction and shame unto my soul. The dread of them was upon me, and I trembled at God's Samuels (1 Sam. xvi. 4).

184. Now, also, the tempter began afresh to mock my soul another way, saying that Christ, indeed, did pity my case, and was sorry for my loss; but forasmuch as I had sinned and transgressed, as I had done, he could by no means help me, nor save me from what I feared; for my sin was not of the nature of theirs for whom he bled and died, neither was it counted with those that were laid to his charge when he hanged on the tree. Therefore, unless he should come down from heaven and die anew for this sin, though, indeed, he did greatly pity me, yet I could have no benefit of him. These things may seem ridiculous to others, even as ridiculous as they were in themselves, but to me they were most tormenting cogitations; every of them augmented my misery, that Jesus Christ should have so much love as to pity me when he could not help me; nor did I think that the reason why he could not help me was because his merits were weak, or his grace and salvation spent on them already, but because his faithfulness to his threatening would not let him extend his mercy to me. Besides, I thought, as I have already hinted, that my sin was not within the bounds of that pardon that was wrapped up in a promise; and if not, then I knew assuredly, that it was more easy for heaven and earth to pass away than for me to have eternal life. So that the ground of all these fears of mine did arise from a steadfast belief that I had of the stability of the holy Word of God, and, also, from my being misinformed of the nature of my sin.

* C 815

185. But, oh! how this would add to my affliction, to conceit that I should be guilty of such a sin for which he did not die. These thoughts would so confound me, and imprison me, and tie me up from faith, that I knew not what to do; but, oh! thought I, that he would come down again! Oh! that the work of man's redemption was yet to be done by Christ! How would I pray him and entreat him to count and reckon this sin amongst the rest for which he died! But this scripture would strike me down as dead, "Christ being raised from the dead dieth no more; death hath no more dominion over him" (Rom. vi. 9).

186. Thus, by the strange and unusual assaults of the tempter, was my soul, like a broken vessel, driven as with the winds, and tossed sometimes headlong into despair, sometimes upon the covenant of works, and sometimes to wish that the new covenant, and the conditions thereof, might, so far forth as I thought myself concerned, be turned another way and changed. But in all these I was but as those that justle against the rocks; more broken, scattered, and rent. Oh, the unthought of imaginations, frights, fears, and terrors that are affected by a thorough application of guilt, yielded to desperation! this is the man that hath "his dwelling among the tombs" with the dead; that is, always crying out and "cutting himself with stones" (Mark v. 2–5). But I say, all in vain; desperation will not comfort him, the old covenant will not save him; nay, heaven and earth shall pass away before one jot or tittle of the Word and law of grace shall fall or be removed. This I saw, this I felt, and under this I groaned; yet this advantage I got thereby, namely, a further confirmation of the certainty of the way of salvation, and that the Scriptures were the Word of God! Oh! I cannot now express what then I saw and felt of the steadiness of Jesus Christ, the rock of man's salvation; what was done could not be undone, added to, nor altered I saw, indeed, that sin might drive the soul beyond Christ, even the sin which is unpardonable; but woe to him that was so driven, for the Word would shut him out.

187. Thus was I always sinking, whatever I did think or do. So one day I walked to a neighbouring town, and sat down upon a settle in the street, and fell into a very deep pause about the most fearful state my sin had brought me

to; and, after long musing, I lifted up my head, but methought I saw as if the sun that shineth in the heavens did grudge to give light, and as if the very stones in the street, and tiles upon the houses, did bend themselves against me; methought that they all combined together to banish me out of the world; I was abhorred of them, and unfit to dwell among them, or be partaker of their benefits, because I had sinned against the Saviour. O how happy, now, was every creature over what I was; for they stood fast and kept their station, but I was gone and lost.

188. Then breaking out in the bitterness of my soul, I said to myself, with a grievous sigh, How can God comfort such a wretch as I? I had no sooner said it but this returned upon me, as an echo doth answer a voice, This sin is not unto death. At which I was as if I had been raised out of a grave, and cried out again, Lord, how couldest thou find out such a word as this? for I was filled with admiration at the fitness, and, also, at the unexpectedness of the sentence, the fitness of the Word, the rightness of the timing of it, the power, and sweetness, and light, and glory that came with it, also, was marvellous to me to find. I was now, for the time, out of doubt as to that about which I so much was in doubt before; my fears before were, that my sin was not pardonable, and so that I had no right to pray, to repent, etc., or that if I did, it would be of no advantage or profit to me. But now, thought I, if this sin is not unto death, then it is pardonable; therefore, from this I have encouragement to come to God, by Christ, for mercy, to consider the promise of forgiveness as that which stands with open arms to receive me, as well as others. This, therefore, was a great easement to my mind; to wit, that my sin was pardonable, that it was not the sin unto death (1 John v. 16, 17). None but those that know what my trouble, by their own experience, was, can tell what relief came to my soul by this consideration; it was a release to me from my former bonds, and a shelter from my former storm. I seemed now to stand upon the same ground with other sinners, and to have as good right to the Word and prayer as any of them.

189. Now, I say, I was in hopes that my sin was not unpardonable, but that there might be hopes for me to obtain

forgiveness. But, oh, how Satan did now lay about him for
to bring me down again! But he could by no means do it,
neither this day nor the most part of the next, for this
sentence stood like a mill-post at my back; yet, towards the
evening of the next day, I felt this word begin to leave me
and to withdraw its supportation from me, and so I returned
to my old fears again, but with a great deal of grudging and
peevishness, for I feared the sorrow of despair; nor could
my faith now longer retain this word.

190. But the next day, at evening, being under many
fears, I went to seek the Lord; and as I prayed, I cried, and
my soul cried to him in these words, with strong cries: O
Lord, I beseech thee, show me that thou hast loved me
with everlasting love (Jer. xxxi. 3). I had no sooner said it
but, with sweetness, this returned upon me, as an echo or
sounding again, "I have loved thee with an everlasting love."
Now I went to bed at quiet; also, when I awaked the next
morning, it was fresh upon my soul—and I believed it.

191. But yet the tempter left me not; for it could not be
so little as an hundred times that he that day did labour
to break my peace. Oh! the combats and conflicts that I
did then meet with as I strove to hold by this word; that of
Esau would fly in my face like to lightning. I should be
sometimes up and down twenty times in an hour, yet God
did bear me up and keep my heart upon this word, from
which I had also, for several days together, very much
sweetness and comfortable hopes of pardon; for thus it was
made out to me, I loved thee whilst thou wast committing
this sin, I loved thee before, I love thee still, and I will
love thee for ever.

192. Yet I saw my sin most barbarous, and a filthy
crime, and could not but conclude, and that with great
shame and astonishment, that I had horribly abused the
holy Son of God; wherefore, I felt my soul greatly to love and
pity him, and my bowels to yearn towards him; for I saw
he was still my Friend, and did reward me good for evil;
yea, the love and affection that then did burn within to my
Lord and Saviour Jesus Christ did work, at this time, such
a strong and hot desire of revengement upon myself for the
abuse I had done unto him, that, to speak as then I thought,
had I had a thousand gallons of blood within my veins,

I could freely then have spilt it all at the command and feet of this my Lord and Saviour.

193. And as I was thus in musing and in my studies, considering how to love the Lord and to express my love to him, that saying came in upon me, "If thou, Lord, shouldest mark iniquities, O Lord, who shall stand? But *there is* forgiveness with thee, that thou mayest be feared" (Ps. cxxx. 3, 4). These were good words to me, especially the latter part thereof; to wit, that there is forgiveness with the Lord, that he might be feared; that is, as then I understood it, that he might be loved and had in reverence; for it was thus made out to me, that the great God did set so high an esteem upon the love of his poor creatures, that rather than he would go without their love he would pardon their transgressions.

194. And now was that word fulfilled on me, and I was also refreshed by it, Then shall they be ashamed and confounded, "and never open their mouth any more because of their shame, when I am pacified toward them for all that they have done, saith the Lord God" (Ezek. xvi. 63). Thus was my soul at this time, and, as I then did think, for ever, set at liberty from being again afflicted with my former guilt and amazement.

195. But before many weeks were over I began to despond again, fearing lest, notwithstanding all that I had enjoyed, that yet I might be deceived and destroyed at the last; for this consideration came strong into my mind, that whatever comfort and peace I thought I might have from the Word of the promise of life, yet unless there could be found in my refreshment a concurrence and agreement in the Scriptures, let me think what I will thereof, and hold it never so fast, I should find no such thing at the end; "for the Scripture cannot be broken" (John x. 35).

196. Now began my heart again to ache and fear I might meet with disappointment at the last; wherefore I began, with all seriousness, to examine my former comfort, and to consider whether one that had sinned as I have done, might with confidence trust upon the faithfulness of God, laid down in those words by which I had been comforted and on which I had leaned myself. But now were brought those sayings to my mind, "For *it is* impossible for those who were once

enlightened, and have tasted of the heavenly gift, and were made partakers of the Holy Ghost, and have tasted the good word of God, and the powers of the world to come, if they shall fall away, to renew them again unto repentance" (Heb. vi. 4–6). "For if we sin wilfully after that we have received the knowledge of the truth, there remaineth no more sacrifice for sins, but a certain fearful looking for of judgment and fiery indignation, which shall devour the adversaries" (Heb. x. 26, 27). Even "as Esau, who for one morsel of meat sold his birthright; for ye know how that afterward, when he would have inherited the blessing, he was rejected; for he found no place of repentance, though he sought it carefully with tears" (Heb. xii. 16, 17).

197. Now was the word of the gospel forced from my soul, so that no promise or encouragement was to be found in the Bible for me; and now would that saying work upon my spirit to afflict me, "Rejoice not, O Israel, for joy as *other* people" (Hos. ix. 1). For I saw indeed there was cause of rejoicing for those that held to Jesus; but as for me, I had cut myself off by my transgressions, and left myself neither foot-hold, nor hand-hold, amongst all the stays and props in the precious word of life.

198. And truly I did now feel myself to sink into a gulf, as an house whose foundation is destroyed; I did liken myself, in this condition, unto the case of a child that was fallen into a mill-pit, who, though it could make some shift to scrabble and spraul in the water, yet because it could find neither hold for hand nor foot, therefore at last it must die in that condition. So soon as this fresh assault had fastened on my soul, that scripture came into my heart, "This *is* for *many* days" (Dan. x. 14). And indeed I found it was so; for I could not be delivered, nor brought to peace again, until well-nigh two years and an half were completely finished. Wherefore these words, though in themselves they tended to discouragement, yet to me, who feared this condition would be eternal, they were at sometimes as an help and refreshment to me.

199. For, thought I, many days are not for ever, many days will have an end, therefore seeing I was to be afflicted, not a few, but many days, yet I was glad it was but for many days. Thus, I say, I could recal myself some-

times, and give myself a help, for as soon as ever the words came into my mind at first, I knew my trouble would be long; yet this would be but sometimes, for I could not always think on this, nor ever be helped by it, though I did.

200. Now, while these Scriptures lay before me, and laid sin anew at my door, that saying in the eighteenth of Luke, with others, did encourage me to prayer. Then the tempter again laid at me very sore, suggesting, That neither the mercy of God, nor yet the blood of Christ, did at all concern me, nor could they help me for my sin; therefore it was in vain to pray. Yet, thought I, I will pray. But, said the tempter, your sin is unpardonable. Well, said I, I will pray. It is to no boot, said he. Yet, said I, I will pray. So I went to prayer to God; and while I was at prayer, I uttered words to this effect, Lord, Satan tells me that neither thy mercy, nor Christ's blood, is sufficient to save my soul; Lord, shall I honour thee most, by believing thou wilt and canst? or him, by believing thou neither wilt nor canst? Lord, I would fain honour thee, by believing thou wilt and canst.

201. And as I was thus before the Lord, that scripture fastened on my heart, "O woman, great *is* thy faith" (Matt. xv. 28), even as if one had clapped me on the back, as I was on my knees before God. Yet I was not able to believe this, that this was a prayer of faith, till almost six months after; for I could not think that I had faith, or that there should be a word for me to act faith on; therefore I should still be as sticking in the jaws of desperation, and went mourning up and down in a sad condition, crying, Is his mercy clean gone? Is his mercy clean gone for ever? And I thought sometimes, even when I was groaning in these expressions, they did seem to make a question whether it was or no; yet I greatly feared it was.

202. There was nothing now that I longed for more than to be put out of doubt, as to this thing in question; and, as I was vehemently desiring to know if there was indeed hopes for me, these words came rolling into my mind, "Will the Lord cast off for ever? And will he be favourable no more? Is his mercy clean gone for ever? Doth his promise fail for evermore? Hath God forgotten to be gracious? Hath he in anger shut up his tender mercies?" (Ps. lxxvii. 7–9). And all the while they run in my mind, methought I had this

still as the answer, It is a question whether he had or no;
it may be he hath not. Yea, the interrogatory seemed to
me to carry in it a sure affirmation that indeed he had not,
nor would so cast off, but would be favourable; that his
promise doth not fail, and that he had not forgotten to be
gracious, nor would in anger shut up his tender mercy.
Something, also, there was upon my heart at the same time,
which I now cannot call to mind; which, with this text, did
sweeten my heart, and made me conclude that his mercy
might not be quite gone, nor clean gone for ever.

203. At another time, I remember I was again much under
the question, Whether the blood of Christ was sufficient to
save my soul? In which doubt I continued from morning
till about seven or eight at night; and at last, when I was,
as it were, quite worn out with fear, lest it should not lay
hold on me, these words did sound suddenly within my
heart, He is able. But methought this word ABLE was spoke
so loud unto me; it showed such a great word, it seemed to
be writ in great letters, and gave such a justle to my fear
and doubt, I mean for the time it tarried with me, which
was about a day, as I never had from that all my life, either
before or after that (Heb. vii. 25).

204. But one morning, when I was again at prayer, and
trembling under the fear of this, that no word of God could
help me, that piece of a sentence darted in upon me, "My
grace is sufficient." At this methought I felt some stay, as
if there might be hopes. But, oh, how good a thing it is for
God to send his Word! For about a fortnight before I was
looking on this very place, and then I thought it could not
come near my soul with comfort, therefore I threw down
my book in a pet. Then I thought it was not large enough
for me; no, not large enough; but now, it was as if it had
arms of grace so wide that it could not only enclose me,
but many more besides.

205. By these words I was sustained, yet not without
exceeding conflicts, for the space of seven or eight weeks;
for my peace would be in and out, sometimes twenty times
a day; comfort now, and trouble presently; peace now, and
before I could go a furlong as full of fear and guilt as ever
heart could hold; and this was not only now and then,
but my whole seven weeks' experience; for this about the

sufficiency of grace, and that of Esau's parting with his birthright, would be like a pair of scales within my mind, sometimes one end would be uppermost, and sometimes again the other; according to which would be my peace or trouble.

206. Therefore I still did pray to God, that he would come in with this scripture more fully on my heart; to wit, that he would help me to apply the whole sentence, for as yet I could not: that he gave, I gathered; but farther I could not go, for as yet it only helped me to hope there might be mercy for me, "My grace is sufficient"; and though it came no farther, it answered my former question; to wit, that there was hope; yet, because "for thee" was left out, I was not contented, but prayed to God for that also. Wherefore, one day as I was in a meeting of God's people, full of sadness and terror, for my fears again were strong upon me; and as I was now thinking my soul was never the better, but my case most sad and fearful, these words did, with great power, suddenly break in upon me, "My grace is sufficient for thee, my grace is sufficient for thee, my grace is sufficient for thee," three times together; and, oh! methought that every word was a mighty word unto me; as *my*, and *grace*, and *sufficient*, and *for thee*; they were then, and sometimes are still, far bigger than others be.

207. At which time my understanding was so enlightened, that I was as though I had seen the Lord Jesus look down from heaven through the tiles upon me, and direct these words unto me. This sent me mourning home, it broke my heart, and filled me full of joy, and laid me low as the dust; only it stayed not long with me, I mean in this glory and refreshing comfort, yet it continued with me for several weeks, and did encourage me to hope. But so soon as that powerful operation of it was taken off my heart, that other about Esau returned upon me as before; so my soul did hang as in a pair of scales again, sometimes up and sometimes down, now in peace, and anon again in terror.

208. Thus I went on for many weeks, sometimes comforted, and sometimes tormented; and, especially at some times, my torment would be very sore, for all those scriptures forenamed in the Hebrews, would be set before me, as the only sentences that would keep me out of heaven. Then, again,

I should begin to repent that ever that thought went through me, I should also think thus with myself, Why, how many scriptures are there against me? There are but three or four: and cannot God miss them, and save me for all them? Sometimes, again, I should think, Oh! if it were not for these three or four words, now how might I be comforted? And I could hardly forbear, at some times, but to wish them out of the book.

209. Then methought I should see as if both Peter, and Paul, and John, and all the writers, did look with scorn upon me, and hold me in derision; and as if they said unto me, All our words are truth, one of as much force as another. It is not we that have cut you off, but you have cast away yourself; there is none of our sentences that you must take hold upon but these, and such as these: "It is impossible; there remains no more sacrifice for sin" (Heb. vi.). And "it had been better for them not to have known" the will of God, "than, after they have known *it*, to turn from the holy commandment delivered unto them" (2 Pet. ii. 21). "For the Scriptures cannot be broken."

210. These, as the elders of the city of refuge, I saw were to be the judges both of my case and me, while I stood, with the avenger of blood at my heels, trembling at their gate for deliverance, also with a thousand fears and mistrusts, I doubted that they would shut me out for ever (Josh. xx. 3, 4).

211. Thus was I confounded, not knowing what to do, nor how to be satisfied in this question, Whether the scriptures could agree in the salvation of my soul? I quaked at the apostles, I knew their words were true, and that they must stand for ever.

212. And I remember one day, as I was in diverse frames of spirit, and considering that these frames were still according to the nature of the several scriptures that came in upon my mind; if this of grace, then was I quiet; but if that of Esau, then tormented; Lord, thought I, if both these scriptures would meet in my heart at once, I wonder which of them would get the better of me. So methought I had a longing mind that they might come both together upon me; yea, I desired of God they might.

213. Well, about two or three days after, so they did indeed; they bolted both upon me at a time, and did work

and struggle strangely in me for a while; at last, that about Esau's birthright began to wax weak, and withdraw, and vanish; and this about the sufficiency of grace prevailed with peace and joy. And as I was in a muse about this thing, that scripture came home upon me, "Mercy rejoiceth against judgment" (Jas. ii. 13).

214. This was a wonderment to me; yet truly I am apt to think it was of God; for the word of the law and wrath must give place to the word of life and grace; because, though the word of condemnation be glorious, yet the word of life and salvation doth far exceed in glory (2 Cor. iii. 8–12; Mark ix. 5–7). Also, that Moses and Elias must both vanish, and leave Christ and his saints alone.

215. This scripture did also most sweetly visit my soul, "And him that cometh to me I will in no wise cast out" (John vi. 37). Oh, the comfort that I have had from this word, "in no wise"! as who should say, by no means, for no thing, whatever he hath done. But Satan would greatly labour to pull this promise from me, telling of me that Christ did not mean me, and such as I, but sinners of a lower rank, that had not done as I had done. But I should answer him again, Satan, here is in this word no such exception; but "him that comes," HIM, any him; "him that cometh to me I will in no wise cast out." And this I well remember still, that of all the sleights that Satan used to take this scripture from me, yet he never did so much as put this question, But do you come aright? And I have thought the reason was, because he thought I knew full well what coming aright was; for I saw that to come aright was to come as I was, a vile and ungodly sinner, and to cast myself at the feet of mercy, condemning myself for sin. If ever Satan and I did strive for any word of God in all my life, it was for this good word of Christ; he at one end and I at the other. Oh, what work did we make! It was for this in John, I say, that we did so tug and strive; he pulled and I pulled; but, God be praised, I got the better of him, I got some sweetness from it.

216. But, notwithstanding all these helps and blessed words of grace, yet that of Esau's selling of his birthright would still at times distress my conscience; for though I had been most sweetly comforted, and that but just before,

yet when that came into my mind, it would make me fear again, I could not be quite rid thereof, it would every day be with me: wherefore now I went another way to work, even to consider the nature of this blasphemous thought; I mean, if I should take the words at the largest, and give them their own natural force and scope, even every word therein. So when I had thus considered, I found, that if they were fairly taken, they would amount to this, that I had freely left the Lord Jesus Christ to his choice, whether he would be my Saviour or no; for the wicked words were these, Let him go if he will. Then that scripture gave me hope, "I will never leave thee nor forsake thee" (Heb. xiii. 5). O Lord, said I, but I have left thee. Then it answered again, "But I will not leave thee." For this I thank God also.

217. Yet I was grievously afraid he should, and found it exceeding hard to trust him, seeing I had so offended him. I could have been exceeding glad that this thought had never befallen, for then I thought I could, with more ease and freedom abundance, have leaned upon his grace. I see it was with me, as it was with Joseph's brethren; the guilt of their own wickedness did often fill them with fears that their brother would at last despise them (Gen. l. 15–17).

218. But above all the scriptures that I yet did meet with, that in the twentieth of Joshua was the greatest comfort to me, which speaks of the slayer that was to flee for refuge. And if the avenger of blood pursue the slayer, then, saith Moses, they that are the elders of the city of refuge shall not deliver him into his hand, because he smote his neighbour unwittingly, and hated him not aforetime. Oh, blessed be God for this word; I was convinced that I was the slayer; and that the avenger of blood pursued me, that I felt with great terror; only now it remained that I inquire whether I have right to enter the city of refuge. So I found that he must not, who lay in wait to shed blood: it was not the wilful murderer, but he who unwittingly did it, he who did unawares shed blood; not of spite, or grudge, or malice, he that shed it unwittingly, even he who did not hate his neighbour before. Wherefore,

219. I thought verily I was the man that must enter, because I had smitten my neighbour unwittingly, and hated him not aforetime. I hated him not aforetime; no, I prayed

unto him, was tender of sinning against him; yea, and against this wicked temptation I had strove for a twelvemonth before; yea, and also when it did pass through my heart, it did in spite of my teeth: wherefore I thought I had right to enter this city, and the elders, which are the apostles, were not to deliver me up. This, therefore, was great comfort to me; and did give me much ground of hope.

220. Yet being very critical, for my smart had made me that I knew not what ground was sure enough to bear me, I had one question that my soul did much desire to be resolved about; and that was, Whether it be possible for any soul that hath indeed sinned the unpardonable sin, yet after that to receive though but the least true spiritual comfort from God through Christ? The which, after I had much considered, I found the answer was, No, they could not; and that for these reasons:

221. First, Because those that have sinned that sin, they are debarred a share in the blood of Christ, and being shut out of that, they must needs be void of the least ground of hope, and so of spiritual comfort; for to such "there remaineth no more sacrifice for sins" (Heb. x. 26). Secondly, Because they are denied a share in the promise of life; they shall never be forgiven, "neither in this world, neither in that which is to come" (Matt. xii. 32). Thirdly, The Son of God excludes them also from a share in his blessed intercession, being for ever ashamed to own them both before his holy Father, and the blessed angels in heaven (Mark viii. 38).

222. When I had, with much deliberation, considered of this matter, and could not but conclude that the Lord had comforted me, and that too after this my wicked sin; then, methought, I durst venture to come nigh unto those most fearful and terrible scriptures, with which all this while I had been so greatly affrighted, and on which, indeed, before I durst scarce cast mine eye, yea, had much ado an hundred times to forbear wishing of them out of the Bible; for I thought they would destroy me; but now, I say, I began to take some measure of encouragement to come close to them, to read them, and consider them, and to weigh their scope and tendency.

223. The which, when I began to do, I found their visage changed; for they looked not so grimly on me as before I

thought they did. And, first, I came to the sixth of the
Hebrews, yet trembling for fear it should strike me; which
when I had considered, I found that the falling there intended
was a falling quite away; that is, as I conceived, a falling from,
and an absolute denial of the gospel of remission of sins by
Christ; for from them the apostle begins his argument
(ver. 1–3). Secondly, I found that this falling away must
be openly, even in the view of the world, even so as "to
put Christ to an open shame." Thirdly, I found that those
he there intended were for ever shut up of God, both in
blindness, hardness, and impenitency: it is impossible they
should be renewed again unto repentance. By all these
particulars, I found, to God's everlasting praise, my sin was
not the sin in this place intended.

First, I confessed I was fallen, but not fallen away, that is,
from the profession of faith in Jesus unto eternal life.
Secondly, I confessed that I had put Jesus Christ to shame
by my sin, but not to open shame; I did not deny him before
men, nor condemn him as a fruitless one before the world.
Thirdly, Nor did I find that God had shut me up, or denied
me to come, though I found it hard work indeed to come
to him by sorrow and repentance. Blessed be God for
unsearchable grace.

224. Then I considered that in the tenth of the Hebrews,
and found that the wilful sin there mentioned is not every
wilful sin, but that which doth throw off Christ, and then his
commandments too. Secondly, That must also be done
openly, before two or three witnesses, to answer that of the
law (ver. 28). Thirdly, This sin cannot be committed, but
with great despite done to the Spirit of grace; despising
both the dissuasions from that sin, and the persuasions to
the contrary. But the Lord knows, though this my sin was
devilish, yet it did not amount to these.

225. And as touching that in the twelfth of the Hebrews,
about Esau's selling his birthright, though this was that
which killed me, and stood like a spear against me; yet now
I did consider, First, That his was not a hasty thought
against the continual labour of his mind, but a thought
consented to and put in practice likewise, and that too after
some deliberation (Gen. xxv.). Secondly, It was a public
and open action, even before his brother, if not before many

more; this made his sin of a far more heinous nature than otherwise it would have been. Thirdly, He continued to slight his birthright: "He did eat and drink, and went his way; thus Esau despised *his* birthright" (ver. 34). Yea, twenty years after, he was found to despise it still. "And Esau said, I have enough, my brother; keep that thou hast unto thyself" (Gen. xxxiii. 9).

226. Now as touching this, that Esau sought a place of repentance; thus I thought, first, This was not for the birthright, but for the blessing; this is clear from the apostle, and is distinguished by Esau himself; "he took away my birthright (that is, formerly); and, behold, now he hath taken away my blessing" (Gen. xxvii. 36). Secondly, Now, this being thus considered, I came again to the apostle, to see what might be the mind of God, in a New Testament style and sense, concerning Esau's sin; and so far as I could conceive, this was the mind of God, That the birthright signified regeneration, and the blessing the eternal inheritance; for so the apostle seems to hint, "Lest there *be* any profane person, as Esau, who for one morsel of meat sold his birthright"; as if he should say, Lest there be any person amongst you that shall cast off all those blessed beginnings of God that at present are upon him, in order to a new birth, lest they become as Esau, even be rejected afterwards, when they would inherit the blessing.

227. For many there are who, in the day of grace and mercy, despise those things which are indeed the birthright to heaven, who yet, when the deciding day appears, will cry as loud as Esau, "Lord, Lord, open to us"; but then, as Isaac would not repent, no more will God the Father, but will say, I have blessed these, yea, and they shall be blessed; but as for you, depart from me, all ye workers of iniquity (Gen. xxvii. 33; Luke xiii. 25-7).

228. When I had thus considered these scriptures, and found that thus to understand them was not against, but according to other scriptures; this still added further to my encouragement and comfort, and also gave a great blow to that objection, to wit, that the scripture could not agree in the salvation of my soul. And now remained only the hinder part of the tempest, for the thunder was gone beyond me, only some drops did still remain, that now and then would

fall upon me; but because my former frights and anguish were very sore and deep, therefore it did oft befal me still, as it befalleth those that have been scared with fire, I thought every voice was Fire, fire; every little touch would hurt my tender conscience.

229. But one day, as I was passing in the field, and that too with some dashes on my conscience, fearing lest yet all was not right, suddenly this sentence fell upon my soul, Thy righteousness is in heaven; and methought withal, I saw, with the eyes of my soul, Jesus Christ at God's right hand; there, I say, is my righteousness; so that wherever I was, or whatever I was a-doing, God could not say of me, He wants my righteousness, for that was just before him. I also saw, moreover, that it was not my good frame of heart that made my righteousness better, nor yet my bad frame that made my righteousness worse; for my righteousness was Jesus Christ himself, the same yesterday, and to-day, and for ever (Heb. xiii. 8).

230. Now did my chains fall off my legs indeed, I was loosed from my affliction and irons, my temptations also fled away; so that, from that time, those dreadful scriptures of God left off to trouble me; now went I also home rejoicing, for the grace and love of God. So when I came home, I looked to see if I could find that sentence, Thy righteousness is in heaven; but could not find such a saying, wherefore my heart began to sink again, only that was brought to my remembrance, he "of God is made unto us wisdom, and righteousness, and sanctification, and redemption"; by this word I saw the other sentence true (1 Cor. i. 30).

231. For by this scripture, I saw that the man Christ Jesus, as he is distinct from us, as touching his bodily presence, so he is our righteousness and sanctification before God. Here, therefore, I lived for some time, very sweetly at peace with God through Christ; Oh, methought, Christ! Christ! there was nothing but Christ that was before my eyes, I was not now only for looking upon this and the other benefits of Christ apart, as of his blood, burial, or resurrection, but considered him as a whole Christ! As he in whom all these, and all other his virtues, relations, offices, and operations met together, and that as he sat on the right hand of God in heaven.

232. It was glorious to me to see his exaltation, and the worth and prevalency of all his benefits, and that because of this: now I could look from myself to him, and should reckon that all those graces of God that now were green in me, were yet but like those cracked groats and fourpence-halfpennies that rich men carry in their purses, when their gold is in their trunks at home! Oh, I saw my gold was in my trunk at home! In Christ, my Lord and Saviour! Now Christ was all; all my wisdom, all my righteousness, all my sanctification, and all my redemption.

233. Further, the Lord did also lead me into the mystery of union with the Son of God, that I was joined to him, that I was flesh of his flesh, and bone of his bone, and now was that a sweet word to me in Eph. v. 30. By this also was my faith in him, as my righteousness, the more confirmed to me; for if he and I were one, then his righteousness was mine, his merits mine, his victory also mine. Now could I see myself in heaven and earth at once; in heaven by my Christ, by my head, by my righteousness and life, though on earth by my body or person.

234. Now I saw Christ Jesus was looked on of God, and should also be looked upon by us, as that common or public person, in whom all the whole body of his elect are always to be considered and reckoned; that we fulfilled the law by him, rose from the dead by him, got the victory over sin, death, the devil, and hell, by him; when he died, we died; and so of his resurrection. "Thy dead *men* shall live, *together with* my dead body shall they arise," saith he (Is. xxvi. 19). And again, "After two days will he revive us: in the third day he will raise us up, and we shall live in his sight" (Hos. vi. 2); which is now fulfilled by the sitting down of the Son of man on the right hand of the Majesty in the heavens, according to that to the Ephesians, he "hath raised *us* up together, and made *us* sit together in heavenly *places* in Christ Jesus" (Eph. ii. 6).

235. Ah, these blessed considerations and scriptures, with many other of a like nature, were in those days made to spangle in mine eyes, so that I have cause to say, "Praise ye the Lord. Praise God in his sanctuary: praise him in the firmament of his power. Praise him for his mighty acts: praise him according to his excellent greatness" (Ps. cl. 1, 2).

236. Having thus, in few words, given you a taste of the sorrow and affliction that my soul went under, by the guilt and terror that this my wicked thought did lay me under; and having given you also a touch of my deliverance therefrom, and of the sweet and blessed comfort that I met with afterwards, which comfort dwelt about a twelvemonth with my heart, to my unspeakable admiration; I will now, God willing, before I proceed any farther, give you in a word or two, what, as I conceive, was the cause of this temptation; and also after that, what advantage, at the last, it became unto my soul.

237. For the causes, I conceived they were principally two: of which two also I was deeply convinced all the time this trouble lay upon me. The first was, for that I did not, when I was delivered from the temptation that went before, still pray to God to keep me from temptations that were to come; for though, as I can say in truth, my soul was much in prayer before this trial seized me, yet then I prayed only, or at the most, principally for the removal of present troubles, and for fresh discoveries of his love in Christ, which I saw afterwards was not enough to do; I also should have prayed that the great God would keep me from the evil that was to come.

238. Of this I was made deeply sensible by the prayer of holy David, who, when he was under present mercy, yet prayed that God would hold him back from sin and temptation to come; "Then," saith he, "shall I be upright, I shall be innocent from the GREAT transgression" (Ps. xix. 13). By this very word was I galled and condemned, quite through this long temptation.

239. That also was another word that did much condemn me for my folly, in the neglect of this duty (Heb. iv. 16), "Let us therefore come boldly unto the throne of grace, that we may obtain mercy, and find grace to help in time of need." This I had not done, and therefore was suffered thus to sin and fall, according to what is written, "Pray that ye enter not into temptation." And truly this very thing is to this day of such weight and awe upon me, that I dare not, when I come before the Lord, go off my knees, until I entreat him for help and mercy against the temptations that are to come; and I do beseech thee, reader, that thou

learn to beware of my negligence, by the affliction that for this thing I did for days, and months, and years, with sorrow undergo.

240. Another cause of this temptation was, that I had tempted God; and on this manner did I do it. Upon a time my wife was great with child, and before her full time was come, her pangs, as of a woman in travail, were fierce and strong upon her, even as if she would have immediately fallen in labour, and been delivered of an untimely birth. Now, at this very time it was that I had been so strongly tempted to question the being of God; wherefore, as my wife lay crying by me, I said, but with all secrecy imaginable, even thinking in my heart, Lord, if thou wilt now remove this sad affliction from my wife, and cause that she be troubled no more therewith this night, and now were her pangs just upon her, then I shall know that thou canst discern the most secret thoughts of the heart.

241. I had no sooner said it in my heart, but her pangs were taken from her, and she was cast into a deep sleep, and so she continued till morning; at this I greatly marvelled, not knowing what to think; but after I had been awake a good while, and heard her cry no more, I fell to sleeping also. So when I waked in the morning, it came upon me again, even what I had said in my heart the last night, and how the Lord had showed me that he knew my secret thoughts, which was a great astonishment unto me for several weeks after.

242. Well, about a year and a half afterwards, that wicked sinful thought, of which I have spoken before, went through my wicked heart, even this thought, Let Christ go if he will; so when I was fallen under guilt for this, the remembrance of my other thought, and of the effect thereof, would also come upon me with this retort, which also carried rebuke along with it, Now you may see that God doth know the most secret thoughts of the heart.

243. And with this, that of the passages that were betwixt the Lord and his servant Gideon fell upon my spirit; how because that Gideon tempted God with his fleece, both wet and dry, when he should have believed and ventured upon his word, therefore the Lord did afterwards so try him, as to send him against an innumerable company of enemies;

and that too, as to outward appearance, without any strength or help (Judges vi., vii.). Thus he served me, and that justly, for I should have believed his word, and not have put an IF upon the all-seeingness of God.

244. And now to show you something of the advantages that I also gained by this temptation; and first, By this I was made continually to possess in my soul a very wonderful sense both of the being and glory of God, and of his beloved Son; in the temptation that went before, my soul was perplexed with unbelief, blasphemy, hardness of heart, questions about the being of God, Christ, the truth of the Word, and certainty of the world to come; I say, then I was greatly assaulted and tormented with atheism; but now the case was otherwise, now was God and Christ continually before my face, though not in a way of comfort, but in a way of exceeding dread and terror. The glory of the holiness of God did at this time break me to pieces; and the bowels and compassion of Christ did break me as on the wheel; for I could not consider him but as a lost and rejected Christ, the remembrance of which was as the continual breaking of my bones.

245. The Scriptures now also were wonderful things unto me; I saw that the truth and verity of them were the keys of the kingdom of heaven; those that the Scriptures favour they must inherit bliss, but those that they oppose and condemn must perish evermore. Oh! this word, "For the Scripture cannot be broken," would rend the caul of my heart; and so would that other, "Whose soever sins ye remit, they are remitted unto them; and whose soever sins ye retain, they are retained." Now I saw the apostles to be the elders of the city of refuge (Josh. xx. 4), those that they were to receive in, were received to life; but those that they shut out were to be slain by the avenger of blood.

246. Oh! one sentence of the Scriptures did more afflict and terrify my mind, I mean those sentences that stood against me, as sometimes I thought they every one did, more I say, than an army of forty thousand men that might have come against me. Woe be to him against whom the Scriptures bend themselves.

247. By this temptation I was made to see more into the nature of the promises than ever I was before; for I lying

now trembling under the mighty hand of God, continually torn and rent by the thunderings of his justice; this made me, with careful heart and watchful eye, with great seriousness, to turn over every leaf, and with much diligence, mixed with trembling, to consider every sentence, together with its natural force and latitude.

248. By this temptation, also, I was greatly beaten off my former foolish practice, of putting by the word of promise when it came into my mind; for now, though I could not suck that comfort and sweetness from the promise as I had done at other times, yea, like to a man a-sinking, I should catch at all I saw; formerly I thought I might not meddle with the promise unless I felt its comfort, but now it was no time thus to do, the avenger of blood too hardly did pursue me.

249. Now therefore I was glad to catch at that word, which yet I feared I had no ground or right to own; and even to leap into the bosom of that promise, that yet I feared did shut its heart against me. Now also I should labour to take the Word as God had laid it down, without restraining the natural force of one syllable thereof. O what did I now see in that blessed sixth of John, "And him that cometh to me I will in no wise cast out" (ver. 37). Now I began to consider with myself, that God had a bigger mouth to speak with than I had heart to conceive with. I thought also with myself that he spake not his words in haste, or in unadvised heat, but with infinite wisdom and judgment, and in very truth and faithfulness (2 Sam. iii. 18).

250. I should in these days, often in my greatest agonies, even flounce towards the promise, as the horses do towards sound ground that yet stick in the mire, concluding, though as one almost bereft of his wits through fear, on this I will rest and stay, and leave the fulfilling of it to the God of heaven that made it. Oh! many a pull hath my heart had with Satan for that blessed sixth of John. I did not now, as at other times, look principally for comfort, though, O how welcome would it have been unto me! But now a word, a word to lean a weary soul upon, that I might not sink for ever! it was that I hunted for.

251. Yea, often when I have been making to the promise, I have seen as if the Lord would refuse my soul for ever.

I was often as if I had run upon the pikes, and as if the Lord had thrust at me to keep me from him as with a flaming sword. Then I should think of Esther, who went to petition the king contrary to the law (Es. iv. 16). I thought also of Benhadad's servants, who went with ropes upon their heads to their enemies for mercy (1 Kings xx. 31). The woman of Canaan also, that would not be daunted, though called dog by Christ (Matt. xv. 20-8); and the man that went to borrow bread at midnight (Luke xi. 5-8), were great encouragements unto me.

252. I never saw those heights and depths in grace, and love, and mercy, as I saw after this temptation. Great sins do draw out great grace; and where guilt is most terrible and fierce there the mercy of God in Christ, when showed to the soul, appears most high and mighty. When Job had passed through his captivity, he had "twice as much as he had before" (Job xlii. 10). Blessed be God for Jesus Christ our Lord. Many other things I might here make observation of, but I would be brief, and therefore shall at this time omit them, and do pray God that my harms may make others fear to offend, lest they also be made to bear the iron yoke as I did.

I had two or three times, at or about my deliverance from this temptation, such strange apprehensions of the grace of God, that I could hardly bear up under it, it was so out of measure amazing, when I thought it could reach me, that I do think, if that sense of it had abode long upon me, it would have made me incapable for business.

253. Now I shall go forward to give you a relation of other of the Lord's dealings with me, of his dealings with me at sundry other seasons, and of the temptations I then did meet withal. I shall begin with what I met with when I first did join in fellowship with the people of God in Bedford. After I had propounded to the church that my desire was to walk in the order and ordinances of Christ with them, and was also admitted by them; while I thought of that blessed ordinance of Christ, which was his last supper with his disciples before his death, that scripture, "This do in remembrance of me" (Luke xxii. 19), was made a very precious word unto me; for by it the Lord did come down upon my conscience with the discovery of his death for my sins; and

as I then felt, did as if he plunged me in the virtue of the same. But, behold, I had not been long a partaker at that ordinance, but such fierce and sad temptations did attend me at all times therein, both to blaspheme the ordinance, and to wish some deadly thing to those that then did eat thereof; that, lest I should at any time be guilty of consenting to these wicked and fearful thoughts, I was forced to bend myself all the while to pray to God to keep me from such blasphemies; and also to cry to God to bless the bread and cup to them as it went from mouth to mouth. The reason of this temptation I have thought since was, because I did not, with that reverence as became me, at first approach to partake thereof.

254. Thus I continued for three-quarters of a year, and could never have rest nor ease; but at last the Lord came in upon my soul with that same scripture by which my soul was visited before; and after that I have been usually very well and comfortable in the partaking of that blessed ordinance, and have, I trust, therein discerned the Lord's body as broken for my sins, and that his precious blood hath been shed for my transgressions.

255. Upon a time I was somewhat inclining to a consumption, wherewith, about the spring, I was suddenly and violently seized with much weakness in my outward man, insomuch that I thought I could not live. Now began I afresh to give myself up to a serious examination after my state and condition for the future, and of my evidences for that blessed world to come; for it hath, I bless the name of God, been my usual course, as always, so especially in the day of affliction, to endeavour to keep my interest in the life to come clear before my eye.

256. But I had no sooner began to recal to mind my former experience of the goodness of God to my soul, but there came flocking into my mind an innumerable company of my sins and transgressions, amongst which these were at this time most to my affliction, namely, my deadness, dulness, and coldness in holy duties; my wanderings of heart, of my wearisomeness in all good things, my want of love to God, his ways, and people, with this at the end of all, Are these the fruits of Christianity? are these the tokens of a blessed man?

257. At the apprehension of these things my sickness was doubled upon me, for now was I sick in my inward man, my soul was clogged with guilt; now also was my former experience of God's goodness to me quite taken out of my mind, and hid as if it had never been, nor seen. Now was my soul greatly pinched between these two considerations, Live I must not, Die I dare not; now I sunk and fell in my spirit, and was giving up all for lost; but as I was walking up and down in the house, as a man in a most woful state, that word of God took hold of my heart, Ye are "justified freely by his grace, through the redemption that is in Christ Jesus" (Rom. iii. 24). But oh, what a turn it made upon me!

258. Now was I as one awakened out of some troublesome sleep and dream, and listening to this heavenly sentence, I was as if I had heard it thus expounded to me: Sinner, thou thinkest that because of thy sins and infirmities I cannot save thy soul, but behold my Son is by me, and upon him I look, and not on thee, and will deal with thee according as I am pleased with him. At this I was greatly lightened in my mind, and made to understand that God could justify a sinner at any time; it was but his looking upon Christ, and imputing of his benefits to us, and the work was forthwith done.

259. And as I was thus in a muse, that scripture also came with great power upon my spirit, "Not by works of righteousness which we have done, but according to his mercy he saved us," etc. (Tit. iii. 5; 2 Tim. i. 9). Now was I got on high; I saw myself within the arms of grace and mercy; and though I was before afraid to think of a dying hour, yet now I cried, Let me die. Now death was lovely and beautiful in my sight; for I saw we shall never live indeed till we be gone to the other world. Oh, methought this life is but a slumber in comparison of that above; at this time also I saw more in those words, "Heirs of God" (Rom. viii. 17), than ever I shall be able to express while I live in this world. "Heirs of God"! God himself is the portion of the saints. This I saw and wondered at, but cannot tell you what I saw.

260. Again, as I was at another time very ill and weak, all that time also the tempter did beset me strongly, for I find he is much for assaulting the soul when it begins to

approach towards the grave, then is his opportunity, labouring to hide from me my former experience of God's goodness; also setting before me the terrors of death and the judgment of God, insomuch that at this time, through my fear of miscarrying for ever, should I now die, I was as one dead before death came, and was as if I had felt myself already descending into the pit; methought, I said, there was no way, but to hell I must; but behold, just as I was in the midst of those fears, these words of the angels carrying Lazarus into Abraham's bosom darted in upon me, as who should say, So it shall be with thee when thou dost leave this world. This did sweetly revive my spirit, and help me to hope in God; which, when I had with comfort mused on a while, that word fell with great weight upon my mind, "O death, where *is* thy sting? O grave, where *is* thy victory?" (1 Cor. xv. 55). At this I became both well in body and mind at once, for my sickness did presently vanish, and I walked comfortably in my work for God again.

261. At another time, though just before I was pretty well and savoury in my spirit, yet suddenly there fell upon me a great cloud of darkness, which did so hide from me the things of God and Christ, that I was as if I had never seen or known them in my life; I was also so overrun in my soul, with a senseless, heartless frame of spirit, that I could not feel my soul to move or stir after grace and life by Christ; I was as if my loins were broken, or as if my hands and feet had been tied or bound with chains. At this time also I felt some weakness to seize upon my outward man, which made still the other affliction the more heavy and uncomfortable to me.

262. After I had been in this condition some three or four days, as I was sitting by the fire, I suddenly felt this word to sound in my heart, I must go to Jesus; at this my former darkness and atheism fled away, and the blessed things of heaven were set within my view. While I was on this sudden thus overtaken with surprise, Wife, said I, is there ever such a scripture, I must go to Jesus? She said she could not tell, therefore I sat musing still to see if I could remember such a place; I had not sat above two or three minutes but that came bolting in upon me, "And to an innumerable company of angels," and withal, Hebrews the twelfth, about the mount Sion, was set before mine eyes (ver. 22-4).

263. Then with joy I told my wife, O now I know, I know! But that night was a good night to me, I never had but few better; I longed for the company of some of God's people that I might have imparted unto them what God had showed me. Christ was a precious Christ to my soul that night; I could scarce lie in my bed for joy, and peace, and triumph, through Christ; this great glory did not continue upon me until morning, yet that twelfth of the author to the Hebrews (ver. 22-4) was a blessed scripture to me for many days together after this.

264. The words are these, "Ye are come unto mount Sion, and unto the city of the living God, the heavenly Jerusalem, and to an innumerable company of angels, to the general assembly and church of the firstborn, which are written in heaven, and to God the Judge of all, and to the spirits of just men made perfect, and to Jesus the mediator of the new covenant, and to the blood of sprinkling, that speaketh better things than *that of* Abel." Through this blessed sentence the Lord led me over and over, first to this word, and then to that, and showed me wonderful glory in every one of them. These words also have oft since this time been great refreshment to my spirit. Blessed be God for having mercy on me.

A BRIEF ACCOUNT OF THE AUTHOR'S CALL TO THE WORK OF THE MINISTRY

265. And now I am speaking my experience, I will in this place thrust in a word or two concerning my preaching the Word, and of God's dealing with me in that particular also. For after I had been about five or six years awakened, and helped myself to see both the want and worth of Jesus Christ our Lord, and also enabled to venture my soul upon him, some of the most able among the saints with us, I say the most able for judgment and holiness of life, as they conceived, did perceive that God had counted me worthy to understand something of his will in his holy and blessed Word, and had given me utterance, in some measure, to express what I saw to others for edification; therefore they

desired me, and that with much earnestness, that I would
be willing, at sometimes, to take in hand, in one of the
meetings, to speak a word of exhortation unto them.

266. The which, though at the first it did much dash and
abash my spirit, yet being still by them desired and in-
treated, I consented to their request, and did twice at two
several assemblies, but in private, though with much weakness and infirmity, discover my gift amongst them; at which
they not only seemed to be, but did solemnly protest, as
in the sight of the great God, they were both affected and
comforted, and gave thanks to the Father of mercies for the
grace bestowed on me.

267. After this, sometimes when some of them did go into
the country to teach, they would also that I should go with
them; where, though as yet I did not, nor durst not, make
use of my gift in an open way, yet more privately still as I
came amongst the good people in those places, I did sometimes speak a word of admonition unto them also; the which,
they as the other received, with rejoicing, at the mercy of
God to me-ward, professing their souls were edified thereby.

268. Wherefore, to be brief, at last, being still desired by
the church, after some solemn prayer to the Lord, with
fasting, I was more particularly called forth, and appointed
to a more ordinary and public preaching the word, not only
to, and amongst them that believed, but also to offer the
gospel to those who had not yet received the faith thereof;
about which time I did evidently find in my mind a secret
pricking forward thereto; though I bless God, not for desire
of vain glory, for at that time I was most sorely afflicted with
the fiery darts of the devil concerning my eternal state.

269. But yet could not be content, unless I was found in
the exercise of my gift, unto which also I was greatly ani-
mated, not only by the continual desires of the godly, but
also by that saying of Paul to the Corinthians, "I beseech
you, brethren, (ye know the household of Stephanas, that
it is the firstfruits of Achaia, and *that* they have addicted
themselves to the ministry of the saints,) that ye submit
yourselves unto such, and to every one that helpeth with
us, and laboureth" (1 Cor. xvi. 15, 16).

270. By this text I was made to see that the Holy Ghost
never intended that men who have gift and abilities should

bury them in the earth, but rather did command and stir up such to the exercise of their gift, and also did commend those that were apt and ready so to do, "They have addicted themselves to the ministry of the saints." This scripture, in these days, did continually run in my mind, to encourage me and strengthen me in this my work for God; I have also been encouraged from several other scriptures and examples of the godly, both specified in the Word and other ancient histories (Acts viii. 4; xviii. 24, 25; I Pet. iv. 10; Rom. xii. 6; Foxe's *Acts and Monuments*).

271. Wherefore, though of myself, of all the saints the most unworthy, yet I, but with great fear and trembling at the sight of my own weakness, did set upon the work, and did according to my gift, and the proportion of my faith, preach that blessed gospel that God had showed me in the holy Word of truth; which, when the country understood, they came in to hear the Word by hundreds, and that from all parts, though upon sundry and divers accounts.

272. And I thank God he gave unto me some measure of bowels and pity for their souls, which also did put me forward to labour with great diligence and earnestness, to find out such a word as might, if God would bless it, lay hold of and awaken the conscience, in which also the good Lord had respect to the desire of his servant; for I had not preached long before some began to be touched by the Word, and to be greatly afflicted in their minds at the apprehension of the greatness of their sin, and of their need of Jesus Christ.

273. But I at first could not believe that God should speak by me to the heart of any man, still counting myself unworthy; yet those who thus were touched would love me and have a peculiar respect for me; and though I did put it from me, that they should be awakened by me, still they would confess it, and affirm it before the saints of God; they would also bless God for me, unworthy wretch that I am! and count me God's instrument that showed to them the way of salvation.

274. Wherefore, seeing them in both their words and deeds to be so constant, and also in their hearts so earnestly pressing after the knowledge of Jesus Christ, rejoicing that ever God did send me where they were; then I began to conclude it might be so, that God had owned in his work such a foolish

one as I, and then came that word of God to my heart with
much sweet refreshment, "The blessing of him that was
ready to perish came upon me; and I caused the widow's
heart to sing for joy" (Job xxix. 13).

275. At this therefore I rejoiced, yea, the tears of those
whom God did awaken by my preaching would be both
solace and encouragement to me; for I thought on those
sayings, "Who is he that maketh me glad but the same
which is made sorry by me?" (2 Cor. ii. 2); and again, Though
"I be not an apostle to others, yet, doubtless, I am to you:
for the seal of mine apostleship are ye in the Lord" (1 Cor.
ix. 2). These things, therefore, were as another argument
unto me that God had called me to, and stood by me in
this work.

276. In my preaching of the Word, I took special notice
of this one thing, namely, that the Lord did lead me to
begin where his Word begins with sinners; that is, to condemn all flesh, and to open and allege that the curse of God,
by the law, doth belong to and lay hold on all men as they
come into the world, because of sin. Now this part of my
work I fulfilled with great sense; for the terrors of the law,
and guilt for my transgressions, lay heavy on my conscience.
I preached what I felt, what I smartingly did feel, even
that under which my poor soul did groan and tremble
to astonishment.

277. Indeed I have been as one sent to them from the
dead; I went myself in chains to preach to them in chains;
and carried that fire in my own conscience that I persuaded
them to beware of. I can truly say, and that without dissembling, that when I have been to preach, I have gone
full of guilt and terror even to the pulpit door, and there
it hath been taken off, and I have been at liberty in my
mind until I have done my work, and then immediately,
even before I could get down the pulpit stairs, I have been
as bad as I was before; yet God carried me on, but surely
with a strong hand, for neither guilt nor hell could take me
off my work.

278. Thus I went for the space of two years, crying out
against men's sins, and their fearful state because of them.
After which the Lord came in upon my own soul with some
staid peace and comfort through Christ; for he did give me

many sweet discoveries of his blessed grace through him. Wherefore now I altered in my preaching, for still I preached what I saw and felt; now therefore I did much labour to hold forth Jesus Christ in all his offices, relations, and benefits unto the world; and did strive also to discover, to condemn, and remove those false supports and props on which the world doth both lean, and by them fall and perish. On these things also I staid as long as on the other.

279. After this, God led me into something of the mystery of union with Christ; wherefore that I discovered and showed to them also. And when I had travelled through these three chief points of the Word of God, about the space of five years or more, I was caught in my present practice and cast into prison, where I have lain above as long again, to confirm the truth by way of suffering, as I was before in testifying of it according to the Scriptures in a way of preaching.

280. When I have been preaching, I thank God, my heart hath often all the time of this and the other exercise, with great earnestness, cried to God that he would make the Word effectual to the salvation of the soul; still being grieved lest the enemy should take the Word away from the conscience, and so it should become unfruitful. Wherefore I did labour so to speak the Word, as that thereby, if it were possible, the sin and person guilty might be particularised by it.

281. Also, when I have done the exercise, it hath gone to my heart to think the Word should now fall as rain on stony places, still wishing from my heart, O that they who have heard me speak this day did but see as I do what sin, death, hell, and the curse of God is; and also what the grace, and love, and mercy of God is, through Christ, to men in such a case as they are, who are yet estranged from him. And, indeed, I did often say in my heart before the Lord, That if to be hanged up presently before their eyes would be a means to awaken them, and confirm them in the truth, I gladly should be contented.

282. For I have been in my preaching, especially when I have been engaged in the doctrine of life by Christ, without works, as if an angel of God had stood by at my back to encourage me. Oh, it hath been with such power and heavenly evidence upon my own soul, while I have been labouring to unfold it, to demonstrate it, and to fasten it upon the con-

sciences of others, that I could not be contented with saying, I believe, and am sure; methought I was more than sure, if it be lawful so to express myself, that those things which then I asserted were true.

283. When I went first to preach the Word abroad, the doctors and priests of the country did open wide against me. But I was persuaded of this, not to render railing for railing, but to see how many of their carnal professors I could convince of their miserable state by the law, and of the want and worth of Christ; for, thought I, This shall answer for me in time to come, when they shall be for my hire before their faces (Gen. xxx. 33).

284. I never cared to meddle with things that were controverted, and in dispute amongst the saints, especially things of the lowest nature; yet it pleased me much to contend with great earnestness for the word of faith and the remission of sins by the death and sufferings of Jesus; but I say, as to other things, I should let them alone, because I saw they engendered strife, and because that they neither, in doing nor in leaving undone, did commend us to God to be his. Besides, I saw my work before me did run in another channel even to carry an awakening word; to that therefore did I stick and adhere.

285. I never endeavoured to, nor durst make use of other men's lines (Rom. xv. 18), though I condemn not all that do, for I verily thought, and found by experience, that what was taught me by the Word and Spirit of Christ, could be spoken, maintained, and stood to by the soundest and best established conscience; and though I will not now speak all that I know in this matter, yet my experience hath more interest in that text of Scripture than many amongst men are aware (Gal. i. 11, 12).

286. If any of those who were awakened by my ministry did after that fall back, as sometimes too many did, I can truly say their loss hath been more to me than if one of my own children, begotten of my body, had been going to its grave; I think, verily, I may speak it without an offence to the Lord, nothing hath gone so near me as that, unless it was the fear of the loss of the salvation of my own soul. I have counted as if I had goodly buildings and lordships in those places where my children were born; my heart hath

been so wrapped up in the glory of this excellent work, that
I counted myself more blessed and honoured of God by this
than if he had made me the emperor of the Christian world,
or the lord of all the glory of the earth without it! O these
words, "He which converteth the sinner from the error of
his way shall save a soul from death" (Jas. v. 20). "The
fruit of the righteous *is* a tree of life; and he that winneth
souls *is* wise" (Prov. xi. 30). "They that be wise shall shine
as the brightness of the firmament; and they that turn
many to righteousness as the stars for ever and ever"
(Dan. xii. 3). "For what is our hope, or joy, or crown of
rejoicing? *Are* not even ye in the presence of our Lord Jesus
Christ at his coming? For ye are our glory and joy" (1 Thess.
ii. 19, 20). These, I say, with many others of a like nature,
have been great refreshments to me.

287. I have observed, that where I have had a work to
do for God, I have had first, as it were, the going of God
upon my spirit to desire I might preach there. I have also
observed that such and such souls in particular have been
strongly set upon my heart, and I stirred up to wish for their
salvation; and that these very souls have, after this, been
given in as the fruits of my ministry. I have also observed,
that a word cast in by the by hath done more execution in
a sermon than all that was spoken besides; sometimes also
when I have thought I did no good, then I did the most
of all; and at other times when I thought I should catch
them I have fished for nothing.

288. I have also observed, that where there hath been a
work to do upon sinners, there the devil hath begun to roar
in the hearts, and by the mouths of his servants. Yea, oftentimes when the wicked world hath raged most, there hath
been souls awaked by the Word. I could instance particulars,
but I forbear.

289. My great desire in my fulfilling my ministry was to
get into the darkest places of the country, even amongst
those people that were farthest off of profession; yet not
because I could not endure the light, for I feared not to
show my gospel to any, but because I found my spirit leaned
most after awakening and converting work, and the Word
that I carried did lead itself most that way also; "yea, so
have I strived to preach the gospel, not where Christ was

named, lest I should build upon another man's foundation"
(Rom. xv. 20).

290. In my preaching I have really been in pain, and
have, as it were, travailed to bring forth children to God;
neither could I be satisfied unless some fruits did appear in
my work. If I were fruitless it mattered not who commended
me; but if I were fruitful, I cared not who did condemn.
I have thought of that, "He that winneth souls *is* wise"
(Prov. xi. 30); and again, "Lo, children *are* an heritage of
the Lord; *and* the fruit of the womb *is his* reward. As arrows
in the hand of a mighty man, so *are* children of the youth.
Happy *is* the man that hath filled his quiver full of them;
they shall not be ashamed, but they shall speak with the
enemies in the gate" (Ps. cxxvii. 3–5).

291. It pleased me nothing to see people drink in opinions
if they seemed ignorant of Jesus Christ, and the worth of
their own salvation, sound conviction for sin, especially for
unbelief, and an heart set on fire to be saved by Christ, with
strong breathing after a truly sanctified soul; that it was that
delighted me; those were the souls I counted blessed.

292. But in this work, as in all other, I had my temptations attending me, and that of diverse kinds, as sometimes
I should be assaulted with great discouragement therein,
fearing that I should not be able to speak the Word at all
to edification; nay, that I should not be able to speak sense
unto the people; at which times I should have such a strange
faintness and strengthlessness seize upon my body that
my legs have scarce been able to carry me to the place
of exercise.

293. Sometimes, again, when I have been preaching, I
have been violently assaulted with thoughts of blasphemy,
and strongly tempted to speak the words with my mouth
before the congregation. I have also at some times, even
when I have begun to speak the Word with much clearness,
evidence, and liberty of speech, yet been before the ending
of that opportunity so blinded, and so estranged from the
things I have been speaking, and have also been so straitened
in my speech, as to utterance before the people, that I have
been as if I had not known or remembered what I have
been about, or as if my head had been in a bag all the time
of the exercise.

294. Again, when as sometimes I have been about to preach upon some smart and scorching portion of the Word, I have found the tempter suggest, What, will you preach this? this condemns yourself; of this your own soul is guilty; wherefore preach not of it at all; or if you do, yet so mince it as to make way for your own escape; lest instead of awakening others, you lay that guilt upon your own soul, as you will never get from under.

295. But, I thank the Lord, I have been kept from consenting to these so horrid suggestions, and have rather, as Samson, bowed myself with all my might, to condemn sin and transgression wherever I found it, yea, though therein also I did bring guilt upon my own conscience! "Let me die," thought I, "with the Philistines" (Judges xvi. 29, 30), rather than deal corruptly with the blessed Word of God, "Thou that teachest another, teachest not thou thyself?" It is far better that thou do judge thyself, even by preaching plainly to others, than that thou, to save thyself, imprison the truth in unrighteousness; blessed be God for his help also in this.

296. I have also, while found in this blessed work of Christ, been often tempted to pride and liftings up of heart; and though I dare not say I have not been infected with this, yet truly the Lord, of his precious mercy, hath so carried it towards me, that, for the most part, I have had but small joy to give way to such a thing; for it hath been my every day's portion to be let into the evil of my own heart, and still made to see such a multitude of corruptions and infirmities therein, that it hath caused hanging down of the head under all my gifts and attainments; I have felt this thorn in the flesh, the very mercy of God to me (2 Cor. xii. 7–9).

297. I have had also, together with this, some notable place or other of the Word presented before me, which word hath contained in it some sharp and piercing sentence concerning the perishing of the soul, notwithstanding gifts and parts; as, for instance, that hath been of great use unto me, "Though I speak with the tongues of men and of angels, and have not charity, I am become as sounding brass, and a tinkling cymbal" (1 Cor. xiii. 1, 2).

298. A tinkling cymbal is an instrument of music, with

which a skilful player can make such melodious and heart-inflaming music, that all who hear him play can scarcely hold from dancing; and yet behold the cymbal hath not life, neither comes the music from it, but because of the art of him that plays therewith; so then the instrument at last may come to naught and perish, though, in times past, such music hath been made upon it.

299. Just thus I saw it was and will be with them who have gifts, but want saving grace, they are in the hand of Christ, as the cymbal in the hand of David; and as David could, with the cymbal, make that mirth in the service of God, as to elevate the hearts of the worshippers, so Christ can use these gifted men, as with them to affect the souls of his people in his church; yet when he hath done all, hang them by as lifeless, though sounding cymbals.

300. This consideration, therefore, together with some others, were, for the most part, as a maul on the head of pride, and desire of vain glory; what, thought I, shall I be proud because I am a sounding brass? Is it so much to be a fiddle? Hath not the least creature that hath life, more of God in it than these? Besides, I knew it was love should never die, but these must cease and vanish; so I concluded, a little grace, a little love, a little of the true fear of God, is better than all these gifts; yea, and I am fully convinced of it, that it is possible for a soul that can scarce give a man an answer, but with great confusion as to method, I say it is possible for them to have a thousand times more grace, and so to be more in the love and favour of the Lord than some who, by virtue of the gift of knowledge, can deliver themselves like angels.

301. Thus, therefore, I came to perceive, that though gifts in themselves were good to the thing for which they are designed, to wit, the edification of others; yet empty and without power to save the soul of him that hath them, if they be alone; neither are they, as so, any sign of a man's state to be happy, being only a dispensation of God to some, of whose improvement, or non-improvement, they must, when a little love more is over, give an account to him that is ready to judge the quick and the dead.

302. This showed me, too, that gifts being alone, were dangerous, not in themselves, but because of those evils that

attend them that have them, to wit, pride, desire of vain glory, self-conceit, etc., all which were easily blown up at the applause and commendation of every unadvised Christian, to the endangering of a poor creature to fall into the condemnation of the devil.

303. I saw therefore that he that hath gifts had need be let into a sight of the nature of them, to wit, that they come short of making of him to be in a truly saved condition, lest he rest in them, and so fall short of the grace of God.

304. He hath also cause to walk humbly with God, and be little in his own eyes, and to remember withal, that his gifts are not his own, but the church's; and that by them he is made a servant to the church; and he must give at last an account of his stewardship unto the Lord Jesus; and to give a good account, will be a blessed thing.

305. Let all men therefore prize a little with the fear of the Lord; gifts indeed are desirable, but yet great grace and small gifts are better than great gifts and no grace. It doth not say, the Lord gives gifts and glory, but the Lord gives grace and glory; and blessed is such an one to whom the Lord gives grace, true grace, for that is a certain forerunner of glory.

306. But when Satan perceived that his thus tempting and assaulting of me would not answer his design, to wit, to overthrow my ministry, and make it ineffectual, as to the ends thereof; then he tried another way, which was to stir up the minds of the ignorant and malicious, to load me with slanders and reproaches; now therefore I may say, that what the devil could devise, and his instruments invent, was whirled up and down the country against me, thinking, as I said, that by that means they should make my ministry to be abandoned.

307. It began therefore to be rumoured up and down among the people, that I was a witch, a jesuit, a highwayman, and the like.

308. To all which, I shall only say, God knows that I am innocent. But as for mine accusers, let them provide themselves to meet me before the tribunal of the Son of God, there to answer for all these things, with all the rest of their iniquities, unless God shall give them repentance for them, for the which I pray with all my heart.

309. But that which was reported with the boldest con-

fidence, was, that I had my misses, my whores, my bastards, yea, two wives at once, and the like. Now these slanders, with the other, I glory in, because but slanders, foolish, or knavish lies, and falsehoods cast upon me by the devil and his seed; and should I not be dealt with thus wickedly by the world, I should want one sign of a saint, and a child of God. "Blessed are ye (said the Lord Jesus) when men shall revile you, and persecute you, and shall say all manner of evil against you falsely for my sake; rejoice, and be exceeding glad, for great *is* your reward in heaven; for so persecuted they the prophets which were before you" (Matt. v. 11).

310. These things, therefore, upon mine own account, trouble me not; no, though they were twenty times more than they are. I have a good conscience, and whereas they speak evil of me, as an evil doer, they shall be ashamed that falsely accuse my good conversation in Christ.

311. So then, what shall I say to those that have thus bespattered me? Shall I threaten them? Shall I chide them? Shall I flatter them? Shall I intreat them to hold their tongues? No, not I, were it not for that these things make them ripe for damnation, that are the authors and abettors, I would say unto them, Report it, because it will increase my glory.

312. Therefore I bind these lies and slanders to me as an ornament, it belongs to my Christian profession to be vilified, slandered, reproached and reviled; and since all this is nothing else, as my God and my conscience do bear me witness, I rejoice in reproaches for Christ's sake.

313. I also calling all those fools, or knaves, that have thus made it anything of their business to affirm any of the things afore-named of me, namely, that I have been naught with other women, or the like. When they have used to the utmost of their endeavours, and made the fullest inquiry that they can, to prove against me truly, that there is any woman in heaven, or earth, or hell, that can say, I have at any time, in any place, by day or night, so much as attempted to be naught with them; and speak I thus, to beg mine enemies into a good esteem of me? no, not I: I will in this beg relief of no man; believe or disbelieve me in this, all is a case to me.

314. My foes have missed their mark in this their shooting at me. I am not the man. I wish that they themselves be guiltless. If all the fornicators and adulterers in England were hanged by the neck till they be dead, JOHN BUNYAN, the object of their envy, would be still alive and well. I know not whether there be such a thing as a woman breathing under the copes of the whole heaven, but by their apparel, their children, or by common fame, except my wife.

315. And in this I admire the wisdom of God, that he made me shy of women from my first conversion until now. Those know, and can also bear me witness, with whom I have been most intimately concerned, that it is a rare thing to see me carry it pleasant towards a woman; the common salutation of a woman I abhor, it is odious to me in whomsoever I see it. Their company alone, I cannot away with. I seldom so much as touch a woman's hand, for I think these things are not so becoming me. When I have seen good men salute those women that they have visited, or that have visited them, I have at times made my objection against it, and when they have answered, that it was but a piece of civility, I have told them, it is not a comely sight; some indeed have urged the holy kiss; but then I have asked why they made baulks, why they did salute the most handsome, and let the ill-favoured go; thus, how laudable soever such things have been in the eyes of others, they have been unseemly in my sight.

316. And now for a wind up in this matter, I calling not only men, but angels, to prove me guilty of having carnally to do with any woman save my wife, nor am I afraid to do it a second time, knowing that I cannot offend the Lord in such a case, to call God for a record upon my soul, that in these things I am innocent. Not that I have been thus kept, because of any goodness in me more than any other, but God has been merciful to me, and has kept me; to whom I pray that he will keep me still, not only from this, but from every evil way and work, and preserve me to his heavenly kingdom. *Amen*.

317. Now as Satan laboured by reproaches and slanders, to make me vile among my countrymen, that, if possible, my preaching might be made of none effect, so there was added hereto a long and tedious imprisonment, that thereby

I might be frighted from my service for Christ, and the world terrified, and made afraid to hear me preach, of which I shall in the next place give you a brief account.

A BRIEF ACCOUNT OF THE AUTHOR'S
IMPRISONMENT

318. Having made profession of the glorious gospel of Christ a long time, and preached the same about five years, I was apprehended at a meeting of good people in the country, among whom, had they let me alone, I should have preached that day, but they took me away from amongst them, and had me before a justice; who, after I had offered security for my appearing at the next sessions, yet committed me, because my sureties would not consent to be bound that I should preach no more to the people.

319. At the sessions after, I was indicted for an upholder and maintainer of unlawful assemblies and conventicles, and for not conforming to the national worship of the Church of England; and after some conference there with the justices, they taking my plain dealing with them for a confession, as they termed it, of the indictment, did sentence me to perpetual banishment, because I refused to conform. So being again delivered up to the jailer's hands, I was had home to prison again, and there have lain now complete twelve years, waiting to see what God would suffer these men to do with me.

320. In which condition I have continued with much content, through grace, but have met with many turnings and goings upon my heart, both from the Lord, Satan, and my own corruptions; by all which, glory be to Jesus Christ, I have also received among many things, much conviction, instruction, and understanding, of which at large I shall not here discourse; only give you in a hint or two, a word that may stir up the godly to bless God, and to pray for me; and also to take encouragement, should the case be their own, not to fear what man can do unto them.

321. I never had in all my life so great an inlet into the Word of God as now; those Scriptures that I saw nothing in before, are made in this place and state to shine upon

me; Jesus Christ also was never more real and apparent than now; here I have seen him and felt him indeed: O that word, We have not preached unto you cunningly devised fables (2 Pet. i. 16); and that, God raised Christ from the dead, and gave him glory, that your faith and hope might be in God (1 Pet. i. 21), were blessed words unto me in this my imprisoned condition.

322. These three or four scriptures also have been great refreshment in this condition to me: John xiv. 1–4; John xvi. 33; Col. iii. 3, 4; Heb. xii. 22–4. So that sometimes when I have been in the savour of them, I have been able to laugh at destruction, and to fear neither the horse nor his rider (Job xxxix. 18). I have had sweet sights of the forgiveness of my sins in this place, and of my being with Jesus in another world: O, "the mount Zion, the heavenly Jerusalem, the innumerable company of angels, and God the judge of all, and the spirits of just men made perfect, and to Jesus" (Heb. xii. 22–4), have been sweet unto me in this place: I have seen THAT here, that I am persuaded I shall never, while in this world, be able to express; I have seen a truth in that scripture, "Whom having not seen, ye love; in whom, though now ye see *him* not, yet believing, ye rejoice with joy unspeakable and full of glory" (1 Pet. i. 8).

323. I never knew what it was for God to stand by me at all turns, and at every offer of Satan to afflict me, etc., as I have found him since I came in hither; for look how fears have presented themselves, so have supports and encouragements, yea, when I have started, even as it were at nothing else but my shadow, yet God, as being very tender of me, hath not suffered me to be molested, but would with one scripture and another strengthen me against all; insomuch that I have often said, Were it lawful, I could pray for greater trouble, for the greater comfort's sake (Eccles. vii. 14; 2 Cor. i. 5).

324. Before I came to prison, I saw what was a-coming, and had especially two considerations warm upon my heart; the first was how to be able to endure, should my imprisonment be long and tedious; the second was how to be able to encounter death, should that be here my portion; for the first of these, that scripture, Col. i. 11, was great information to me, namely, to pray to God to be "strengthened with

all might, according to his glorious power, unto all patience and longsuffering with joyfulness." I could seldom go to prayer before I was imprisoned, but not for so little as a year together, this sentence, or sweet petition, would, as it were, thrust itself into my mind, and persuade me, that if ever I would go through long-suffering, I must have all patience, especially if I would endure it joyfully.

325. As to the second consideration, that saying, 2 Cor. i. 9, was of great use to me, "But we had the sentence of death in ourselves, that we should not trust in ourselves, but in God which raiseth the dead." By this scripture I was made to see, that if ever I would suffer rightly, I must first pass a sentence of death upon everything that can properly be called a thing of this life, even to reckon myself, my wife, my children, my health, my enjoyments, and all, as dead to me, and myself as dead to them. "He that loveth father or mother, son or daughter, more than me, is not worthy of me" (Matt. x. 37).

326. The second was, to live upon God that is invisible; as Paul said in another place, the way not to faint, is to "look not at the things which are seen, but at the things which are not seen: for the things which are seen *are* temporal; but the things which are not seen *are* eternal" (2 Cor. iv. 18). And thus I reasoned with myself; if I provide only for a prison, then the whip comes at unawares; and so does also the pillory; again, if I provide only for these, then I am not fit for banishment; further, if I conclude that banishment is the worst, then if death come I am surprised. So that I see the best way to go through sufferings is to trust in God through Christ, as touching the world to come; and as touching this world, to count "the grave my house, to make my bed in darkness, and to say to corruption, Thou *art* my father, and to the worm, *Thou art* my mother and my sister." That is, to familiarise these things to me.

327. But notwithstanding these helps, I found myself a man, and compassed with infirmities; the parting with my wife and poor children hath oft been to me in this place as the pulling the flesh from my bones, and that not only because I am somewhat too too fond of those great mercies, but also because I should have often brought to my mind the many hardships, miseries and wants that my poor family was like

to meet with, should I be taken from them, especially my poor blind child, who lay nearer my heart than all I had besides; O the thoughts of the hardship I thought my blind one might go under, would break my heart to pieces.

328. Poor child, thought I, what sorrow art thou like to have for thy portion in this world? Thou must be beaten, must beg, suffer hunger, cold, nakedness, and a thousand calamities, though I cannot now endure the wind should blow upon thee. But yet recalling myself, thought I, I must venture you all with God, though it goeth to the quick to leave you. Oh, I saw in this condition I was as a man who was pulling down his house upon the head of his wife and children; yet thought I, I must do it, I must do it. And now I thought on those two milch kine that were to carry the ark of God into another country, and to leave their calves behind them (1 Sam. vi. 10-12).

329. But that which helped me in this temptation was divers considerations, of which three in special here I will name; the first was the consideration of those two scriptures, "Leave thy fatherless children, I will preserve *them* alive, and let thy widows trust in me"; and again, "The Lord said, Verily it shall *be* well with thy remnant; verily I will cause the enemy to entreat thee *well* in the time of evil," etc. (Jer. xlix. 11; xv. 11).

330. I had also this consideration, that if I should now venture all for God, I engaged God to take care of my concernments; but if I forsook him and his ways, for fear of any trouble that should come to me or mine, then I should not only falsify my profession, but should count also that my concernments were not so sure, if left at God's feet, while I stood to and for his name, as they would be, if they were under my own tuition, though with the denial of the way of God. This was a smarting consideration, and was as spurs unto my flesh. That scripture also greatly helped it to fasten the more upon me, where Christ prays against Judas, that God would disappoint him in all his selfish thoughts, which moved him to sell his master: pray read it soberly, Ps. cix. 6-20.

331. I had also another consideration, and that was, the dread of the torments of hell, which I was sure they must partake of, that for fear of the cross, do shrink from their profession of Christ, his words, and laws, before the sons of

men: I thought also of the glory that he had prepared for those that, in faith, and love, and patience, stood to his ways before them. These things, I say, have helped me, when the thoughts of the misery that both myself and mine, might for the sake of my profession be exposed to, hath lain pinching on my mind.

332. When I have indeed conceited that I might be banished for my profession, then I have thought of that scripture, "They were stoned, they were sawn asunder, were tempted, were slain with the sword; they wandered about in sheepskins and goatskins; being destitute, afflicted, tormented, of whom the world was not worthy" (Heb. xi. 37), for all they thought they were too bad to dwell and abide amongst them. I have also thought of that saying, "The Holy Ghost witnesseth in every city, that bonds and afflictions abide me." I have verily thought that my soul and it have sometimes reasoned about the sore and sad estate of a banished and exiled condition, how they are exposed to hunger, to cold, to perils, to nakedness, to enemies, and a thousand calamities; and at last, it may be, to die in a ditch, like a poor forlorn and desolate sheep. But I thank God, hitherto I have not been moved by these most delicate reasonings, but have rather, by them, more approved my heart to God.

333. I will tell you a pretty business; I was once above all the rest in a very sad and low condition for many weeks; at which time also I being but a young prisoner, and not acquainted with the laws, had this lay much upon my spirit, That my imprisonment might end at the gallows for aught that I could tell. Now, therefore, Satan laid hard at me to beat me out of heart, by suggesting thus unto me, But how if when you come indeed to die, you should be in this condition; that is, as not to savour the things of God, nor to have any evidence upon your soul for a better state hereafter? For indeed at that time all the things of God were hid from my soul.

334. Wherefore, when I at first began to think of this, it was a great trouble to me; for I thought with myself, that in the condition I now was in, I was not fit to die, neither indeed did think I could, if I should be called to it: besides, I thought with myself, if I should make a scrabbling

shift to clamber up the ladder, yet I should either with quaking, or other symptoms of faintings, give occasion to the enemy to reproach the way of God and his people, for their timorousness. This therefore lay with great trouble upon me, for methought I was ashamed to die with a pale face, and tottering knees, for such a cause as this.

335. Wherefore, I prayed to God that he would comfort me, and give me strength to do and suffer what he should call me to; yet no comfort appeared, but all continued hid: I was also at this time so really possessed with the thought of death, that oft I was as if I was on the ladder with a rope about my neck; only this was some encouragement to me, I thought I might now have an opportunity to speak my last words to a multitude, which I thought would come to see me die; and, thought I, if it must be so, if God will but convert one soul by my very last words, I shall not count my life thrown away, nor lost.

336. But yet all the things of God were kept out of my sight, and still the tempter followed me with, But whither must you go when you die? What will become of you? Where will you be found in another world? What evidence have you for heaven and glory, and an inheritance among them that are sanctified? Thus was I tossed for many weeks, and knew not what to do; at last this consideration fell with weight upon me, That it was for the Word and way of God that I was in this condition, wherefore I was engaged not to flinch a hair's breadth from it.

337. I thought also, that God might choose whether he would give me comfort now or at the hour of death, but I might not therefore choose whether I would hold my profession or no: I was bound, but he was free: yea, it was my duty to stand to his word, whether he would ever look upon me or no, or save me at the last: wherefore, thought I, the point being thus, I am for going on, and venturing my eternal state with Christ, whether I have comfort here or no; if God doth not come in, thought I, I will leap off the ladder even blindfold into eternity, sink or swim, come heaven, come hell, Lord Jesus, if thou wilt catch me, do; if not, I will venture for thy name.

338. I was no sooner fixed upon this resolution, but that word dropped upon me, "Doth Job serve God for naught?"

As if the accuser had said, Lord, Job is no upright man, he
serves thee for by-respects: hast thou not made a hedge
about him, etc. "But put forth thine hand now, and touch
all that he hath, and he will curse thee to thy face." How
now, thought I, is this the sign of an upright soul, to desire
to serve God, that will serve God for nothing rather than
give out? Blessed be God, then, I hope I have an upright
heart, for I am resolved, God giving me strength, never to
deny my profession, though I have nothing at all for my
pains; and as I was thus considering, that scripture was
set before me, Ps. xliv. 12–26.

339. Now was my heart full of comfort, for I hoped it was
sincere: I would not have been without this trial for much;
I am comforted every time I think of it, and I hope I shall
bless God for ever for the teaching I have had by it. Many
more of the dealings of God towards me I might relate, but
these, "Out of the spoils won in battles have I dedicated to
maintain the house of the Lord" (1 Chron. xxvi. 27).

THE CONCLUSION

1. Of all the temptations that ever I met with in my life,
to question the being of God, and truth of his gospel, is the
worst, and the worst to be borne; when this temptation comes,
it takes away my girdle from me, and removeth the foundation from under me. Oh, I have often thought of that word,
"Have your loins girt about with truth"; and of that, "When
the foundations are destroyed, what can the righteous do?"

2. Sometimes, when, after sin committed, I have looked
for sore chastisement from the hand of God, the very next
that I have had from him hath been the discovery of his
grace. Sometimes, when I have been comforted, I have
called myself a fool for my so sinking under trouble. And
then, again, when I have been cast down, I thought I was
not wise to give such way to comfort. With such strength
and weight have both these been upon me.

3. I have wondered much at this one thing, that though
God doth visit my soul with never so blessed a discovery of

himself, yet I have found again, that such hours have attended me afterwards, that I have been in my spirit so filled with darkness, that I could not so much as once conceive what that God and that comfort was with which I have been refreshed.

4. I have sometimes seen more in a line of the Bible than I could well tell how to stand under, and yet at another time the whole Bible hath been to me as dry as a stick; or rather, my heart hath been so dead and dry unto it, that I could not conceive the least drachm of refreshment, though I have looked it all over.

5. Of all tears, they are the best that are made by the blood of Christ; and of all joy, that is the sweetest that is mixed with mourning over Christ. Oh! it is a goodly thing to be on our knees, with Christ in our arms, before God. I hope I know something of these things.

6. I find to this day seven abominations in my heart: (1) Inclinings to unbelief. (2) Suddenly to forget the love and mercy that Christ manifesteth. (3) A leaning to the works of the law. (4) Wanderings and coldness in prayer. (5) To forget to watch for that I pray for. (6) Apt to murmur because I have no more, and yet ready to abuse what I have. (7) I can do none of those things which God commands me, but my corruptions will thrust in themselves, "When I would do good, evil is present with me."

7. These things I continually see and feel, and am afflicted and oppressed with; yet the wisdom of God doth order them for my good. (1) They make me abhor myself. (2) They keep me from trusting my heart. (3) They convince me of the insufficiency of all inherent righteousness. (4) They show me the necessity of flying to Jesus. (5) They press me to pray unto God. (6) They show me the need I have to watch and be sober. (7) And provoke me to look to God, through Christ, to help me, and carry me through this world. Amen.

A RELATION OF THE IMPRISONMENT OF MR. JOHN BUNYAN, MINISTER OF THE GOSPEL AT BEDFORD, IN NOVEMBER 1660. HIS EXAMINATION BEFORE THE JUSTICES; HIS CONFERENCE WITH THE CLERK OF THE PEACE; WHAT PASSED BETWEEN THE JUDGES AND HIS WIFE WHEN SHE PRESENTED A PETITION FOR HIS DELIVERANCE, ETC.

The relation of my imprisonment in the month of November 1660, when, by the good hand of my God, I had for five or six years together, without any interruption, freely preached the blessed gospel of our Lord Jesus Christ ; and had also, through his blessed grace, some encouragement by his blessing thereupon ; the devil, that old enemy of man's salvation, took his opportunity to inflame the hearts of his vassals against me, insomuch that at the last I was laid out for by the warrant of a justice, and was taken and committed to prison. The relation thereof is as followeth :

Upon the 12th of this instant November 1660, I was desired by some of the friends in the country to come to teach at Samsell, by Harlington, in Bedfordshire. To whom I made a promise, if the Lord permitted, to be with them on the time aforesaid. The justice hearing thereof, whose name is Mr. Francis Wingate, forthwith issued out his warrant to take me, and bring me before him, and in the meantime to keep a very strong watch about the house where the meeting should be kept, as if we that were to meet together in that place did intend to do some fearful business, to the destruction of the country; when, alas, the constable, when he came in, found us only with our Bibles in our hands, ready to speak and hear the Word of God; for we were just about to begin our exercise. Nay, we had begun in prayer for the blessing of God upon our opportunity, intending to have preached the Word of the Lord unto them there present; but the constable coming in prevented us; so that I was taken and forced to depart the room. But had I been minded to have played the coward, I could have escaped, and kept out of his hands. For when I was come to my friend's house, there was whispering that that day I should be taken, for there was a warrant out to take me; which when my friend heard, he being somewhat timorous, questioned whether we had best have our meeting or not; and whether it might not be better for me to depart, lest they should take me and have me before the justice, and after that send me to prison, for he knew better than I what spirit they were of, living by them; to whom I said, No, by no means, I will not stir, neither will I have the meeting dismissed for this. Come, be of good cheer, let us not be daunted; our cause is good, we need not be ashamed of it; to preach God's Word is so good a work, that we shall be well rewarded, if we suffer for that; or to this purpose; but as for my friend, I think he was more afraid of [for] me, than of himself. After this I walked into the close, where, I somewhat seriously considering the matter, this came into my mind, That I had showed myself hearty and courageous in my preaching, and had, blessed be grace, made it my business to encourage others; therefore, thought I, if I should now run, and make an escape, it will be of a very ill savour in the country. For what will my weak and newly converted brethren think of it, but that I was not so strong in deed as I was in word? Also I feared that if I should run, now there was a warrant out for me, I might by so doing make them afraid to stand, when great words only should be spoken to them. Besides, I thought, that seeing God of his mercy should choose me to go upon the forlorn hope in this country; that is, to be the first that should be opposed, for the gospel; if I should fly, it might be a discouragement to the whole body that might follow after. And further, I thought the world thereby would take occasion at my cowardliness, to have blasphemed the gospel, and to have had some ground to suspect worse of me and my profession than I deserved. These things with others considered by me, I came in again to the house, with a full resolution to keep the meeting, and not to go away, though I could have been gone about an hour before the officer apprehended me; but I would not; for I was resolved to see the utmost of what they could say or do unto me. For blessed be the Lord, I knew of no evil that I had said or done. And so, as aforesaid, I began the meeting. But being prevented by the constable's coming in with his warrant to take me, I could not proceed. But before I went away, I spake some few words of counsel and encouragement to the people, declaring to them, that they saw we were prevented of our opportunity to speak and hear the Word of God, and were like to suffer for the same: desiring them that they should not be discouraged, for it was a mercy to suffer upon so good account. For we might have been apprehended as thieves or murderers, or for other wickedness; but blessed be God it was not so, but we suffer as Christians for well doing: and we had better be the persecuted than the persecutors, etc. But the constable and the justice's man waiting on us would not be at quiet till they had me away, and that we departed the house. But because the justice was not at home that day, there was a friend of mine engaged for me to bring me to the constable on the morrow morning. Otherwise the constable must have charged a watch with me, or have secured me some other ways, my crime was so great. So on the next morning we went to the constable, and so to the justice. He asked the constable what we did, where we were met together, and what we had with us? I trow he meant whether we had armour or not; but when the constable told him, that there were only met a few of us together to preach and hear the Word, and no sign of anything else, he could not well tell what to say: yet because he had sent for me, he did adventure to put out a few proposals to me, which were to this effect, namely, What I did there? and why I did not content myself with following my calling? for it was against the law, that such as I should be admitted to do as I did.

John Bunyan. To which I answered, that the intent of my coming thither, and to other places, was to instruct and counsel people to forsake their sins, and close in with Christ, lest they did miserably perish; and that I could do both these without confusion, to wit, follow my calling, and preach the Word also.

At which words, he was in a chafe, as it appeared; for he said that he would break the neck of our meetings.

Bun. I said, it may be so. Then he wished me to get sureties to be bound for me, or else he would send me to the jail.

My sureties being ready, I called them in, and when the bond for my appearance was made, he told them, that they were bound to keep me from preaching; and that if I did preach, their bonds would be forfeited. To which I answered, that then I should break them; for I should not leave speaking the Word of God: even to counsel, comfort, exhort, and teach the people among whom I came; and I thought this to be a work that had no hurt in it: but was rather worthy of commendation than blame.

Wingate. Whereat he told me, that if they would not be so bound, my mittimus must be made, and I sent to the jail, there to lie to the quarter-sessions.

Now while my mittimus was making, the justice was withdrawn; and in comes an old enemy to the truth, Dr. Lindale, who, when he was come in, fell to taunting at me with many reviling terms.

Bun. To whom I answered, that I did not come thither to talk with him, but with the justice. Whereat he supposed that I had nothing to say for myself, and triumphed as if he had got the victory; charging and condemning me for meddling with that for which I could show no warrant; and asked me, if I had taken the oaths? and if I had not, it was pity but that I should be sent to prison, etc.

I told him, that if I was minded, I could answer to any sober question that he should put to me. He then urged me again, how I could prove it lawful for me to preach, with a great deal of confidence of the victory.

But at last, because he should see that I could answer him if I listed, I cited to him that verse in Peter, which saith, "As every man hath received the gift, even so let him minister the same," etc.

Lind. Aye, saith he, to whom is that spoken?

Bun. To whom? said I; why, to every man that hath received a gift from God. Mark, saith the apostle, "As every man that hath received a gift from God," etc. And again, "You may all prophesy one by one." Whereat the man was a little stopt, and went a softlier pace: but not being willing to lose the day, he began again, and said:

Lind. Indeed I do remember that I have read of one Alexander a coppersmith, who did much oppose and disturb the apostles;—aiming, it is like, at me, because I was a tinker.

Bun. To which I answered, that I also had read of very many priests and pharisees that had their hands in the blood of our Lord Jesus Christ.

Lind. Aye, saith he, and you are one of those scribes and pharisees: for you, with a pretence, make long prayers to devour widows' houses.

Bun. I answered, that if he had got no more by preaching and praying than I had done, he would not be so rich as he now was. But that scripture coming into my mind, "Answer not a fool according to his folly," I was as sparing of my speech as I could, without prejudice to truth.

Now by this time my mittimus was made, and I committed to the constable to be sent to the jail in Bedford, etc.

But as I was going, two of my brethren met with me by the way, and desired the constable to stay, supposing that they should prevail with the justice, through the favour of a pretended friend, to let me go at liberty. So we did stay, while they went to the justice; and after much discourse with him, it came to this; that if I would come to him again, and say some certain words to him, I should be released. Which when they told me, I said if the words were such that might be said with a good conscience, I should, or, else, I should not. So through their importunity I went back again, but not believing that I should be delivered: for I feared their spirit was too full of opposition to the truth to let me go, unless I should in something or other dishonour my God, and wound my conscience. Wherefore, as I went, I lifted up my heart to God for light and strength to be kept, that I might not do anything that might either dishonour him, or wrong my own soul, or be a grief or discouragement to any that was inclining after the Lord Jesus Christ.

Well, when I came to the justice again, there was Mr. Foster of Bedford, who coming out of another room, and seeing of me by the light of the candle, for it was dark night when I came thither, he said unto me, Who is there? John Bunyan? with such seeming affection, as if he would have leaped on my neck and kissed me, which made me somewhat wonder, that such a man as he, with whom I had so little acquaintance, and, besides, that had ever been a close opposer of the ways of God, should carry himself so full of love to me; but, afterwards, when I saw what he did, it caused me to remember those sayings, "Their tongues are smoother than oil, but their words are drawn swords." And again, "Beware of men," etc. When I had answered him, that blessed be God I was well, he said, What is the occasion of your being here? or to that purpose. To whom I answered, that I was at a meeting of people a little way off, intending to speak a word of exhortation to them; but the justice hearing thereof, said I, was pleased to send his warrant to fetch me before him, etc.

Foster. So, said he, I understand; but well, if you will promise to call the people no more together, you shall have your liberty to go home; for my brother is very loath to send you to prison, if you will be but ruled.

Bun. Sir, said I, pray what do you mean by calling the people together? My business is not anything among them, when they are come together, but to exhort them to look after the salvation of their souls, that they may be saved, etc.

Fost. Saith he, We must not enter into explication or dispute now; but if you will say you will call the people no more together, you may have your liberty; if not, you must be sent away to prison.

Bun. Sir, said I, I shall not force or compel any man to hear me; but yet, if I come into any place where there is a people met together, I should, according to the best of my skill and wisdom, exhort and counsel them to seek out after the Lord Jesus Christ, for the salvation of their souls.

Fost. He said, that was none of my work; I must follow my calling; and if I would but leave off preaching, and follow my calling, I should have the justice's favour, and be acquitted presently.

Bun. To whom I said, that I could follow my calling and that too, namely, preaching the Word; and I did look upon it as my duty to do them both, as I had an opportunity.

Fost. He said, to have any such meetings was against the law; and, therefore, he would have me leave off, and say I would call the people no more together.

Bun. To whom I said, that I durst not make any further promise; for my conscience would not suffer me to do it. And again, I did look upon it as my duty to do as much good as I could, not only in my trade, but also in communicating to all people, wheresoever I came, the best knowledge I had in the Word.

Fost. He told me that I was the nearest the Papists of any, and that he would convince me of immediately.

Bun. I asked him wherein?

Fost. He said, in that we understood the Scriptures literally.

Bun. I told him that those that were to be understood literally, we understood them so; but for those that were to be understood otherwise, we endeavoured so to understand them.

Fost. He said, Which of the Scriptures do you understand literally?

Bun. I said this, "He that believeth shall be saved." This was to be understood just as it is spoken; that whosoever believeth in Christ shall, according to the plain and simple words of the text, be saved.

Fost. He said that I was ignorant, and did not understand the Scriptures; for how, said he, can you understand them when you know not the original Greek, etc.

Bun. To whom I said, that if that was his opinion, that none could understand the Scriptures but those that had the original Greek, etc., then but a very few of the poorest sort should be saved; this is harsh; yet the Scripture saith, "That God hides these things from the wise and prudent," that is, from the learned of the world, "and reveals them to babes and sucklings."

Fost. He said there were none that heard me but a company of foolish people.

Bun. I told him that there were the wise as well as the foolish that do hear me; and again, those that are most commonly counted foolish by the world are the wisest before God; also, that God had rejected the wise, and mighty, and noble, and chosen the foolish and the base.

Fost. He told me that I made people neglect their calling; and that God had commanded people to work six days, and serve him on the seventh.

Bun. I told him that it was the duty of people, both rich and poor, to look out for their souls on those days as well as for their bodies; and that God would have his people "exhort one another daily, while it is called to-day."

Fost. He said again that there was none but a company of poor, simple, ignorant people that came to hear me.

Bun. I told him that the foolish and ignorant had most need of teaching and information; and, therefore, it would be profitable for me to go on in that work.

Fost. Well, said he, to conclude, but will you promise that you will not call the people together any more? and then you may be released and go home.

Bun. I told him that I durst say no more than I had said; for I durst not leave off that work which God had called me to.

So he withdrew from me, and then came several of the justice's servants to me, and told me that I stood so much upon a nicety. Their master, they said, was willing to let me go; and if I would but say I would call the people no more together, I might have my liberty, etc.

Bun. I told them there were more ways than one in which a man might be said to call the people together. As, for instance, if a man get upon the market-place, and there read a book, or the like, though he do not say to the people, Sirs, come hither and hear; yet if they come to him because he reads, he, by his very reading, may be said to call them together; because they would not have been there to hear if he had not been there to read. And seeing this might be termed a calling the people together, I durst not say I would not call them together; for then, by the same argument, my preaching might be said to call them together.

Wing. and Fost. Then came the justice and Mr. Foster to me again; we had a little more discourse about preaching, but because the method of it is out of my mind, I pass it; and when they saw that I was at a point, and would not be moved nor persuaded,

Mr. Foster, the man that did at the first express so much love to me, told the justice that then he must send me away to prison. And that he would do well, also, if he would present all those that were the cause of my coming among them to meetings. Thus we parted.

And, verily, as I was going forth of the doors, I had much ado to forbear saying to them that I carried the peace of God along with me; but I held my peace, and, blessed be the Lord, went away to prison, with God's comfort in my poor soul.

After I had lain in the jail five or six days, the brethren sought means, again, to get me out by bondsmen; for so ran my mittimus, that I should lie there till I could find sureties. They went to a justice at Elstow, one Mr. Crumpton, to desire him to take bond for my appearing at the quarter-sessions. At the first he told them he would; but afterwards he made a demur at the business, and desired first to see my mittimus, which run to this purpose: That I went about to several conventicles in this country, to the great disparagement of the government of the Church of England, etc. When he had seen it, he said that there might be something more against me than was expressed in my mittimus; and that he was but a young man, and, therefore, he durst not do it. This my jailer told me; whereat I was not at all daunted, but rather glad, and saw evidently that the Lord had heard me; for before I went down to the justice, I begged of God that if I might do more good by being at liberty than in prison, that then I might be set at liberty; but if not, his will be done; for I was not altogether without hopes but that my imprisonment might be an awakening to the saints in the country, therefore I could not tell well which to choose; only I, in that manner, did commit the thing to God. And verily, at my return, I did meet my God sweetly in the prison again, comforting of me and satisfying of me that it was his will and mind that I should be there.

When I came back again to prison, as I was musing at the slender answer of the justice, this word dropt in upon my heart with some life, "For he knew that for envy they had delivered him."

Thus have I, in short, declared the manner and occasion of my being in prison; where I lie waiting the good will of God, to do with me as he pleaseth; knowing that not one hair of my head can fall to the ground without the will of my Father which is in heaven. Let the rage and malice of men be never so great, they can do no more, nor go no farther, than God permits them; but when they have done their worst, "We know that all things work together for good to them that love God" (Rom. viii. 28).

Farewell.

Here is the Sum of my Examination before Justice Keelin, Justice Chester, Justice Blundale, Justice Beecher, and Justice Snagg, etc.

After I had lain in prison above seven weeks, the quarter-sessions was to be kept in Bedford, for the county thereof, unto which I was to be brought; and when my jailer had set me before those justices, there was a bill of indictment preferred against me. The extent thereof was as followeth: "That John Bunyan, of the town of Bedford, labourer, being a person of such and such conditions, he hath, since such a time, devilishly and perniciously abstained from coming to church to hear Divine service, and is a common upholder of several unlawful meetings and conventicles, to the great disturbance and distraction of the good subjects of this kingdom, contrary to the laws of our sovereign lord the King, etc.

The Clerk. When this was read, the clerk of the sessions said unto me, What say you to this?

Bun. I said, that as to the first part of it, I was a common frequenter of the church of God. And was also, by grace, a member with the people over whom Christ is the Head.

Keelin. But, saith Justice Keelin, who was the judge in that court? Do you come to church, you know what I mean; to the parish church, to hear Divine service?

Bun. I answered, No, I did not.

Keel. He asked me why?

Bun. I said, Because I did not find it commanded in the Word of God.

Keel. He said, We were commanded to pray.

Bun. I said, But not by the Common Prayer Book.

Keel. He said, How then?

Bun. I said, With the Spirit. As the apostle saith, "I will pray with the Spirit with understanding" (1 Cor. xiv. 15).

Keel. He said, We might pray with the Spirit, and with understanding, and with the Common Prayer Book also.

Bun. I said that the prayers in the Common Prayer Book were such as were made by other men, and not by the motions of the Holy Ghost, within our hearts; and as I said, the apostle saith, he will pray with the Spirit, and with the understanding; not with the Spirit and the Common Prayer Book.

Another Justice. What do you count prayer? Do you think it is to say a few words over before or among a people?

Bun. I said, No, not so; for men might have many elegant or excellent words, and yet not pray at all; but when a man prayeth, he doth, through a sense of those things which he wants, which sense is begotten by the Spirit, pour out his heart before God through Christ; though his words be not so many and so excellent as others are.

Justices. They said, That was true.

Bun. I said, This might be done without the Common Prayer Book.

Another. One of them said (I think it was Justice Blundale, or Justice Snagg), How should we know that you do not write out your prayers first, and then read them afterwards to the people? This he spake in a laughing way.

Bun. I said, It is not our use to take a pen and paper, and write a few words thereon, and then go and read it over to a company of people.

But how should we know it? said he.

Bun. Sir, it is none of our custom, said I.

Keel. But, said Justice Keelin, it is lawful to use Common Prayer, and such-like forms: for Christ taught his disciples to pray, as John also taught his disciples. And further, said he, cannot one man teach another to pray? "Faith comes by hearing"; and one man may convince another of sin, and therefore prayers made by men, and read over, are good to teach, and help men to pray.

While he was speaking these words, God brought that word into my mind, in the eighth of the Romans, at the 26th verse. I say, God brought it, for I thought not on it before: but as he was speaking, it came so fresh into my mind, and was set so evidently before me, as if the Scripture had said, Take me, take me; so when he had done speaking,

Bun. I said, Sir, the Scripture saith, that it is the Spirit that helpeth our infirmities; for we know not what we should pray for as we ought: but the Spirit itself maketh intercession for us, with sighs and groanings which cannot be uttered. Mark, said I, it doth not say the Common Prayer Book teacheth us how to pray, but the Spirit. And it is

E 815

"the Spirit that helpeth our infirmities," saith the apostle; he doth not say it is the Common Prayer Book.

And as to the Lord's prayer, although it be an easy thing to say, "Our Father," etc., with the mouth, yet there are very few that can, in Spirit, say the two first words in that prayer; that is, that can call God their Father, as knowing what it is to be born again, and as having experience, that they are begotten of the Spirit of God; which if they do not, all is but babbling, etc.

Keel. Justice Keelin said, that that was a truth.

Bun. And I say further, As to your saying that one man may convince another of sin, and that faith comes by hearing, and that one man may tell another how he should pray, etc., I say men may tell each other of their sins, but it is the Spirit that must convince them.

And though it be said that "faith comes by hearing," yet it is the Spirit that worketh faith in the heart through hearing, or else they are not profited by hearing (Heb. iv. 12).

And that though one man may tell another how he should pray, yet, as I said before, he cannot pray, nor make his condition known to God, except the Spirit help. It is not the Common Prayer Book that can do this. It is the Spirit that showeth us our sins, and the Spirit that showeth us a Saviour (John xvi. 16); and the Spirit that stirreth up in our hearts desires to come to God, for such things as we stand in need of (Matt. xi. 27), even sighing out our souls unto him for them with "groans which cannot be uttered." With other words to the same purpose. At this they were set.

Keel. But, says Justice Keelin, what have you against the Common Prayer Book?

Bun. I said, Sir, if you will hear me, I shall lay down my reasons against it.

Keel. He said, I should have liberty; but first, said he, let me give you one caution; take heed of speaking irreverently of the Common Prayer Book; for if you do so, you will bring great damage upon yourself.

Bun. So I proceeded, and said, My first reason was, because it was not commanded in the Word of God, and therefore I could not use it.

Another. One of them said, Where do you find it commanded in the Scripture, that you should go to Elstow, or

Bedford, and yet it is lawful to go to either of them, is it not?

Bun. I said, To go to Elstow, or Bedford, was a civil thing, and not material, though not commanded, and yet God's Word allowed me to go about my calling, and therefore if it lay there, then to go thither, etc. But to pray was a great part of the Divine worship of God, and therefore it ought to be done according to the rule of God's Word.

Another. One of them said, He will do harm; let him speak no further.

Keel. Justice Keelin said, No, no, never fear him, we are better established than so; he can do no harm; we know the Common Prayer Book hath been ever since the apostles' time, and is lawful for it to be used in the church.

Bun. I said, Show me the place in the epistles where the Common Prayer Book is written, or one text of Scripture that commands me to read it, and I will use it. But yet, notwithstanding, said I, they that have a mind to use it, they have their liberty; that is, I would not keep them from it; but for our parts, we can pray to God without it. Blessed be his name.

With that, one of them said, Who is your God? Beelzebub? Moreover, they often said that I was possessed with the spirit of delusion, and of the devil. All which sayings I passed over; the Lord forgive them! And further, I said, Blessed be the Lord for it, we are encouraged to meet together, and to pray, and exhort one another; for we have had the comfortable presence of God among us. For ever blessed be his holy name!

Keel. Justice Keelin called this pedlar's French, saying, that I must leave off my canting. The Lord open his eyes!

Bun. I said, that we ought to "exhort one another daily, while it is called to-day," etc. (Heb. iii. 13).

Keel. Justice Keelin said, that I ought not to preach; and asked me where I had my authority? with other such-like words.

Bun. I said, that I would prove that it was lawful for me, and such as I am, to preach the Word of God.

Keel. He said unto me, By what scripture?

I said, By that in the first epistle of Peter, chap. iv., the 10th verse, and Acts xviii., with other scriptures, which he would not suffer me to mention. But said, Hold; not so many, which is the first?

Bun. I said, This: "As every man hath received the gift, *even so* minister the same one to another, as good stewards of the manifold grace of God. If any man speak, *let him speak* as the oracles of God," etc.

Keel. He said, Let me a little open that scripture to you: "As every man hath received the gift"; that is, said he, as everyone hath received a trade, so let him follow it. If any man have received a gift of tinkering, as thou hast done, let him follow his tinkering. And so other men their trades; and the divine his calling, etc.

Bun. Nay, sir, said I, but it is most clear, that the apostle speaks here of preaching the Word; if you do but compare both the verses together, the next verse explains this gift what it is, saying, "If any man speak, *let him speak* as the oracles of God." So that it is plain, that the Holy Ghost doth not so much in this place exhort to civil callings, as to the exercising of those gifts that we have received from God. I would have gone on, but he would not give me leave.

Keel. He said, We might do it in our families, but not otherwise.

Bun. I said, If it was lawful to do good to some, it was lawful to do good to more. If it was a good duty to exhort our families, it is good to exhort others; but if they held it a sin to meet together to seek the face of God, and exhort one another to follow Christ, I should sin still; for so we should do.

Keel. He said he was not so well versed in Scripture as to dispute, or words to that purpose. And said, moreover, that they could not wait upon me any longer; but said to me, Then you confess the indictment, do you not? Now, and not till now, I saw I was indicted.

Bun. I said, This I confess, we have had many meetings together, both to pray to God, and to exhort one another, and that we had the sweet comforting presence of the Lord among us for our encouragement; blessed be his name therefor. I confessed myself guilty no otherwise.

Keel. Then, said he, hear your judgment. You must be had back again to prison, and there lie for three months following; and at three months' end, if you do not submit to go to church to hear Divine service, and leave your preaching, you must be banished the realm: and if, after such a day as shall be appointed you to be gone, you shall be found in this realm, etc., or be found to come over again without special licence from the king, etc., you must stretch by the neck for it, I tell you plainly; and so he bid my jailer have me away.

Bun. I told him, as to this matter, I was at a point with him; for if I was out of prison to-day I would preach the gospel again to-morrow, by the help of God.

Another. To which one made me some answer; but my jailer pulling me away to be gone, I could not tell what he said.

Thus I departed from them; and I can truly say, I bless the Lord Jesus Christ for it, that my heart was sweetly refreshed in the time of my examination; and also afterwards, at my returning to the prison. So that I found Christ's words more than bare trifles, where he saith, "I will give you a mouth and wisdom, which all your adversaries shall not be able to gainsay nor resist" (Luke xxi. 15). And that his peace no man can take from us.

Thus have I given you the substance of my examination. The Lord make these profitable to all that shall read or hear them. Farewell.

The Substance of some Discourse had between the Clerk of the Peace and myself, when he came to admonish me, according to the tenor of that Law by which I was in Prison

When I had lain in prison other twelve weeks, and now not knowing what they intended to do with me, upon the 3rd of April, 1661, comes Mr. Cobb unto me, as he told me, being sent by the justices to admonish me; and demanded of me submittance to the Church of England, etc. The extent of our discourse was as followeth:

Cobb. When he was come into the house he sent for me out of my chamber; who, when I was come unto him, he said, Neighbour Bunyan, how do you do?

Bun. I thank you, sir, said I, very well, blessed be the Lord.

Cobb. Saith he, I come to tell you that it is desired you would submit yourself to the laws of the land, or else at the next sessions it will go worse with you, even to be sent away out of the nation, or else worse than that.

Bun. I said that I did desire to demean myself in the world, both as becometh a man and a Christian.

Cobb. But, saith he, you must submit to the laws of the land, and leave off those meetings which you was wont to have; for the statute law is directly against it; and I am sent to you by the justices to tell you that they do intend to prosecute the law against you if you submit not.

Bun. I said, Sir, I conceive that that law by which I am in prison at this time doth not reach or condemn either me or the meetings which I do frequent; that law was made against those that, being designed to do evil in their meetings, make the exercise of religion their pretence, to cover their wickedness. It doth not forbid the private meetings of those that plainly and simply make it their only end to worship the Lord, and to exhort one another to edification. My end in meeting with others is simply to do as much good as I can, by exhortation and counsel, according to that small measure of light which God hath given me, and not to disturb the peace of the nation.

Cobb. Everyone will say the same, said he; you see the late insurrection at London, under what glorious pretences they went; and yet, indeed, they intended no less than the ruin of the kingdom and commonwealth.

Bun. That practice of theirs I abhor, said I; yet it doth not follow that, because they did so, therefore all others will do so. I look upon it as my duty to behave myself under the king's government, both as becomes a man and a Christian, and if an occasion were offered me, I should willingly manifest my loyalty to my prince, both by word and deed.

Cobb. Well, said he, I do not profess myself to be a man that can dispute; but this I say, truly, neighbour Bunyan, I would have you consider this matter seriously, and submit yourself; you may have your liberty to exhort your neighbour in private discourse, so be you do not call together an assembly of people; and, truly, you may do much good to the church of Christ, if you would go this way; and this you may do, and the law not abridge you of it. It is your private meetings that the law is against.

Bun. Sir, said I, if I may do good to one by my discourse, why may I not do good to two? and if to two, why not to four, and so to eight? etc.

Cobb. Aye, saith he, and to a hundred, I warrant you.

Bun. Yes, sir, said I, I think I should not be forbid to do as much good as I can.

Cobb. But, saith he, you may but pretend to do good, and indeed, notwithstanding, do harm, by seducing the people; you are, therefore, denied your meeting so many together, lest you should do harm.

Bun. And yet, said I, you say the law tolerates me to discourse with my neighbour; surely there is no law tolerates me to seduce anyone; therefore, if I may, by the law, discourse with one, surely it is to do him good; and if I, by discoursing, may do good to one, surely, by the same law, I may do good to many.

Cobb. The law, saith he, doth expressly forbid your private meetings; therefore they are not to be tolerated.

Bun. I told him that I would not entertain so much uncharitableness of that Parliament in the 35th of Elizabeth, or of the queen herself, as to think they did, by that law, intend the oppressing of any of God's ordinances, or the interrupting any in the way of God; but men may, in the wresting of it, turn it against the way of God; but take the law in itself, and it only fighteth against those that drive at mischief in their hearts and meetings, making religion only their cloak, colour, or pretence; for so are the words of the statute: "If any meetings, under colour or pretence of religion," etc.

Cobb. Very good; therefore the king, seeing that pretences are usually in and among people, as to make religion their pretence only, therefore he, and the law before him, doth forbid such private meetings, and tolerates only public; you may meet in public.

Bun. Sir, said I, let me answer you in a similitude: Set the case that, at such a wood corner, there did usually come forth thieves, to do mischief; must there therefore a law be made that everyone that cometh out there shall be killed? May there not come out true men as well as thieves out from thence? Just thus it is in this case; I do think they may be many that may design the destruction of the commonwealth; but it does not follow therefore that all private meetings are unlawful; those that transgress, let them be punished. And if at any time I myself should do any act in my conversation as doth not become a man and Christian, let me bear the punishment. And as for your saying I may meet in public, if I may be suffered, I would gladly do it. Let me have but meeting enough in public, and I shall care the less to have them in private. I do not meet in private because I am afraid to have meetings in public. I bless the Lord that my heart is at that point, that if any man can lay anything to my charge, either in doctrine or practice, in this particular, that can be proved error or heresy, I am willing to disown it, even in the very market-place; but if it be truth, then to stand to it to the last drop of my blood. And, sir, said I, you ought to commend me for so doing. To err and to be a heretic are two things; I am no heretic, because I will not stand refractorily to defend any one thing that is contrary to the Word. Prove anything which I hold to be an error, and I will recant it.

Cobb. But, goodman Bunyan, said he, methinks you need not stand so strictly upon this one thing, as to have meetings of such public assemblies. Cannot you submit, and, notwithstanding, do as much good as you can, in a neighbourly way, without having such meetings?

Bun. Truly, sir, said I, I do not desire to commend myself, but to think meanly of myself; yet when I do most despise myself, taking notice of that small measure of light which God hath given me, also that the people of the Lord, by their own saying, are edified thereby. Besides, when I see that the Lord, through grace, hath in some measure blessed my labour, I dare not but exercise that gift which God hath given me for the good of the people. And I said further, that I would willingly speak in public, if I might.

Cobb. He said, that I might come to the public assemblies and hear. What though you do not preach? you may hear. Do not think yourself so well enlightened, and that you have received a gift so far above others, but that you may hear other men preach. Or to that purpose.

Bun. I told him, I was as willing to be taught as to give

instruction, and I looked upon it as my duty to do both; for, said I, a man that is a teacher, he himself may learn also from another that teacheth, as the apostle saith: "Ye may all prophesy, one by one, that all may learn" (1 Cor. xiv. 31). That is, every man that hath received a gift from God, he may dispense it, that others may be comforted; and when he hath done, he may hear and learn, and be comforted himself of others.

Cobb. But, said he, what if you should forbear awhile, and sit still, till you see further how things will go?

Bun. Sir, said I, Wyclif saith, that he which leaveth off preaching and hearing of the Word of God for fear of excommunication of men, he is already excommunicated of God, and shall in the day of judgment be counted a traitor to Christ.

Cobb. Aye, saith he, they that do not hear shall be so counted indeed; do you, therefore, hear.

Bun. But, sir, said I, he saith, he that shall leave off either preaching or hearing, etc. That is, if he hath received a gift of edification, it is his sin, if he doth not lay it out in a way of exhortation and counsel, according to the proportion of his gift; as well as to spend his time altogether in hearing others preach.

Cobb. But, said he, how shall we know that you have received a gift?

Bun. Said I, Let any man hear and search, and prove the doctrine by the Bible.

Cobb. But will you be willing, said he, that two indifferent persons shall determine the case, and will you stand by their judgment?

Bun. I said, Are they infallible?

Cobb. He said, No.

Bun. Then, said I, it is possible my judgment may be as good as theirs. But yet I will pass by either, and in this matter be judged by the Scriptures; I am sure that is infallible, and cannot err.

Cobb. But, said he, who shall be judge between you, for you take the Scriptures one way, and they another?

Bun. I said, The Scripture should, and that by comparing one scripture with another; for that will open itself, if it be rightly compared. As, for instance, if under the different apprehensions of the word Mediator, you would know the truth of it, the Scriptures open it, and tell us that he that is a mediator must take up the business between two, and "a mediator is not a mediator of one, but God is one," and "*there is* one mediator between God and men, even the man Christ Jesus" (Gal. iii. 20; 1 Tim. ii. 5). So likewise the Scripture calleth Christ a complete, or perfect, or able high priest. That is opened in that he is called man, and also God. His blood also is discovered to be effectually efficacious by the same things. So the Scripture, as touching the matter of meeting together, etc., doth likewise sufficiently open itself and discover its meaning.

Cobb. But are you willing, said he, to stand to the judgment of the church?

Bun. Yes, sir, said I, to the approbation of the church of God; the church's judgment is best expressed in Scripture. We had much other discourse which I cannot well remember, about the laws of the nation, and submission to government; to which I did tell him, that I did look upon myself as bound in conscience to walk according to all righteous laws, and that whether there was a king or no; and if I did anything that was contrary, I did hold it my duty to bear patiently the penalty of the law, that was provided against such offenders; with many more words to the like effect. And said, moreover, that to cut off all occasions of suspicion from any, as touching the harmlessness of my doctrine in private, I would willingly take the pains to give anyone the notes of all my sermons; for I do sincerely desire to live quietly in my country, and to submit to the present authority.

Cobb. Well, neighbour Bunyan, said he, but indeed I would wish you seriously to consider of these things, between this and the quarter-sessions, and to submit yourself. You may do much good if you continue still in the land; but alas, what benefit will it be to your friends, or what good can you do to them, if you should be sent away beyond the seas into Spain, or Constantinople, or some other remote part of the world? Pray be ruled.

Jailer. Indeed, sir, I hope he will be ruled.

Bun. I shall desire, said I, in all godliness and honesty, to behave myself in the nation, whilst I am in it. And if I must be so dealt withal, as you say, I hope God will help me to bear what they shall lay upon me. I know no evil that I have done in this matter, to be so used. I speak as in the presence of God.

Cobb. You know, saith he, that the Scripture saith, "the powers that be are ordained of God."

Bun. I said, Yes, and that I was to submit to the king as supreme, also to the governors, as to them that are sent by him.

Cobb. Well then, said he, the king then commands you, that you should not have any private meetings; because it is against his law, and he is ordained of God, therefore you should not have any.

Bun. I told him that Paul did own the powers that were in his day, as to be of God; and yet he was often in prison under them for all that. And also, though Jesus Christ told Pilate, that he had no power against him, but of God, yet he died under the same Pilate; and yet, said I, I hope you will not say that either Paul, or Christ, were such as did deny magistracy, and so sinned against God in slighting the ordinance. Sir, said I, the law hath provided two ways of obeying: The one to do that which I, in my conscience, do believe that I am bound to do, actively; and where I cannot obey actively, there I am willing to lie down, and to suffer what they shall do unto me. At this he sat still, and said no more; which, when he had done, I did thank him for his civil and meek discoursing with me; and so we parted.

O that we might meet in heaven!

Farewell.   J. B.

Here followeth a discourse between my Wife and the Judges, with others, touching my Deliverance at the Assizes following; the which I took from her own Mouth

After that I had received this sentence of banishing, or hanging, from them, and after the former admonition, touching the determination of the justices, if I did not recant; just when the time drew nigh, in which I should have abjured, or have done worse, as Mr. Cobb told me, came the time in which the king was to be crowned. Now, at the coronation of kings, there is usually a releasement of divers prisoners, by virtue of his coronation; in which privilege also I should have had my share; but that they took me for a convicted person, and therefore, unless I sued out a pardon, as they called it, I could have no benefit thereby; notwithstanding, yet, forasmuch as the coronation proclamation did give liberty, from the day the king was crowned to that day twelvemonth, to sue them out; therefore, though they would not let me out of prison, as they let out thousands, yet they could not meddle with me, as touching the execution of their sentence; because of the liberty offered for the suing out of pardons. Whereupon I continued in prison till the next assizes, which are called Midsummer assizes, being then kept in August 1661.

Now, at that assizes, because I would not leave any possible means unattempted that might be lawful, I did, by my wife, present a petition to the judges three times, that I might be heard, and that they would impartially take my case into consideration.

The first time my wife went, she presented it to Judge Hale, who very mildly received it at her hand, telling her that he would do her and me the best good he could; but he feared, he said, he could do none. The next day, again, lest they should, through the multitude of business, forget me, we did throw another petition into the coach to Judge Twisdon; who, when he had seen it, snapt her up, and angrily told her that I was a convicted person, and could not be released, unless I would promise to preach no more, etc.

Well, after this, she yet again presented another to Judge Hale, as he sat on the bench, who, as it seemed, was willing to give her audience. Only Justice Chester being present, stept up and said, that I was convicted in the court, and that I was a hot-spirited fellow, or words to that purpose, whereat he waived it, and did not meddle therewith. But yet, my wife being encouraged by the high sheriff, did venture once more into their presence, as the poor widow did to the unjust judge, to try what she could do with them for my liberty, before they went forth of the town. The place where she went to them was to the Swan Chamber, where the two judges, and many justices and gentry of the country, were in company together. She then, coming into the chamber with abashed face, and a trembling heart, began her errand to them in this manner:

Woman. My lord (directing herself to Judge Hale), I make bold to come once again to your lordship, to know what may be done with my husband.

Judge Hale. To whom he said, Woman, I told thee before, I could do thee no good; because they have taken that for a conviction which thy husband spoke at the sessions; and unless there be something done to undo that, I can do thee no good.

Wom. My lord, said she, he is kept unlawfully in prison; they clapped him up before there was any proclamation against the meetings; the indictment also is false. Besides, they never asked him whether he was guilty or no; neither did he confess the indictment.

One of the Justices. Then one of the justices that stood by, whom she knew not, said, My lord, he was lawfully convicted.

Wom. It is false, said she; for when they said to him, Do you confess the indictment? he said only this, that he had been at several meetings, both where there was preaching the Word, and prayer, and that they had God's presence among them.

Judge Twisdon. Whereat Judge Twisdon answered very angrily, saying, What! you think we can do what we list; your husband is a breaker of the peace, and is convicted by the law, etc. Whereupon Judge Hale called for the Statute Book.

Wom. But, said she, my lord, he was not lawfully convicted.

Chester. Then Justice Chester said, My lord, he was lawfully convicted.

Wom. It is false, said she; it was but a word of discourse that they took for a conviction, as you heard before.

Chest. But it is recorded, woman, it is recorded, said Justice Chester; as if it must be of necessity true, because it was recorded. With which words he often endeavoured to stop her mouth, having no other argument to convince her, but "it is recorded, it is recorded."

Wom. My lord, said she, I was a while since at London, to see if I could get my husband's liberty; and there I spoke with my Lord Barkwood, one of the House of Lords, to whom I delivered a petition, who took it of me and presented it to some of the rest of the House of Lords, for my husband's releasement; who, when they had seen it, they said that they

could not release him, but had committed his releasement
to the judges, at the next assizes. This he told me; and now
I come to you to see if anything may be done in this business, and you give neither releasement nor belief. To which
they gave her no answer, but made as if they heard her not.

Chest. Only Justice Chester was often up with this, "He
is convicted," and "It is recorded."

Wom. If it be, it is false, said she.

Chest. My lord, said Justice Chester, he is a pestilent
fellow, there is not such a fellow in the country again.

Twis. What, will your husband leave preaching? If he
will do so, then send for him.

Wom. My lord, said she, he dares not leave preaching, as
long as he can speak.

Twis. See here, what should we talk any more about
such a fellow? Must he do what he lists? He is a breaker
of the peace.

Wom. She told him again, that he desired to live peaceably, and to follow his calling, that his family might be
maintained; and, moreover, said, My lord, I have four small
children that cannot help themselves, of which one is blind,
and have nothing to live upon, but the charity of good
people.

Hale. Hast thou four children? said Judge Hale; thou
art but a young woman to have four children.

Wom. My lord, said she, I am but mother-in-law to them,
having not been married to him yet full two years. Indeed,
I was with child when my husband was first apprehended;
but being young, and unaccustomed to such things, said
she, I being smayed at the news, fell into labour, and so
continued for eight days, and then was delivered, but my
child died.

Hale. Whereat, he looking very soberly on the matter,
said, Alas, poor woman!

Twis. But Judge Twisdon told her, that she made poverty
her cloak; and said, moreover, that he understood I was
maintained better by running up and down a-preaching,
than by following my calling.

Hale. What is his calling? said Judge Hale.

Answer. Then some of the company that stood by said,
A tinker, my lord.

Wom. Yes, said she, and because he is a tinker, and a poor man, therefore he is despised, and cannot have justice.

Hale. Then Judge Hale answered, very mildly, saying, I tell thee, woman, seeing it is so, that they have taken what thy husband spake for a conviction; thou must either apply thyself to the king, or sue out his pardon, or get a writ of error.

Chest. But when Justice Chester heard him give her this counsel; and especially, as she supposed, because he spoke of a writ of error, he chafed, and seemed to be very much offended; saying, My lord, he will preach and do what he lists.

Wom. He preacheth nothing but the Word of God, said she.

Twis. He preach the Word of God! said Twisdon; and withal she thought he would have struck her; he runneth up and down, and doth harm.

Wom. No, my lord, said she, it is not so; God hath owned him, and done much good by him.

Twis. God! said he; his doctrine is the doctrine of the devil.

Wom. My lord, said she, when the righteous Judge shall appear, it will be known that his doctrine is not the doctrine of the devil.

Twis. My lord, said he, to Judge Hale, do not mind her, but send her away.

Hale. Then said Judge Hale, I am sorry, woman, that I can do thee no good; thou must do one of those three things aforesaid; namely, either to apply thyself to the king, or sue out his pardon, or get a writ of error; but a writ of error will be cheapest.

Wom. At which Chester again seemed to be in a chafe, and put off his hat, and as she thought, scratched his head for anger: but when I saw, said she, that there was no prevailing to have my husband sent for, though I often desired them that they would send for him, that he might speak for himself, telling them, that he could give them better satisfaction than I could in what they demanded of him, with several other things, which now I forget; only this I remember, that though I was somewhat timorous at my first entrance into the chamber, yet before I went out, I could not but break forth into tears, not so much because they were so hard-hearted against me and my husband, but to think what a sad account such poor creatures will have to give at the coming of the Lord, when they shall there answer for all things whatsoever they have done in the body, whether it be good or whether it be bad.

So, when I departed from them, the Book of Statute was brought, but what they said of it I know nothing at all, neither did I hear any more from them.

Some Carriages of the Adversaries of God's Truth with me at the next Assizes, which was on the 19th of the First Month, 1662

I shall pass by what befel between these two assizes, how I had, by my jailer, some liberty granted me, more than at the first, and how I followed my wonted course of preaching, taking all occasions that were put into my hand to visit the people of God; exhorting them to be steadfast in the faith of Jesus Christ, and to take heed that they touched not the Common Prayer, etc., but to mind the Word of God, which giveth direction to Christians in every point, being able to make the man of God perfect in all things through faith in Jesus Christ, and thoroughly to furnish him unto all good works (2 Tim. iii. 17). Also, how I, having, I say, somewhat more liberty, did go to see Christians at London; which my enemies hearing of, were so angry, that they had almost cast my jailer out of his place, threatening to indict him, and to do what they could against him. They charged me also, that I went thither to plot and raise division, and make insurrection, which, God knows, was a slander; whereupon my liberty was more straitened than it was before: so that I must not look out of the door. Well, when the next sessions came, which was about the 10th of the eleventh month, I did expect to have been very roundly dealt withal; but they passed me by, and would not call me, so that I rested till the assizes, which was the 19th of the first month following; and when they came, because I had a desire to come before the judge, I desired my jailer to put my name into the calendar among the felons, and made friends of the judge and high sheriff, who promised that I should be called; so that I thought what I had done might have been effectual for the obtaining of my desire; but all was in vain: for when the assizes came, though my name was in the calendar, and also though both the judge and sheriff had promised that I should appear before them, yet the justices and the clerk of the peace did so work it about, that I, notwithstanding, was deferred, and might not appear; and although, I say, I do not know of all their carriages towards me, yet this I know, that the clerk of the peace did discover himself to be one of my greatest opposers: for, first, he came to my jailer, and told him that I must not go down before the judge, and therefore must not be put into the calendar; to whom my jailer said, that my name was in already. He bid him put me out again; my jailer told him that he could not, for he had given the judge a calendar with my name in it, and also the sheriff another. At which he was very much displeased, and desired to see that calendar that was yet in my jailer's hand; who, when he had given it him, he looked on it, and said it was a false calendar; he also took the calendar and blotted out my accusation, as my jailer had writ it. Which accusation I cannot tell what it was, because it was so blotted out; and he himself put in words to this purpose: "That John Bunyan was committed to prison, being lawfully convicted for upholding of unlawful meetings and conventicles," etc. But yet, for all this, fearing that what he had done, unless he added thereto, it would not do; he first run to the clerk of the assizes, then to the justices, and afterwards, because he would not leave any means unattempted to hinder me, he comes again to my jailer, and tells him, that if I did go down before the judge, and was released, he would make him pay my fees, which, he said, was due to him; and further told him, that he would complain of him at the next quarter-sessions for making of false calendars; though my jailer himself, as I afterwards learned, had put in my accusation worse than in itself it was by far. And thus was I hindered and prevented, at that time also, from appearing before the judge, and left in prison. Farewell.

JOHN BUNYAN.

A CONTINUATION OF MR. BUNYAN'S LIFE; BEGINNING WHERE
HE LEFT OFF, AND CONCLUDING WITH THE TIME AND
MANNER OF HIS DEATH AND BURIAL, TOGETHER WITH HIS
TRUE CHARACTER

Reader, the painful and industrious author of this book has
already given you a faithful and very moving relation of the
beginning and middle of the days of his pilgrimage on earth;
and since there yet remains somewhat worthy of notice and
regard, which occurred in the last scene of his life; the which,
for want of time, or fear that some over-censorious people
should impute it to him, as an earnest coveting of praise from
men, he has not left behind him in writing. Wherefore, as a
true friend and long acquaintance of Mr. Bunyan's, that his
good end may be known as well as his evil beginning, I have
taken upon me, from my knowledge, and the best account given
by other of his friends, to piece this to the thread, too soon broke
off, and so lengthen it out to his entering upon eternity.

He has told you at large of his birth and education; the
evil habits and corruptions of his youth; the temptations he
struggled and conflicted so frequently with; the mercies, comforts, and deliverances he found; how he came to take upon
him the preaching of the gospel; the slanders, reproaches, and
imprisonments that attended him; and the progress he notwithstanding made, by the assistance of God's grace, no doubt
to the saving of many souls. Therefore take these things as
he himself has methodically laid them down in the words of
verity; and so I pass on as to what remains.

After his being freed from his twelve years' imprisonment
and upwards, for nonconformity, wherein he had time to furnish the world with sundry good books, etc.; and, by his
patience, to move Dr. Barlow, the then Bishop of Lincoln,
and other churchmen, to pity his hard and unreasonable sufferings, so far as to stand very much his friends in procuring his
enlargement, or there perhaps he had died by the noisomeness
and ill usage of the place; being now, I say, again at liberty,
and having, through mercy, shaken off his bodily fetters, for
those upon his soul were broken before, by the abounding grace
that filled his heart, he went to visit those that had been a
comfort to him in his tribulation, with a Christian-like acknow-
ledgment of their kindness and enlargement of charity; giving
encouragement by his example if it happened to be their hard
haps to fall into affliction or trouble, then to suffer patiently
for the sake of a good conscience, and for the love of God in
Jesus Christ towards their souls; and, by many cordial persuasions, supported some whose spirits began to sink low through
the fear of danger that threatened their worldly concernment,

so that the people found a wonderful consolation in his discourse and admonitions.

As often as opportunity would admit, he gathered them together in convenient places, though the law was then in force against meetings, and fed them with the sincere milk of the Word, that they might grow up in grace thereby. To such as were anywhere taken and imprisoned upon these accounts, he made it another part of his business to extend his charity, and gather relief for such of them as wanted.

He took great care to visit the sick, and strengthen them against the suggestions of the tempter, which at such times are very prevalent; so that they had cause for ever to bless God, who had put into his heart, at such a time, to rescue them from the power of the roaring lion, who sought to devour them; nor did he spare any pains or labour in travel, though to the remote counties, where he knew, or imagined, any people might stand in need of his assistance, insomuch that some of these visitations that he made, which was two or three every year, some, though in jeering manner, no doubt, gave him the epithet of Bishop Bunyan, whilst others envied him for his so earnestly labouring in Christ's vineyard, yet the seed of the Word he, all this while, sowed in the hearts of his congregation, watered with the grace of God, brought forth in abundance, in bringing in disciples to the church of Christ.

Another part of his time he spent in reconciling differences, by which he hindered many mischiefs, and saved some families from ruin; and, in such fallings out, he was uneasy, till he found a means to labour a reconciliation, and become a peace-maker, on whom a blessing is promised in Holy Writ; and, indeed, in doing this good office, he may be said to sum up his days, it being the last undertaking of his life, as will appear in the close of this paper.

When, in the late reign, liberty of conscience was unexpectedly given and indulged to Dissenters of all persuasions, his piercing wit penetrated the veil, and found that it was not for the Dissenters' sake they were so suddenly freed from the prosecutions that had long lain heavy upon them, and set, in a manner, on an equal foot with the Church of England, which the Papists were undermining, and about to subvert. He foresaw all the advantages that could have redounded to the Dissenters, would have been no more than what Poliphemus, the monstrous giant of Sicily, would have allowed Ulysses, viz. That he would eat his men first, and do him the favour of being eaten last. For, although Mr. Bunyan, following the examples of others, did lay hold of this liberty, as an acceptable thing in itself, knowing that God is the only lord of conscience, and that it is good at all times to do according to the dictates of a good conscience, and that the preaching the glad tidings of the gospel is beautiful in the preacher; yet, in all this, he moved with caution and a holy fear, earnestly praying for averting the impendent judgments, which he saw like a black tempest hanging over our heads, for our sins, and ready to break upon us, and that the Ninevites' remedy was now highly necessary. Hereupon, he gathered his congregation at Bedford, where he mostly lived, and had lived, and had spent the greatest part of his life; and there being no convenient place to be had, for the entertainment of so great a confluence of people as followed him, upon the account of his teaching, he consulted with them for the building of a meeting house; to which they made their voluntary contributions, with all cheerfulness and alacrity; and the first time he appeared there to edify, the place was so thronged, that many were constrained to stay without, though the house was very spacious, everyone striving to partake of his instructions, that were of his persuasion; and show their good will towards him, by being present at the opening of the place; and here he lived in much peace and quiet of mind, contenting himself with that little God had bestowed upon him, and sequestering himself from all secular employments, to follow that of his call to the ministry; for, as God said to Moses, he that made the lips and heart, can give eloquence and wisdom, without extraordinary acquirements in a university.

During these things, there were regulators sent into all cities and towns corporate, to new-model the government in the magistracy, etc., by turning out some, and putting in others. Against this, Mr. Bunyan expressed his zeal with some weariness, as foreseeing the bad consequence that would attend it, and laboured with his congregation to prevent their being imposed on in this kind; and when a great man in those days, coming to Bedford upon some such errand, sent for him, as it is supposed, to give him a place of public trust, he would by no means come at him, but sent his excuse.

When he was at leisure from writing and teaching, he often came up to London, and there went among the congregations of the nonconformists, and used his talent to the great good liking of the hearers; and even some, to whom he had been misrepresented, upon the account of his education, were convinced of his worth and knowledge in sacred things, as perceiving him to be a man of sound judgment, delivering himself plainly and powerfully; insomuch that many who came as mere spectators, for novelty's sake, rather than to be edified and improved, went away well satisfied with what they heard, and wondered, as the Jews did at the apostles, viz. whence this man should have these things; perhaps not considering that God more immediately assists those that make it their business industriously and cheerfully to labour in his vineyard.

Thus he spent his latter years, in imitation of his great Lord and Master, the ever-blessed Jesus; he went about doing good, so that the most prying critic, or even malice herself, is defied to find, even upon the narrowest search or observation, any sully or stain upon his reputation with which he may be justly charged; and this we note as a challenge to those that have had the least regard for him, or them of his persuasion, and have, one way or other, appeared in the front of those that oppressed him, and for the turning whose hearts, in obedience to the commission and commandment given him of God, he frequently prayed, and sometimes sought a blessing for them, even with tears, the effects of which they may, peradventure, though undeservedly, have found in their persons, friends, relations, or estates; for God will hear the prayers of the faithful, and answer them, even for those that vex them, as it happened in the case of Job's praying for the three persons that had been grievous in their reproach against him, even in the day of his sorrow.

But yet let me come a little nearer to particulars and periods of time for the better refreshing the memories of those that knew his labour and suffering, and for the satisfaction of all that shall read this book.

After he was sensibly convicted of the wicked state of his life, and converted, he was baptised into the congregation and admitted a member thereof, viz. in the year 1655, and became speedily a very zealous professor; but, upon the return of King Charles to the crown, in 1660, he was, on the 12th of November, taken, as he was edifying some good people that were got together to hear the Word, and confined in Bedford jail for the space of six years, till the Act of Indulgence to Dissenters being allowed, he obtained his freedom by the intercession of some in trust and power that took pity of his sufferings; but within six years afterwards [from his first imprisonment] he was again taken up, viz. in the year 1666, and was then confined for six years more, when even the jailer took such pity of his rigorous sufferings that he did as the Egyptian jailer did to Joseph, put all the care and trust into his hands. When he was taken this last time, he was preaching on these words, viz. "Dost thou believe on the Son of God?" and this imprisonment continued six years; and when this was over, another short affliction, which was an imprisonment of half a year, fell to his share. During these confinements he wrote these following books, viz.: *Of Prayer by the Spirit, The Holy City, Resurrection, Grace Abounding, Pilgrim's Progress*, the first part.

In the last year of his twelve years' imprisonment, the pastor of the congregation at Bedford died, and he was chosen to that care of souls on the 12th of December, 1671. And in this his charge he often had disputes with scholars, that came to oppose him, as supposing him an ignorant person, and thought he argued plainly and by Scripture without phrases and logical expressions; yet he nonplussed one who came to oppose him in his congregation, by demanding whether or no we had the true copies of the original Scriptures; and another, when he was preaching, accused him of uncharitableness, for saying, It was very hard for most to be saved; saying, by that, he went about to exclude most of his congregation; but he confuted him and put him to silence with the parable of the stony ground and other texts out of the 13th of Matthew, in our Saviour's sermon out of a ship, all his method being to keep close to the Scriptures; and what he found not warranted there, himself would not warrant nor determine, unless in such cases as were plain, wherein no doubts or scruples did arise.

But not to make any further mention of this kind, it is well known that this person managed all his affairs with such exactness as if he had made it his study, above all other things, not to give occasion of offence, but rather suffer many inconveniencies to avoid; being never heard to reproach or revile any, what injury soever he received, but rather to rebuke those that did; and as it was in his conversation, so it is manifested in those books he has caused to be published to the world; where, like the archangel disputing with Satan about the body of Moses, as we find it in the epistle of Jude, he brings no railing accusation, but leaves the rebukers, those that persecuted him, to the Lord.

In his family he kept up a very strict discipline in prayer and exhortations; being in this like Joshua, as that good man expresses it, viz. Whatsoever others did, as for me and my house, we will serve the Lord; and, indeed, a blessing waited on his labours and endeavours, so that his wife, as the Psalmist says, was like a pleasant vine upon the walls of his house, and his children like olive branches round his table; for so shall it be with the man that fears the Lord; and though by reason of the many losses he sustained by imprisonment and spoil, of his chargeable sickness, etc., his earthly treasures swelled not to excess, he always had sufficient to live decently and creditably, and with that he had the greatest of all treasures, which is content; for, as the wise man says, that is a continual feast.

But where content dwells, even a poor cottage is a kingly palace; and this happiness he had all his life long, not so much minding this world as knowing he was here as a pilgrim and stranger, and had no tarrying city, but looking for one not made with hands, eternal in the highest heavens; but at length, worn out with sufferings, age, and often teaching, the day of his dissolution drew near, and death, that unlocks the prison of the soul, to enlarge it for a more glorious mansion, put a stop to his acting his part on the stage of mortality; heaven, like earthly princes when it threatens war, being always so kind as to call home its ambassadors before it be denounced; and even the last act or undertaking of his was a labour of love and charity; for it so falling out, that a young gentleman, a neighbour of Mr. Bunyan, happening into the displeasure of his father, and being much troubled in mind upon that account, as also for that he had heard his father purposed to disinherit him, or otherwise deprive him of what he had to leave, he pitched upon Mr. Bunyan as a fit man to make way for his submission, and prepare his father's mind to receive him; and he, as willing to do any good office as it could be requested, as readily under-took it; and so, riding to Reading, in Berkshire, he then there used such pressing arguments and reasons against anger and passion, as also for love and reconciliation, that the father was mollified, and his bowels yearned towards his returning son.

But Mr. Bunyan, after he had disposed all things to the best for accommodation, returning to London, and being overtaken with excessive rains, coming to his lodging extreme wet, fell sick of a violent fever, which he bore with much constancy and patience; and expressed himself as if he desired nothing more than to be dissolved, and to be with Christ, in that case esteeming death as gain, and life only a tedious delaying of felicity expected; and finding his vital strength decay, having settled his mind and affairs, as well as the shortness of his time and the violence of his disease would admit, with a con-stant and Christian patience, he resigned his soul into the hands of his most merciful Redeemer, following his pilgrim from the City of Destruction to the New Jerusalem; his better part having been all along there, in holy contemplation, pantings, and breathings after the hidden manna, and water of life; as by many holy and humble consolations expressed in his letters to several persons, in prison and out of prison, too many to be here inserted at present. He died at the house of one Mr. Straddocks, a grocer, at the Star on Snowhill, in the parish of St. Sepulchre, London, on the 12th of August, 1688, and in the sixtieth year of his age, after ten days' sickness; and was buried in the new burying place near the Artillery Ground; where he sleeps to the morning of the resurrection, in hopes of a glorious rising to an incorruptible immortality of joy and happiness; where no more trouble and sorrow shall afflict him, but all tears be wiped away; when the just shall be incorrupted, as members of Christ their head, and reign with him as kings and priests for ever.

A BRIEF CHARACTER OF MR. JOHN BUNYAN

He appeared in countenance to be of a stern and rough temper; but in his conversation mild and affable, not given to loquacity or much discourse in company, unless some urgent occasion required it; observing never to boast of himself, or his parts, but rather seem low in his own eyes, and submit him-self to the judgment of others; abhorring lying and swearing, being just in all that lay in his power to his word, not seeming to revenge injuries, loving to reconcile differences, and make friendship with all; he had a sharp quick eye, accomplished with an excellent discerning of persons, being of good judgment and quick wit. As for his person, he was tall of stature, strong-boned, though not corpulent, somewhat of a ruddy face, with sparkling eyes, wearing his hair on his upper lip, after the old

British fashion; his hair reddish, but in his latter days, time had sprinkled it with grey; his nose well set, but not declining or bending, and his mouth moderate large; his forehead something high, and his habit always plain and modest. And thus have we impartially described the internal and external parts of a person, whose death hath been much regretted; a person who had tried the smiles and frowns of time; not puffed up in prosperity, nor shaken in adversity, always holding the golden mean.

> "In him at once did three great worthies shine,
> Historian, poet, and a choice divine;
> Then let him rest in undisturbèd dust,
> Until the resurrection of the just."

POSTSCRIPT

In this his pilgrimage, God blessed him with four children, one of which, named Mary, was blind, and died some years before; his other children are Thomas, Joseph, and Sarah; and his wife Elizabeth, having lived to see him overcome his labour and sorrow, and pass from this life to receive the reward of his works, long survived him not, but in 1692 she died; to follow her faithful pilgrim from this world to the other, whither he was gone before her; while his works, which consist of sixty books, remain for the edifying of the reader, and the praise of the author.—*Vale*.

THE LIFE AND DEATH OF
MR. BADMAN

PRESENTED TO THE WORLD IN

A FAMILIAR DIALOGUE BETWEEN MR. WISEMAN
AND MR. ATTENTIVE

THE AUTHOR TO THE READER

Courteous Reader,

As I was considering with myself what I had written
concerning the Progress of the Pilgrim from this world to
glory, and how it had been acceptable to many in this
nation, it came again into my mind to write, as then, of him
that was going to heaven, so now, of the life and death of
the ungodly, and of their travel from this world to hell. The
which in this I have done, and have put it, as thou seest,
under the name and title of Mr. Badman, a name very proper
for such a subject. I have also put it into the form of a
dialogue, that I might with more ease to myself, and pleasure
to the reader, perform the work. And although, as I said,
I have put it forth in this method, yet have I as little as may
be gone out of the road of mine own observation of things.
Yea, I think I may truly say that to the best of my remembrance, all the things that here I discourse of, I mean as
to matter of fact, have been acted upon the stage of this
world, even many times before mine eyes.

Here therefore, courteous reader, I present thee with the
life and death of Mr. Badman indeed; yea, I do trace him
in his life, from his childhood to his death; that thou mayest,
as in a glass, behold with thine own eyes the steps that
take hold of hell; and also discern, while thou art reading
of Mr. Badman's death, whether thou thyself art treading
in his path thereto. And let me entreat thee to forbear
quirking and mocking, for that I say Mr. Badman is dead;
but rather gravely inquire concerning thyself by the Word,
whether thou art one of his lineage or no; for Mr. Badman
has left many of his relations behind him; yea, the very world
is overspread with his kindred. True, some of his relations,
as he, are gone to their place and long home, but thousands
of thousands are left behind; as brothers, sisters, cousins,
nephews, besides innumerable of his friends and associates.
I may say, and yet speak nothing but too much truth in
so saying, that there is scarce a fellowship, a community,

139

or fraternity of men in the world, but some of Mr. Badman's relations are there; yea, rarely can we find a family or household in a town, where he has not left behind him either a brother, nephew, or friend.

The butt therefore, that at this time I shoot at, is wide; and it will be as impossible for this book to go into several families, and not to arrest some, as for the king's messenger to rush into a house full of traitors, and find none but honest men there. I cannot but think that this shot will light upon many, since our fields are so full of this game; but how many it will kill to Mr. Badman's course, and make alive to the Pilgrim's Progress, that is not in me to determine; this secret is with the Lord our God only, and he alone knows to whom he will bless it to so good and so blessed an end. However, I have put fire to the pan, and doubt not but the report will quickly be heard.

I told you before that Mr. Badman had left many of his friends and relations behind him, but if I survive them, as that is a great question to me, I may also write of their lives; however, whether my life be longer or shorter, this is my prayer at present, that God will stir up witnesses against them, that may either convert or confound them; for wherever they live, and roll in their wickedness, they are the pest and plague of that country. England shakes and totters already, by reason of the burden that Mr. Badman and his friends have wickedly laid upon it. Yea, our earth reels and staggereth to and fro like a drunkard, the transgression thereof is heavy upon it.

Courteous reader, I will treat thee now, even at the door and threshold of this house, but only with this intelligence, that Mr. Badman lies dead within. Be pleased therefore, if thy leisure will serve thee, to enter in, and behold the state in which he is laid, betwixt his death-bed and the grave. He is not buried as yet, nor doth he stink, as is designed he shall, before he lies down in oblivion. Now as others have had their funerals solemnised, according to their greatness and grandeur in the world, so likewise Mr. Badman, forasmuch as he deserveth not to go down to his grave with silence, has his funeral state according to his deserts.

Four things are usual at great men's funerals, which we will take leave, and I hope without offence, to allude to, in the funeral of Mr. Badman.

First. They are sometimes, when dead, presented to their friends, by their completely wrought images, as lively as by cunning men's hands they can be; that the remembrance of them may be renewed to their survivors, the remembrance of them and their deeds; and this I have endeavoured to answer in my discourse of Mr. Badman, and therefore I have drawn him forth in his features and actions from his childhood to his grey hairs. Here, therefore, thou hast him lively set forth as in cuts; both as to the minority, flower, and seniority of his age, together with those actions of his life, that he was most capable of doing, in and under those present circumstances of time, place, strength; and the opportunities that did attend him in these.

Second. There is also usual at great men's funerals, those badges and escutcheons of their honour, that they have received from their ancestors, or have been thought worthy of for the deeds and exploits they have done in their life; and here Mr. Badman has his, but such as vary from all men of worth, but so much the more agreeing with the merit of his doings. They all have descended in state, he only as an abominable branch. His deserts are the deserts of sin, and therefore the escutcheons of honour that he has, are only that he died without honour, and at his end became a fool. "Thou shalt not be joined with them in burial. The seed of evil doers shall never be renowned" (Is. xiv. 20).

The funeral pomp therefore of Mr. Badman, is to wear upon his hearse the badges of a dishonourable and wicked life; since "his bones are full *of the sin* of his youth, which shall lie down," as Job says, "with him in the dust." Nor is it fit that any should be his attendants, now at his death, but such as with him conspired against their own souls in their life; persons whose transgressions have made them infamous to all that have or shall know what they have done.

Some notice therefore I have also here in this little discourse given the reader, of them who were his confederates in his life, and attendants at his death; with a hint, either of some high villany committed by them, as also of those judgments that have overtaken and fallen upon them from the just and revenging hand of God. All which are things either fully known by me, as being eye- and ear-witness thereto, or that I have received from such hands, whose relation, as to this, I am bound to believe.

Third. The funerals of persons of quality have been solemnised with some suitable sermon at the time and place of their burial; but that I am not come to as yet, having got no farther than to Mr. Badman's death; but forasmuch as he must be buried, after he hath stunk out his time before his beholders, I doubt not but some such that we read are appointed to be at the burial of Gog, will do this work in my stead; such as shall leave him neither skin nor bone above ground, but shall set a sign by it till the buriers have buried it in the valley of Hamon-gog (Ezek. xxxix.).

Fourth. At funerals there does use to be mourning and lamentation, but here also Mr. Badman differs from others; his familiars cannot lament his departure, for they have not sense of his damnable state; they rather ring him and sing him to hell in the sleep of death, in which he goes thither. Good men count him no loss to the world, his place can well be without him, his loss is only his own, and it is too late for him to recover that damage or loss by a sea of bloody tears, could he shed them. Yea, God has said he will laugh at his destruction; who then shall lament for him, saying, Ah! my brother. He was but a stinking weed in his life; nor was he better at all in his death; such may well be thrown over the wall without sorrow, when once God has plucked them up by the roots in his wrath.

Reader, if thou art of the race, lineage, stock, or fraternity of Mr. Badman, I tell thee, before thou readest this book, thou wilt neither brook the author nor it, because he hath writ of Mr. Badman as he has. For he that condemneth the wicked that die so, passeth also the sentence upon the wicked that live. I therefore expect neither credit of, nor countenance from thee, for this narration of thy kinsman's life. For thy old love to thy friend, his ways, doings, etc., will stir up in thee enmity rather in thy very heart against me. I shall therefore incline to think of thee, that thou wilt rend, burn, or throw it away in contempt; yea, and wish also, that for writing so notorious a truth, some mischief may befal me. I look also to be loaded by thee with disdain, scorn, and contempt; yea, that thou shouldest railingly and vilifyingly say I lie, and am a bespatterer of honest men's lives and deaths. For Mr. Badman, when himself was alive, could not abide to be counted a knave, though his actions told all that went by, that indeed he was such an one. How then should

his brethren that survive him, and that tread in his very
steps, approve of the sentence that by this book is pronounced against him? Will they not rather imitate Korah,
Dathan, and Abiram's friends, even rail at me for condemning
him, as they did at Moses for doing execution?

I know it is ill puddling in the cockatrice's den, and that
they run hazards that hunt the wild boar. The man also that
writeth Mr. Badman's life had need be fenced with a coat
of mail, and with the staff of a spear, for that his surviving
friends will know what he doth; but I have adventured to do
it, and to play, at this time, at the hole of these asps; if they
bite, they bite; if they sting, they sting. Christ sends his
lambs in the midst of wolves, not to do like them, but to
suffer by them for bearing plain testimony against their
bad deeds. But had one not need to walk with a guard, and
to have a sentinel stand at one's door for this? Verily, the
flesh would be glad of such help; yea, a spiritual man, could
he tell how to get it (Acts xxiii.). But I am stript naked of
these, and yet am commanded to be faithful in my service
for Christ. Well then, I have spoken what I have spoken,
and now "come on me what *will*" (Job xiii. 13). True, the
text says, Rebuke a scorner and he will hate thee; and that
he that reproveth a wicked man getteth himself a blot and
shame. But what then? Open rebuke is better than secret
love, and he that receives it shall find it so afterwards.

So then, whether Mr. Badman's friends shall rage or laugh
at what I have writ, I know that the better end of the staff
is mine. My endeavour is to stop a hellish course of life, and
to "save a soul from death" (Jas. v. 20). And if for so doing
I meet with envy from them, from whom in reason I should
have thanks, I must remember the man in the dream, that
cut his way through his armed enemies, and so got into the
beauteous palace; I must, I say, remember him, and do
myself likewise.

Yet four things I will propound to the consideration of
Mr. Badman's friends before I turn my back upon them.

1. Suppose that there be a hell in very deed; not that I
do question it any more than I do whether there be a sun to
shine, but I suppose it for argument sake with Mr. Badman's
friends. I say, suppose there be a hell, and that too such an
one as the Scripture speaks of, one at the remotest distance
from God and life eternal, one where the worm of a guilty

conscience never dies, and where the fire of the wrath of God is not quenched. Suppose, I say, that there is such a hell, prepared of God—as there is indeed—for the body and soul of the ungodly world after this life to be tormented in; I say, do but with thyself suppose it, and then tell me is it not prepared for thee, thou being a wicked man? Let thy conscience speak, I say, is it not prepared for thee, thou being an ungodly man? And dost thou think, wast thou there now, that thou art able to wrestle with the judgment of God? Why then do the fallen angels tremble there? Thy hands cannot be strong, nor can thy heart endure, in that day when God shall deal with thee (Ezek. xxii. 14).

2. Suppose that someone that is now a soul in hell for sin, was permitted to come hither again to dwell, and that they had a grant also, that, upon amendment of life, next time they die, to change that place for heaven and glory. What sayest thou, O wicked man? Would such an one, thinkest thou, run again into the same course of life as before, and venture the damnation that for sin he had already been in? Would he choose again to lead that cursed life that afresh would kindle the flames of hell upon him, and that would bind him up under the heavy wrath of God? O! he would not, he would not; Luke xvi. insinuates it; yea, reason itself awake would abhor it, and tremble at such a thought.

3. Suppose again, that thou that livest and rollest in thy sin, and that as yet hast known nothing but the pleasure thereof, shouldest be by an angel conveyed to some place, where, with convenience, from thence thou mightest have a view of heaven and hell, of the joys of the one and the torments of the other; I say, suppose that from thence thou mightest have such a view thereof as would convince thy reason that both heaven and hell are such realities as by the Word they are declared to be; wouldest thou, thinkest thou, when brought to thy home again, choose to thyself thy former life, to wit, to return to thy folly again? No; if belief of what thou sawest remained with thee, thou wouldest eat fire and brimstone first.

4. I will propound again. Suppose that there was amongst us such a law, and such a magistrate to inflict the penalty, that for every open wickedness committed by thee, so much of thy flesh should with burning pincers be plucked from

thy bones, wouldest thou then go on thy open way of lying, swearing, drinking, and whoring, as thou with delight doest now? Surely, surely, no. The fear of the punishment would make thee forbear; yea, would make thee tremble, even then when thy lusts were powerful, to think what a punishment thou wast sure to sustain so soon as the pleasure was over. But O! the folly, the madness, the desperate madness that is in the hearts of Mr. Badman's friends, who, in despite of the threatenings of a holy and sin-revenging God, and of the outcries and warnings of all good men, yea, that will in despite of the groans and torments of those that are now in hell for sin, go on in a sinful course of life, yea, though every sin is also a step of descent down to that infernal cave (Luke xvi. 24, 28). O! how true is that saying of Solomon, "The heart of the sons of men is full of evil, and madness *is* in their heart while they live, and after that *they go* to the dead" (Eccles. ix. 3). To the dead! that is, to the dead in hell, to the damned dead, the place to which those that have died bad men are gone, and that those that live bad men are like to go to, when a little more sin, like stolen waters, hath been imbibed by their sinful souls.

That which has made me publish this book is,

1. For that wickedness, like a flood, is like to drown our English world. It begins already to be above the tops of the mountains; it has almost swallowed up all; our youth, middle age, old age, and all, are almost carried away of this flood. O debauchery, debauchery, what hast thou done in England! Thou hast corrupted our young men, and hast made our old men beasts; thou hast deflowered our virgins, and hast made matrons bawds. Thou hast made our earth "to reel to and fro like a drunkard"; it is in danger to "be removed like a cottage," yea, it is, because transgression is so heavy upon it, like to fall and rise no more (Is. xxiv. 20). O! that I could mourn for England, and for the sins that are committed therein, even while I see that, without repentance, the men of God's wrath are about to deal with us, each having his "slaughtering weapon in his hand" (Ezek. ix. 1, 2). Well, I have written, and by God's assistance shall pray that this flood may abate in England; and could I but see the tops of the mountains above it, I should think that these waters were abating.

2. It is the duty of those that can to cry out against this

deadly plague, yea, to lift up their voice as with a trumpet against it, that men may be awakened about it, fly from it, as from that which is the greatest of evils. Sin pulled angels out of heaven, pulls men down to hell, and overthroweth kingdoms. Who, that sees a house on fire, will not give the alarm to them that dwell therein? Who, that sees the land invaded, will not set the beacons on a flame? Who, that sees the devils as roaring lions, continually devouring souls, will not make an outcry? But above all, when we see sin, sinful sin, a-swallowing up a nation, sinking of a nation, and bringing its inhabitants to temporal, spiritual, and eternal ruin, shall we not cry out and cry, They are drunk, but not with wine; they stagger, but not with strong drink; they are intoxicated with the deadly poison of sin, which will, if its malignity be not by wholesome means allayed, bring soul and body, and estate, and country, and all, to ruin and destruction?

3. In and by this outcry I shall deliver myself from the ruins of them that perish; for a man can do no more in this matter—I mean a man in my capacity—than to detect and condemn the wickedness, warn the evil doer of the judgment, and fly therefrom myself. But O that I might not only deliver myself! O that many would hear, and turn at this my cry from sin! that they may be secured from the death and judgment that attend it.

Why I have handled the matter in this method is best known to myself. And why I have concealed most of the names of the persons whose sins or punishments I here and there in this book make relation of is, (1) For that neither the sins nor judgments were all alike open; the sins of some were committed, and the judgments executed for them, only in a corner. Not to say that I could not learn some of their names, for could I, I should not have made them public, for this reason. (2) Because I would not provoke those of their relations that survive them; I would not justly provoke them; and yet, as I think, I should, should I have entailed their punishment to their sins, and both to their names, and so have turned them into the world. (3) Nor would I lay them under disgrace and contempt, which would, as I think, unavoidably have happened unto them had I withal inserted their names.

As for those whose names I mention, their crimes or judgments were manifest; public almost as anything of that nature that happeneth to mortal men. Such therefore have published their own shame by their sin, and God his anger, by taking of open vengeance. As Job says, God has struck "them as wicked men in the open sight of others" (Job xxxiv. 26). So that I cannot conceive, since their sin and judgment was so conspicuous, that my admonishing the world thereof should turn to their detriment. For the publishing of these things are, so far as relation is concerned, intended for remembrances, that they may also bethink themselves, repent and turn to God, lest the judgments for their sins should prove hereditary. For the God of heaven hath threatened to visit the iniquity of the fathers upon the children, if they hate him, to the third and fourth generation (Exod. xx. 5).

Nebuchadnezzar's punishment for his pride being open —for he was for his sin driven from his kingly dignity, and from among men too, to eat grass like an ox, and to company with the beasts—Daniel did not stick to tell Belshazzar his son to his face thereof; nor to publish it that it might be read and remembered by the generations to come. The same may be said of Judas and Ananias, etc., for their sin and punishment were known to all the dwellers at Jerusalem (Acts i. 19). Nor is it a sign but of desperate impenitence and hardness of heart, when the offspring or relations of those who have fallen by open, fearful, and prodigious judgments, for their sin, shall overlook, forget, pass by, or take no notice of such high outgoings of God against them and their house. Thus Daniel aggravates Belshazzar's crime, for that he hardened his heart in pride, though he knew that for that very sin and transgression his father was brought down from his height, and made to be a companion for asses. "And thou his son, O Belshazzar," says he, "hast not humbled thine heart, though thou knewest all this" (Dan. v. 22). A home reproof, indeed, but home [reproof] is most fit for an open and a continued in transgression.

Let those, then, that are the offspring or relations of such, who by their own sin, and the dreadful judgments of God, are made to become a sign (Deut. xvi. 9-12), having been swept as dung from off the face of the earth, beware, lest when judgment knocks at their door, for their sins, as it did before at the door of their progenitors, it falls also with as heavy a stroke as on them that went before them

(Num. xvi. 38–40). Lest, I say, they in that day, instead of finding mercy, find for their high, daring, and judgment-affronting sins, judgment without mercy.

To conclude; let those that would not die Mr Badman's death, take heed of Mr. Badman's ways; for his ways bring to his end. Wickedness will not deliver him that is given to it; though they should cloak all with a profession of religion. If it was a transgression of old for a man to wear a woman's apparel, surely it is a transgression now for a sinner to wear a Christian profession for a cloak. Wolves in sheep's clothing swarm in England this day; wolves both as to doctrine, and as to practice too. Some men make a profession, I doubt, on purpose that they may twist themselves into a trade; and thence into an estate; yea, and if need be, into an estate knavishly, by the ruins of their neighbour. Let such take heed, for those that do such things have the greater damnation. Christian, make thy profession shine by a conversation according to the gospel; or else thou wilt damnify religion, bring scandal to thy brethren, and give offence to their enemies; and it would be better that a millstone was hanged about thy neck, and that thou, as so adorned, was cast into the bottom of the sea, than so to do. Christian, a profession according to the gospel is, in these days, a rare thing; seek then after it, put it on, and keep it without spot, and, as becomes thee, white, and clean, and thou shalt be rare Christian.

The prophecy of the last times is, that professing men, for so I understand the text, shall be many of them base (2 Tim. iii.); but continue thou in the things that thou hast learned, not of wanton men, nor of licentious times, but of the Word and doctrine of God, that is, according to godliness; and thou shalt walk with Christ in white. Now, God Almighty gave his people grace, not to hate or malign sinners, nor yet to choose any of their ways, but to keep themselves pure from the blood of all men, by speaking and doing according to that name and those rules that they profess to know and love; for Jesus Christ's sake.

JOHN BUNYAN.

THE LIFE AND DEATH OF
MR. BADMAN

PRESENTED TO THE WORLD IN

A FAMILIAR DIALOGUE BETWEEN MR. WISE-
MAN AND MR. ATTENTIVE

Wiseman. Good morrow, my good neighbour, Mr. Attentive; whither are you walking so early this morning?
Methinks you look as if you were concerned about something more than ordinary. Have you lost any of your cattle,
or what is the matter?

Attentive. Good Sir, good morrow to you. I have not as
yet lost aught, but yet you give a right guess of me, for I
am, as you say, concerned in my heart, but it is because
of the badness of the times. And, Sir, you, as all our neighbours know, are a very observing man, pray, therefore, what
do you think of them?

Wise. Why, I think, as you say, to wit, that they are
bad times, and bad they will be, until men are better; for
they are bad men that make bad times; if men, therefore,
would mend, so would the times. It is a folly to look for
good days so long as sin is so high, and those that study
its nourishment so many. God bring it down, and those that
nourish it, to repentance, and then, my good neighbour,
you will be concerned, not as you are now; now you are
concerned because times are so bad, but then you will be
so because times are so good; now you are concerned so as
to be perplexed, but then you will be concerned so as to lift
up your voice with shouting, for I dare say, could you see
such days, they would make you shout.

Atten. Aye, so they would; such times I have prayed for,
such times I have longed for; but I fear they will be worse
before they be better.

Wise. Make no conclusions, man; for he that hath the hearts of men in his hand can change them from worse to better, and so bad times into good. God give long life to them that are good, and especially to those of them that are capable of doing him service in the world. The ornament and beauty of this lower world, next to God and his wonders, are the men that spangle and shine in godliness.

Now as Mr. Wiseman said this, he gave a great sigh.

Atten. Amen, amen. But why, good Sir, do you sigh so deeply; is it for aught else than that for the which, as you have perceived, I myself am concerned?

Wise. I am concerned, with you, for the badness of the times; but that was not the cause of that sigh, of the which, as I see, you take notice. I sighed at the remembrance of the death of that man for whom the bell tolled at our town yesterday.

Atten. Why, I trow, Mr. Goodman your neighbour is not dead. Indeed I did hear that he had been sick.

Wise. No, no, it is not he. Had it been he, I could not but have been concerned, but yet not as I am concerned now. If he had died, I should only have been concerned for that the world had lost a light; but the man that I am concerned for now was one that never was good, therefore such an one who is not dead only, but damned. He died that he might die, he went from life to death, and then from death to death, from death natural to death eternal. And as he spake this, the water stood in his eyes.

Atten. Indeed, to go from a death-bed to hell is a fearful thing to think on. But, good neighbour Wiseman, be pleased to tell me who this man was, and why you conclude him so miserable in his death?

Wise. Well, if you can stay, I will tell you who he was, and why I conclude thus concerning him.

Atten. My leisure will admit me to stay, and I am willing to hear you out. And I pray God your discourse may take hold on my heart, that I may be bettered thereby. So they agreed to sit down under a tree. Then Mr. Wiseman proceeded as followeth:

Wise. The man that I mean is one Mr. Badman; he has lived in our town a great while, and now, as I said, he is dead. But the reason of my being so concerned at his death is, not for that he was at all related to me, or for that any good conditions died with him, for he was far from them, but for that, as I greatly fear, he hath, as was hinted before, died two deaths at once.

Atten. I perceive what you mean by two deaths at once; and to speak truth, it is a fearful thing thus to have ground to think of any: for although the death of the ungodly and sinners is laid to heart but of few, yet to die in such a state is more dreadful and fearful than any man can imagine. Indeed if a man had no soul, if his state was not truly immortal, the matter would not be so much; but for a man to be so disposed of by his Maker, as to be appointed a sensible being for ever, and for him too to fall into the hands of revenging justice, that will be always, to the utmost extremity that his sin deserveth, punishing of him in the dismal dungeon of hell, this must needs be unutterably sad and lamentable.

Wise. There is no man, I think, that is sensible of the worth of one soul, but must, when he hears of the death of unconverted men, be stricken with sorrow and grief: because, as you said well, that man's state is such that he has a sensible being for ever. For it is sense that makes punishment heavy. But yet sense is not all that the damned have, they have sense and reason too; so then, as sense receiveth punishment with sorrow, because it feels, and bleeds under the same, so by reason, and the exercise thereof, in the midst of torment, all present affliction is aggravated, and that in three manner of ways: (1) Reason will consider thus with himself: For what am I thus tormented? and will easily find it is for nothing but that base and filthy thing, sin; and now will vexation be mixed with punishment, and that will greatly heighten the affliction. (2) Reason will consider thus with himself: How long must this be my state? and will soon return to himself this answer: This must be my state for ever and ever. Now this will greatly increase the torment. (3) Reason will consider thus with himself: What have I lost more than present ease and quiet by my sins that I have committed? and will quickly return himself this answer: I have lost communion with God, Christ, saints, and angels, and a share in heaven and eternal life: and this also must needs greaten the misery of poor damned souls. And this is the case of Mr. Badman.

Atten. I feel my heart even shake at the thoughts of coming into such a state. Hell! who knows that is yet alive, what the torments of hell are? This word HELL gives a very dreadful sound.

Wise. Aye, so it does in the ears of him that has a tender conscience. But if, as you say, and that truly, the very name of hell is so dreadful, what is the place itself, and what are the punishments that are there inflicted, and that without the least intermission, upon the souls of damned men, for ever and ever?

Atten. Well, but passing this; my leisure will admit me to stay, and therefore pray tell me what it is that makes you think that Mr. Badman is gone to hell.

Wise. I will tell you. But first, do you know which of the Badmans I mean?

Atten. Why, was there more of them than one?

Wise. O yes, a great many, both brothers and sisters, and yet all of them the children of a godly parent, the more a great deal is the pity.

Atten. Which of them therefore was it that died?

Wise. The eldest, old in years, and old in sin; but the sinner that dies an hundred years old shall be accursed.

Atten. Well, but what makes you think he is gone to hell?

Wise. His wicked life, and fearful death, especially since the manner of his death was so corresponding with his life.

Atten. Pray let me know the manner of his death, if yourself did perfectly know it.

Wise. I was there when he died; but I desire not to see another such man, while I live, die in such sort as he did.

Atten. Pray therefore let me hear it.

Wise. You say you have leisure and can stay, and therefore, if you please, we will discourse even orderly of him. First, we will begin with his life, and then proceed to his death: because a relation of the first may the more affect you, when you shall hear of the second.

Atten. Did you then so well know his life?

Wise. I knew him of a child. I was a man when he was but a boy, and I made special observation of him from first to last.

Atten. Pray then let me hear from you an account of his life; but be as brief as you can, for I long to hear of the manner of his death.

Wise. I will endeavour to answer your desires, and first, I will tell you, that from a child he was very bad; his very beginning was ominous, and presaged that no good end was, in likelihood, to follow thereupon. There were several sins that he was given to, when but a little one, that manifested him to be notoriously infected with original corruption; for I dare say he learned none of them of his father and mother; nor was he admitted to go much abroad among other children that were vile, to learn to sin of them: nay, contrariwise, if at any time he did get abroad amongst others, he would be as the inventor of bad words, and an example in bad actions. To them all he used to be, as we say, the ringleader and master-sinner from a child.

Atten. This was a bad beginning indeed, and did demonstrate that he was, as you say, polluted, very much polluted with original corruption. For to speak my mind freely, I do confess that it is mine opinion that children come polluted with sin into the world, and that ofttimes the sins of their youth, especially while they are very young, are rather by virtue of indwelling sin, than by examples that are set before them by others. Not but that they learn to sin by example too, but example is not the root, but rather the temptation unto wickedness. The root is sin within; "for from within, out of the heart of men," proceedeth sin (Mark vii. 21).

Wise. I am glad to hear that you are of this opinion, and to confirm what you have said by a few hints from the Word. Man in his birth is compared to an ass, an unclean beast, and to a wretched infant in its blood (Job xi. 12; Ezek. xvi.). Besides, all the first-born of old that were offered unto the Lord, were to be redeemed at the age of a month, and that was before they were sinners by imitation (Exod. xiii. 13; xxxiv. 20). The scripture also affirmeth, that by the sin of one, judgment came upon all; and renders this reason, "for that all have sinned" (Rom. v. 12). Nor is that objection worth a rush, that Christ by his death hath taken away original sin. First, Because it is scriptureless. Secondly, Because it makes them incapable of salvation by

Christ; for none but those that in their own persons are sinners are to have salvation by him. Many other things might be added, but between persons so well agreed as you and I are, these may suffice at present. But when an antagonist comes to deal with us about this matter, then we have for him often other strong arguments, if he be an antagonist worth the taking notice of.

Atten. But, as was hinted before, he used to be the ring-leading sinner, or the master of mischief, among other children; yet these are but generals; pray therefore tell me in particular which were the sins of his childhood.

Wise. I will so. When he was but a child, he was so addicted to lying that his parents scarce knew when to believe he spake true; yea, he would invent, tell, and stand to the lies that he invented and told, and that with such an audacious face, that one might even read in his very countenance the symptoms of a hard and desperate heart this way.

Atten. This was an ill beginning indeed, and argueth that he began to harden himself in sin betimes. For a lie cannot be knowingly told and stood in, and I perceive that this was his manner of way in lying, but he must as it were force his own heart unto it. Yea, he must make his heart hard and bold to do it. Yea, he must be arrived to an exceeding pitch of wickedness thus to do, since all this he did against that good education, that before you seemed to hint he had from his father and mother.

Wise. The want of good education, as you have intimated, is many times a cause why children do so easily, so soon, become bad; especially when there is not only a want of that, but bad examples enough, as, the more is the pity, there is in many families; by virtue of which poor children are trained up in sin, and nursed therein for the devil and hell. But it was otherwise with Mr. Badman, for to my knowledge this his way of lying was a great grief to his parents, for their hearts were much dejected at this beginning of their son; nor did there want counsel and correction from them to him if that would have made him better. He wanted not to be told, in my hearing, and that over and over and over, that "all liars shall have their part in the lake which burneth with fire and brimstone"; and that "whosoever

loveth and maketh a lie," should not have any part in the
new and heavenly Jerusalem (Rev. xxi. 8, 27; xxii. 15).
But all availed nothing with him; when a fit, or an occasion
to lie came upon him, he would invent, tell, and stand to his
lie as stedfastly as if it had been the biggest of truths that he
told, and that with that hardening of his heart and face,
that it would be to those who stood by, a wonder. Nay,
and this he would do when under the rod of correction, which
is appointed by God for parents to use, that thereby they
might keep their children from hell (Prov. xxii. 15; xxiii. 13,14).

Atten. Truly it was, as I said, a bad beginning, he served
the devil betimes; yea, he became nurse to one of his brats,
for a spirit of lying is the devil's brat, "for he is a liar, and
the father of it" (John viii. 44).

Wise. Right, he is the father of it indeed. A lie is begot
by the devil as the father, and is brought forth by the wicked
heart as the mother; wherefore another scripture also saith,
"Why hath Satan filled thine heart to lie," etc. (Acts v. 3, 4).
Yea, he calleth the heart that is big with a lie, an heart that
hath conceived, that is, by the devil. "Why hast thou conceived this thing in thine heart? thou hast not lied unto
men, but unto God." True, his lie was a lie of the highest
nature, but every lie hath the same father and mother as
had the lie last spoken of. "For he is a liar, and the father
of it." A lie then is the brat of hell, and it cannot be in the
heart before the person has committed a kind of spiritual
adultery with the devil. That soul therefore that telleth a
known lie, has lien with, and conceived it by lying with
the devil, the only father of lies. For a lie has only one father
and mother, the devil and the heart. No marvel therefore
if the hearts that hatch and bring forth lies be so much of
complexion with the devil. Yea, no marvel though God and
Christ have so bent their word against liars. A liar is wedded
to the devil himself.

Atten. It seems a marvellous thing in mine eyes, that
since a lie is the offspring of the devil, and since a lie brings
the soul to the very den of devils, to wit, the dark dungeon
of hell, that men should be so desperately wicked as to
accustom themselves to so horrible a thing.

Wise. It seems also marvellous to me, especially when I
observe for how little a matter some men will study, con-

trive, make, and tell a lie. You shall have some that will lie it over and over, and that for a penny profit. Yea, lie and stand in it, although they know that they lie. Yea, you shall have some men that will not stick to tell lie after lie, though themselves get nothing thereby. They will tell lies in their ordinary discourse with their neighbours, also their news, their jests, and their tales, must needs be adorned with lies; or else they seem to bear no good sound to the ear, nor show much to the fancy of him to whom they are told. But alas! what will these liars do, when, for their lies, they shall be tumbled down into hell, to that devil that did beget those lies in their heart, and so be tormented by fire and brimstone, with him, and that for ever and ever, for their lies?

Atten. Can you not give one some example of God's judgments upon liars, that one may tell them to liars when one hears them lie, if perhaps they may by the hearing thereof, be made afraid, and ashamed to lie?

Wise. Examples! why, Ananias and his wife are examples enough to put a stop, one would think, to a spirit addicted thereto, for they both were stricken down dead for telling a lie, and that by God himself, in the midst of a company of people (Acts v.). But if God's threatening of liars with hell-fire, and with the loss of the kingdom of heaven, will not prevail with them to leave off to lie and make lies, it cannot be imagined that a relation of temporal judgments that have swept liars out of the world heretofore, should do it. Now, as I said, this lying was one of the first sins that Mr. Badman was addicted to, and he could make them and tell them fearfully.

Atten. I am sorry to hear this of him, and so much the more, because, as I fear, this sin did not reign in him alone; for usually one that is accustomed to lying, is also accustomed to other evils besides; and if it were not so also with Mr. Badman, it would be indeed a wonder.

Wise. You say true, the liar is a captive slave of more than the spirit of lying; and therefore this Mr. Badman, as he was a liar from a child, so he was also much given to pilfer and steal, so that what he could, as we say, handsomely lay his hands on, that was counted his own, whether they were the things of his fellow-children, or if he could lay hold of anything at a neighbour's house, he would take it away; you must understand me of trifles; for being yet but a child, he attempted no great matter, especially at first. But yet as he grew up in strength and ripeness of wit, so he attempted to pilfer and steal things still of more value than at first. He took at last great pleasure in robbing of gardens and orchards; and as he grew up, to steal pullen from the neighbourhood. Yea, what was his father's could not escape his fingers, all was fish that came to his net, so hardened, at last, was he in this mischief also.

Atten. You make me wonder more and more. What, play the thief too! What, play the thief so soon! He could not but know, though he was but a child, that what he took from others was none of his own. Besides, if his father was a good man, as you say, it could not be but he must also hear from him that to steal was to transgress the law of God, and so to run the hazard of eternal damnation.

Wise. His father was not wanting to use the means to reclaim him, often urging, as I have been told, that saying in the law of Moses, "Thou shalt not steal" (Exod. xx. 15). And also that, "This is the curse that goeth forth over the face of the whole earth; for every one that stealeth shall be cut off," etc. (Zech. v. 3). The light of nature also, though he was little, must needs show him that what he took from others was not his own; and that he would not willingly have been served so himself. But all was to no purpose, let father and conscience say what they would to him, he would go on, he was resolved to go on in his wickedness.

Atten. But his father would, as you intimate, sometimes rebuke him for his wickedness; pray how would he carry it then?

Wise. How! why like to a thief that is found. He would stand gloating, and hanging down his head in a sullen, pouching manner; a body might read, as we used to say, the picture of ill-luck in his face; and when his father did demand his answer to such questions concerning his villany, he would grumble and mutter at him, and that should be all he could get.

Atten. But you said that he would also rob his father, methinks that was an unnatural thing.

Wise. Natural or unnatural, all is one to a thief. Besides, you must think that he had likewise companions to whom he was, for the wickedness that he saw in them, more firmly knit, than either to father or mother. Yea, and what had he cared if father and mother had died for grief for him! Their death would have been, as he would have counted, great release and liberty to him; for the truth is, they and their counsel were his bondage; yea, and if I forget not, I have heard some say that when he was, at times, among his companions he would greatly rejoice to think that his parents were old, and could not live long, and then, quoth he, I shall be mine own man, to do what I list, without their control.

Atten. Then it seems he counted that robbing of his parents was no crime.

Wise. None at all; and therefore he fell directly under that sentence, "Whoso robbeth his father or his mother, and saith it is no transgression, the same is the companion of a destroyer" (Prov. xxviii. 24). And for that he set so light by them as to their persons and counsels, it was a sign that at present he was of a very abominable spirit, and that some judgment waited to take hold of him in time to come (1 Sam. ii. 25).

Atten. But can you imagine what it was, I mean, in his conceit, for I speak not now of the suggestions of Satan, by which doubtless he was put on to do these things; I say what it should be in his conceit, that should make him think that this his manner of pilfering and stealing was no great matter?

Wise. It was for that the things that he stole were small; to rob orchards, and gardens, and to steal pullen, and the like, these he counted tricks of youth, nor would he be beat out of it by all that his friends could say. They would tell him that he must not covet, or desire, and yet to desire is less than to take, even anything, the least thing that was his neighbour's; and that if he did, it would be a transgression of the law; but all was one to him; what through the wicked talk of his companions, and the delusion of his own corrupt heart, he would go on in his pilfering course, and where he thought himself secure, would talk of, and laugh at it when he had done.

Atten. Well, I heard a man once, when he was upon the ladder with the rope about his neck, confess, when ready to be turned off by the hangman, that that which had brought him to that end was his accustoming of himself, when young, to pilfer and steal small things. To my best remembrance he told us, that he began the trade of a thief by stealing of pins and points; and therefore did forewarn all the youth that then were gathered together to see him die, to take heed of beginning, though but with little sins; because by tampering at first with little ones, way is made for the commission of bigger.

Wise. Since you are entered upon stories, I also will tell you one; the which, though I heard it not with mine own ears, yet my author I dare believe. It is concerning one old Tod, that was hanged about twenty years ago, or more, at Hertford, for being a thief. The story is this:

At a summer assizes holden at Hertford, while the judge was sitting upon the bench, comes this old Tod into court, clothed in a green suit, with his leathern girdle in his hand, his bosom open, and all on a dung sweat, as if he had run for his life; and being come in, he spake aloud as follows: My lord, said he, here is the veriest rogue that breathes upon the face of the earth. I have been a thief from a child. When I was but a little one, I gave myself to rob orchards, and to do other such-like wicked things, and I have continued a thief ever since. My lord, there has not been a robbery committed these many years, within so many miles of this place, but I have either been at it, or privy to it.

The judge thought the fellow was mad, but after some conference with some of the justices, they agreed to indict him; and so they did of several felonious actions; to all which he heartily confessed guilty, and so was hanged, with his wife at the same time.

Atten. This is a remarkable story indeed, and you think it is a true one.

Wise. It is not only remarkable, but pat to our purpose. This thief, like Mr. Badman, began his trade betimes; he began too where Mr. Badman began, even at robbing of orchards, and other such things, which brought him, as you may perceive, from sin to sin, till at last it brought him to the public shame of sin, which is the gallows.

As for the truth of this story, the relater told me that he was, at the same time, himself in the court, and stood within

less than two yards of old Tod, when he heard him aloud to
utter the words.

Atten. These two sins, of lying and stealing, were a bad
sign of an evil end.

Wise. So they were, and yet Mr. Badman came not to his
end like old Tod; though I fear to as bad, nay, worse than
was that death of the gallows, though less discerned by
spectators; but more of that by and by. But you talk of
these two sins as if these were all that Mr. Badman was
addicted to in his youth. Alas, alas, he swarmed with sins,
even as a beggar does with vermin, and that when he was
but a boy.

Atten. Why, what other sins was he addicted to, I mean
while he was but a child?

Wise. You need not ask to what other sins was he, but
to what other sins was he not addicted; that is, of such as
suited with his age; for a man may safely say that nothing
that was vile came amiss to him, if he was but capable to
do it. Indeed, some sins there be that childhood knows not
how to be tampering with; but I speak of sins that he was
capable of committing, of which I will nominate two or
three more. And, First, He could not endure the Lord's
day, because of the holiness that did attend it; the beginning
of that day was to him as if he was going to prison, except
he could get out from his father and mother, and lurk in
by-holes among his companions, until holy duties were over.
Reading the Scriptures, hearing sermons, godly conference,
repeating of sermons and prayers, were things that he could
not away with; and, therefore, if his father on such days,
as often he did, though sometimes, notwithstanding his
diligence, he would be sure to give him the slip, did keep
him strictly to the observation of the day, he would plainly
show, by all carriages, that he was highly discontent therewith. He would sleep at duties, would talk vainly with his
brothers, and, as it were, think every godly opportunity
seven times as long as it was, grudging till it was over.

Atten. This his abhorring of that day, was not, I think,
for the sake of the day itself; for as it is a day, it is nothing
else but as other days of the week. But I suppose that the
reason of his loathing of it was for that God hath put sanctity
and holiness upon it; also, because it is the day above all

the days of the week that ought to be spent in holy devotion, in remembrance of our Lord's resurrection from the dead.

Wise. Yes, it was therefore that he was such an enemy to it; even because more restraint was laid upon him on that day, from his own ways, than were possible should be laid upon him on all others.

Atten. Doth not God, by instituting of a day unto holy duties, make great proof how the hearts and inclinations of poor people do stand to holiness of heart, and a conversation in holy duties?

Wise. Yes, doubtless; and a man shall show his heart and his life what they are, more by one Lord's day than by all the days of the week besides. And the reason is, because on the Lord's day there is a special restraint laid upon men as to thoughts and life, more than upon other days of the week besides. Also, men are enjoined on that day to a stricter performance of holy duties, and restraint of worldly business, than upon other days they are; wherefore, if their hearts incline not naturally to good, now they will show it, now they will appear what they are. The Lord's day is a kind of an emblem of the heavenly Sabbath above, and it makes manifest how the heart stands to the perpetuity of holiness, more than to be found in a transient duty does.

On other days, a man may be in and out of holy duties, and all in a quarter of an hour; but now, the Lord's day is, as it were, a day that enjoins to one perpetual duty of holiness. "Remember that thou keep holy the Sabbath day"; which, by Christ, is not abrogated, but changed, into the first of the week, not as it was given in particular to the Jews, but as it was sanctified by him from the beginning of the world (Gen. ii. 2; Exod. xxxi. 13-17; Mark xvi. 1; Acts xx. 7; 1 Cor. xvi. 1, 2; Mark ii. 27, 28; Rev. i. 10); and therefore is a greater proof of the frame and temper of a man's heart, and does more make manifest to what he is inclined, than doth his other performance of duties. There-fore, God puts great difference between them that truly call, and walk in, this day as holy, and count it honourable, upon the account that now they have an opportunity to show how they delight to honour him; in that they have not only an hour, but a whole day, to show it in (Is. lviii. 13). I say, he puts great difference between these, and that other sort that say, When will the Sabbath be gone, that we may be at our worldly business? (Amos viii. 5). The first he calleth a blessed man, but brandeth the other for an unsanctified worldling. And, indeed, to delight ourselves in God's service upon his holy days, gives a better proof of a sanctified nature than to grudge at the coming, and to be weary of the holy duties of such days, as Mr. Badman did.

Atten. There may be something in what you say, for he that cannot abide to keep one day holy to God, to be sure he hath given a sufficient proof that he is an unsanctified man; and, as such, what should he do in heaven? That being the place where a perpetual Sabbath is to be kept to God; I say, to be kept for ever and ever (Heb. iv. 9). And, for aught I know, one reason why one day in seven hath been by our Lord set apart unto holy duties for men, may be to give them conviction that there is enmity in the hearts of sinners to the God of heaven, for he that hateth holiness, hateth God himself. They pretend to love God, and yet love not a holy day, and yet love not to spend that day in one continued act of holiness to the Lord. They had as good say nothing as to call him Lord, Lord, and yet not do the things that he says. And this Mr. Badman was such a one, he could not abide this day, nor any of the duties of it. Indeed, when he could get from his friends, and so spend it in all manner of idleness and profaneness, then he would be pleased well enough; but what was this but a turning the day into night, or other than taking an opportunity at God's forbidding, to follow our callings, to solace and satisfy our lusts and delights of the flesh? I take the liberty to speak thus of Mr. Badman, upon a confidence of what you, Sir, have said of him is true.

Wise. You needed not to have made that apology for your censuring of Mr. Badman, for all that knew him will confirm what you say of him to be true. He could not abide either that day, or anything else that had the stamp or image of God upon it. Sin, sin, and to do the thing that was naught, was that which he delighted in, and that from a little child.

Atten. I must say again I am sorry to hear it, and that for his own sake, and also for the sake of his relations, who must needs be broken to pieces with such doings as these.

For, for these things' sake comes the wrath of God upon the children of disobedience (Eph. v. 6). And, doubtless, he must be gone to hell, if he died without repentance; and to beget a child for hell is sad for parents to think on.

Wise. Of his dying, as I told you, I will give you a relation anon; but now we are upon his life, and upon the manner of his life in his childhood, even of the sins that attended him then, some of which I have mentioned already; and, indeed, I have mentioned but some, for yet there are more to follow, and those not at all inferior to what you have already heard.

Atten. Pray what were they?

Wise. Why he was greatly given, and that while a lad, to grievous swearing and cursing; yea, he then made no more of swearing and cursing than I do of telling my fingers. Yea, he would do it without provocation thereto. He counted it a glory to swear and curse, and it was as natural to him as to eat, and drink, and sleep.

Atten. O what a young villain was this! Here is, as the apostle says, a yielding of "members, *as* instruments of unrighteousness unto sin," indeed (Rom. vi. 13)! This is proceeding from evil to evil with a witness. This argueth that he was a black-mouthed young wretch indeed.

Wise. He was so; and yet, as I told you, he counted above all this kind of sinning to be a badge of his honour; he reckoned himself a man's fellow when he had learned to swear and curse boldly.

Atten. I am persuaded that many do think as you have said, that to swear is a thing that does bravely become them, and that it is the best way for a man, when he would put authority or terror into his words, to stuff them full of the sin of swearing.

Wise. You say right, else, as I am persuaded, men would not so usually belch out their blasphemous oaths as they do; they take a pride in it; they think that to swear is gentleman-like; and, having once accustomed themselves unto it, they hardly leave it all the days of their lives.

Atten. Well, but now we are upon it, pray show me the difference between swearing and cursing; for there is a difference, is there not?

Wise. Yes; there is a difference between swearing and

cursing. Swearing, vain swearing, such as young Badman accustomed himself unto. Now, vain and sinful swearing is a light and wicked calling of God, etc., to witness to our vain and foolish attesting of things, and those things are of two sorts. 1. Things that we swear, are or shall be done. 2. Things so sworn to, true or false.

1. Things that we swear, are or shall be done. Thou swearest thou hast done such a thing, that such a thing is so, or shall be so; for it is no matter which of these it is that men swear about, if it be done lightly, and wickedly, and groundlessly, it is vain, because it is a sin against the third commandment, which says, "Thou shalt not take the name of the Lord thy God in vain" (Exod. xx. 7). For this is a vain using of that holy and sacred name, and so a sin for which, without sound repentance, there is not, nor can be rightly expected, forgiveness.

Atten. Then it seems, though as to the matter of fact, a man swears truly, yet if he sweareth lightly and groundlessly, his oath is evil, and he by it under sin.

Wise. Yes, a man may say, "The Lord liveth," and that is true, and yet in so saying "swear falsely"; because he sweareth vainly, needlessly, and without a ground (Jer. v. 2). To swear groundedly and necessarily, which then a man does when he swears as being called thereto of God, that is tolerated by the Word. But this was none of Mr. Badman's swearing, and therefore that which now we are not concerned about.

Atten. I perceive by the prophet that a man may sin in swearing to a truth. They therefore must needs most horribly sin that swear to confirm their jests and lies; and, as they think, the better to beautify their foolish talking.

Wise. They sin with a high hand; for they presume to imagine that God is as wicked as themselves, to wit, that he is an avoucher of lies to be true. For, as I said before, to swear is to call God to witness; and to swear to a lie is to call God to witness that that lie is true. This, therefore, must needs offend; for it puts the highest affront upon the holiness and righteousness of God, therefore his wrath must sweep them away (Zech. v. 3). This kind of swearing is put in with lying, and killing, and stealing, and committing adultery; and therefore must not go unpunished (Jer. vii. 9; Hos. iv. 2, 3). For if God "will not hold him guiltless that taketh his name in vain," which a man may do when he swears to a truth, as I have showed before, how can it be imagined that he should hold such guiltless, who, by swearing, will appeal to God for lies that be not true, or that swear out of their frantic and bedlam madness? It would grieve and provoke a sober man to wrath, if one should swear to a notorious lie and avouch that that man would attest it for a truth; and yet thus do men deal with the holy God. They tell their jestings, tales, and lies, and then swear by God that they are true. Now, this kind of swearing was as common with young Badman, as it was to eat when he was an hungered, or to go to bed when it was night.

Atten. I have often mused in my mind, what it should be that should make men so common in the use of the sin of swearing, since those that be wise will believe them never the sooner for that.

Wise. It cannot be anything that is good, you may be sure; because the thing itself is abominable. (1) Therefore it must be from the promptings of the spirit of the devil within them. (2) Also it flows sometimes from hellish rage, when the tongue hath set on fire of hell even the whole course of nature (Jas. iii. 6–9). (3) But commonly, swearing flows from that daring boldness that biddeth defiance to the law that forbids it. (4) Swearers think, also, that by their belching of their blasphemous oaths out of their black and polluted mouths, they show themselves the more valiant men. (5) And imagine also, that by these outrageous kind of villanies, they shall conquer those that at such a time they have to do with, and make them believe their lies to be true. (6) They also swear frequently to get gain thereby, and when they meet with fools they overcome them this way. But if I might give advice in this matter, no buyer should lay out one farthing with him that is a common swearer in his calling; especially with such an oath-master that endeavoureth to swear away his commodity to another, and that would swear his chapman's money into his own pocket.

Atten. All these causes of swearing, so far as I can perceive, flow from the same root as do the oaths themselves, even from a hardened and desperate heart. But, pray, show me now how wicked cursing is to be distinguished from this kind of swearing.

Wise. Swearing, as I said, hath immediately to do with the name of God, and it calls upon him to be witness to the truth of what is said; that is, if they that swear, swear by him. Some, indeed, swear by idols, as by the mass, by our lady, by saints, beasts, birds, and other creatures; but the usual way of our profane ones in England is to swear by God, Christ, faith, and the like. But, however, or by whatever they swear, cursing is distinguished from swearing thus.

To curse, to curse profanely, it is to sentence another or ourself, for or to evil; or to wish that some evil might happen to the person or thing under the curse unjustly.

It is to sentence for or to evil, that is, without a cause. Thus Shimei cursed David; he sentenced him for and to evil unjustly, when he said to him, "Come out, come out, thou bloody man, and thou man of Belial. The Lord hath returned upon thee all the blood of the house of Saul, in whose stead thou hast reigned, and the Lord hath delivered the kingdom into the hand of Absalom thy son; and, behold, thou *art taken* in thy mischief, because thou *art* a bloody man" (2 Sam. xvi. 7, 8).

This David calls "a grievous curse." "And behold," saith he to Solomon his son, "*thou hast* with thee Shimei . . . a Benjamite . . . which cursed me with a grievous curse in the day when I went to Mahanaim" (1 Kings ii. 8).

But what was this curse? Why, First, It was a wrong sentence past upon David; Shimei called him bloody man, man of Belial, when he was not. Secondly, He sentenced him to the evil that at present was upon him for being a bloody man, that is, against the house of Saul, when that present evil overtook David for quite another thing. And we may thus apply it to the profane ones of our times, who in their rage and envy have little else in their mouths but a sentence against their neighbour for and to evil unjustly. How common is it with many, when they are but a little offended with one, to cry, Hang him, Damn him, Rogue? This is both a sentencing of him for and to evil, and is in itself a grievous curse.

2. The other kind of cursing is to wish that some evil might happen to and overtake this or that person or thing. And this kind of cursing Job counted a grievous sin. "Neither have I suffered (says he) my mouth to sin by wishing a

curse to his soul"; or consequently to body or estate (Job xxxi. 30). This then is a wicked cursing, to wish that evil might either befal another or ourselves. And this kind of cursing young Badman accustomed himself unto. (1) He would wish that evil might befal others; he would wish their necks broken, or that their brains were out, or that the pox or plague was upon them, and the like; all which is a devilish kind of cursing, and is become one of the common sins of our age. (2) He would also as often wish a curse to himself, saying, Would I might be hanged, or burned, or that the devil might fetch me, if it be not so, or the like. We count the Damn-me-blades to be great swearers, but when in their hellish fury they say, God damn me, God perish me, or the like, they rather curse than swear; yea, curse themselves, and that with a wish that damnation might light upon themselves; which wish and curse of theirs in a little time they will see accomplished upon them, even in hell fire, if they repent them not of their sins.

Atten. But did this young Badman accustom himself to such filthy kind of language?

Wise. I think I may say that nothing was more frequent in his mouth, and that upon the least provocation. Yea, he was so versed in such kind of language, that neither father, nor mother, nor brother, nor sister, nor servant, no, nor the very cattle that his father had, could escape these curses of his. I say that even the brute beasts, when he drove them or rid upon them, if they pleased not his humour, they must be sure to partake of his curse. He would wish their necks broke, their legs broke, their guts out, or that the devil might fetch them, or the like; and no marvel, for he that is so hardy to wish damnation or other bad curses to himself, or dearest relations, will not stick to wish evil to the silly beast in his madness.

Atten. Well, I see still that this Badman was a desperate villain. But pray, sir, since you have gone thus far, now show me whence this evil of cursing ariseth, and also what dishonour it bringeth to God; for I easily discern that it doth bring damnation to the soul.

Wise. This evil of cursing ariseth in general from the desperate wickedness of the heart, but particularly from, (1) Envy, which is, as I apprehend, the leading sin to witchcraft. (2) It also ariseth from pride, which was the sin of the fallen angels. (3) It ariseth, too, from scorn and contempt of others. (4) But for a man to curse himself, must needs arise from desperate madness (Job xv.; Eccles. vii. 22).

The dishonour that it bringeth to God is this. It taketh away from his authority, in whose power it is only to bless and curse; not to curse wickedly, as Mr. Badman, but justly and righteously, giving by his curse, to those that are wicked, the due reward of their deeds.

Besides, these wicked men, in their wicked cursing of their neighbour, etc., do even curse God himself in his handiwork (Jas. iii. 9). Man is God's image, and to curse wickedly the image of God is to curse God himself. Therefore as when men wickedly swear, they rend and tear God's name, and make him, as much as in them lies, the avoucher and approver of all their wickedness; so he that curseth and condemneth in this sort his neighbour, or that wisheth him evil, curseth, condemneth, and wisheth evil to the image of God, and, consequently, judgeth and condemneth God himself. Suppose that a man should say with his mouth, I wish that the king's picture was burned; would not this man's so saying render him as an enemy to the person of the king? Even so it is with them that, by cursing, wish evil to their neighbour, or to themselves, they contemn the image, even the image of God himself.

Atten. But do you think that the men that do thus, do think that they do so vilely, so abominably?

Wise. The question is not what men do believe concerning their sin, but what God's Word says of it. If God's Word says that swearing and cursing are sins, though men should count them for virtues, their reward will be a reward for sin, to wit, the damnation of the soul. To curse another, and to swear vainly and falsely, are sins against the light of nature. (1) To curse is so, because whoso curseth another, knows that at the same time he would not be so served himself. (2) To swear also is a sin against the same law; for nature will tell me that I should not lie, and therefore much less swear to confirm it. Yea, the heathens have looked upon swearing to be a solemn ordinance of God, and therefore not to be lightly or vainly used by men, though to confirm a matter of truth (Gen. xxxi. 43–55).

Atten. But I wonder, since cursing and swearing are such evils in the eyes of God, that he doth not make some examples to others, for their committing such wickedness.

Wise. Alas! so he has, a thousand times twice told, as may be easily gathered by any observing people in every age and country. I could present you with several myself; but waiving the abundance that might be mentioned, I will here present you with two. One was that dreadful judgment of God upon one N. P. at Wimbleton in Surrey; who, after a horrible fit of swearing at and cursing of some persons that did not please him, suddenly fell sick, and in little time died raving, cursing, and swearing.

But above all, take that dreadful story of Dorothy Mately, an inhabitant of Ashover, in the county of Derby. This Dorothy Mately, saith the relater, was noted by the people of the town to be a great swearer, and curser, and liar, and thief; just like Mr. Badman. And the labour that she did usually follow was to wash the rubbish that came forth of the lead mines, and there to get sparks of lead ore; and her usual way of asserting of things was with these kind of imprecations: I would I might sink into the earth if it be not so; or, I would God would make the earth open and swallow me up. Now upon the 23rd of March, 1660, this Dorothy was washing of ore upon the top of a steep hill, about a quarter of a mile from Ashover, and was there taxed by a lad for taking of two single pence out of his pocket, for he had laid his breeches by, and was at work in his drawers; but she violently denied it; wishing that the ground might swallow her up if she had them: she also used the same wicked words on several other occasions that day.

Now one George Hodgkinson, of Ashover, a man of good report there, came accidentally by where this Dorothy was, and stood still awhile to talk with her, as she was washing her ore; there stood also a little child by her tub-side, and another a distance from her, calling aloud to her to come away; wherefore the said George took the girl by the hand to lead her away to her that called her: but behold, they had not gone above ten yards from Dorothy, but they heard her crying out for help; so looking back, he saw the woman, and her tub, and sieve twirling round, and sinking into the ground. Then said the man, Pray to God to pardon thy sin, for thou art never like to be seen alive any longer. So she and her tub twirled round and round, till they sunk about three yards into the earth, and then for a while staid. Then she called for help again; thinking, as she said, she should stay there. Now the man, though greatly amazed, did begin to think which way to help her; but immediately a great stone which appeared in the earth, fell upon her head, and broke her skull, and then the earth fell in upon her, and covered her. She was afterwards digged up, and found about four yards within ground, with the boy's two single pence in her pocket, but her tub and sieve could not be found.

Atten. You bring to my mind a sad story, the which I will relate unto you. The thing is this: About a bow-shot from where I once dwelt, there was a blind ale-house, and the man that kept it had a son, whose name was Edward. This Edward was, as it were, a half fool, both in his words and manner of behaviour. To this blind ale-house certain jovial companions would once or twice a week come, and this Ned, for so they called him, his father would entertain his guests withal; to wit, by calling for him to make them sport by his foolish words and gestures. So when these boon blades came to this man's house, the father would call for Ned. Ned, therefore, would come forth; and the villain was devilishly addicted to cursing, yea, to cursing his father and mother, and anyone else that did cross him. And because, though he was a half fool, he saw that his practice was pleasing, he would do it with the more audaciousness.

Well, when these brave fellows did come at their times to this tippling-house, as they call it, to fuddle and make merry, then must Ned be called out; and because his father was best acquainted with Ned, and best knew how to provoke him, therefore he would usually ask him such questions, or command him such business, as would be sure to provoke him indeed. Then would he, after his foolish manner, curse his father most bitterly; at which the old man would laugh, and so would the rest of the guests, as at that which pleased them best, still continuing to ask that Ned still might be provoked to curse, that they might still be provoked to laugh. This was the mirth with which the old man did use to entertain his guests.

The curses wherewith this Ned did use to curse his father,

and at which the old man would laugh, were these, and such like; the devil take you—the devil fetch you; he would also wish him plagues and destructions many. Well, so it came to pass, through the righteous judgment of God, that Ned's wishes and curses were in a little time fulfilled upon his father; for not many months passed between them after this manner, but the devil did indeed take him, possess him, and also in a few days carried him out of this world by death; I say Satan did take him and possess him; I mean, so it was judged by those that knew him, and had to do with him in that his lamentable condition. He could feel him like a live thing go up and down in his body; but when tormenting time was come, as he had often tormenting fits, then he would lie like an hard bump in the soft place of his chest, I mean I saw it so, and so would rend and tear him, and make him roar till he died away.

I told you before that I was an ear- and eye-witness of what I here say; and so I was. I have heard Ned in his roguery cursing his father, and his father laughing thereat most heartily; still provoking of Ned to curse, that his mirth might be increased. I saw his father also, when he was possessed, I saw him in one of his fits, and saw his flesh, as it was thought, by the devil gathered up on a heap, about the bigness of half an egg, to the unutterable torture and affliction of the old man. There was also one Freeman, who was more than an ordinary doctor, sent for, to cast out this devil; and I was there when he attempted to do it; the manner thereof was this: They had the possessed into an out-room, and laid him on his belly upon a form, with his head hanging over the form's end. Then they bound him down thereto; which done, they set a pan of coals under his mouth, and put something therein which made a great smoke; by this means, as it was said, to fetch out the devil. There, therefore, they kept the man till he was almost smothered in the smoke, but no devil came out of him; at which Freeman was somewhat abashed, the man greatly afflicted, and I made to go away wondering and fearing. In a little time, therefore, that which possessed the man, carried him out of the world, according to the cursed wishes of his son. And this was the end of this hellish mirth.

Wise. These were all sad judgments.

Atten. These were dreadful judgments indeed.

Wise. Aye, and they look like the threatening of that text, though chiefly it concerned Judas, "As he loved cursing, so let it come unto him; as he delighteth not in blessing, so let it be far from him. As he clothed himself with cursing, like as with a garment, so let it come into his bowels like water, and like oil into his bones" (Ps. cix. 17, 18).

Atten. It is a fearful thing for youth to be trained up in a way of cursing and swearing.

Wise. Trained up in them! that I cannot say Mr. Badman was, for his father hath ofttimes in my hearing bewailed the badness of his children, and of this naughty boy in particular. I believe that the wickedness of his children made him, in the thoughts of it, go many a night with heavy heart to bed, and with as heavy a one to rise in the morning. But all was one to his graceless son, neither wholesome counsel, nor fatherly sorrow, would make him mend his manners.

There are some indeed that do train up their children to swear, curse, lie, and steal, and great is the misery of such poor children whose hard hap it is to be ushered into the world by, and to be under the tuition too of such ungodly parents. It had been better for such parents had they not begat them, and better for such children had they not been born. O! methinks for a father or a mother to train up a child in that very way that leadeth to hell and damnation, what thing so horrible! But Mr. Badman was not by his parents so brought up.

Atten. But methinks, since this young Badman would not be ruled at home, his father should have tried what good could have been done of him abroad, by putting him out to some man of his acquaintance, that he knew to be able to command him, and to keep him pretty hard to some employ; so should he, at least, have been prevented of time to do those wickednesses that could not be done without time to do them in.

Wise. Alas! his father did so; he put him out betimes to one of his own acquaintance, and entreated him of all love that he would take care of his son, and keep him from extravagant ways. His trade also was honest and commodious; he had besides a full employ therein, so that this young Badman had no vacant seasons nor idle hours yielded him by his calling, therein to take opportunities to do badly; but all was one to him, as he had begun to be vile in his father's house, even so he continued to be when he was in the house of his master.

Atten. I have known some children, who, though they have been very bad at home, yet have altered much when they have been put out abroad; especially when they have fallen into a family where the governors thereof have made conscience of maintaining of the worship and service of God therein; but perhaps that might be wanting in Mr. Badman's master's house.

Wise. Indeed some children do greatly mend when put under other men's roofs; but, as I said, this naughty boy did not so; nor did his badness continue because he wanted a master that both could and did correct it. For his master was a very good man, a very devout person; one that frequented the best soul means, that set up the worship of God in his family, and also that walked himself thereafter. He was also a man very meek and merciful, one that did never over-drive young Badman in business, nor that kept him at it at unseasonable hours.

Atten. Say you so! This is rare. I for my part can see but few that can parallel, in these things, with Mr. Badman's master.

Wise. Nor I neither, yet Mr. Badman had such an one; for, for the most part, masters are nowadays such as mind nothing but their worldly concerns, and if apprentices do but answer their commands therein, soul and religion may go whither they will. Yea, I much fear that there have been many towardly lads put out by their parents to such masters that have quite undone them as to the next world.

Atten. The more is the pity. But, pray, now you have touched upon this subject, show me how many ways a master may be the ruin of his poor apprentice.

Wise. Nay, I cannot tell you of all the ways, yet some of them I will mention. Suppose, then, that a towardly lad be put to be an apprentice with one that is reputed to be a godly man, yet that lad may be ruined many ways; that is, if his master be not circumspect in all things that respect both God and man, and that before his apprentice.

1. If he be not moderate in the use of his apprentice; if

he drives him beyond his strength; if he holds him to work at unseasonable hours; if he will not allow him convenient time to read the Word, to pray, etc. This is the way to destroy him; that is, in those tender beginnings of good thoughts, and good beginnings about spiritual things.

2. If he suffers his house to be scattered with profane and wicked books, such as stir up to lust, to wantonness, such as teach idle, wanton, lascivious discourse, and such as have a tendency to provoke to profane drollery and jesting; and lastly, such as tend to corrupt and pervert the doctrine of faith and holiness. All these things will eat as doth a canker, and will quickly spoil, in youth, etc., those good beginnings that may be putting forth themselves in them.

3. If there be a mixture of servants, that is, if some very bad be in the same place, that is a way also to undo such tender lads; for they that are bad and sordid servants will be often, and they have an opportunity too, to be distilling and fomenting of their profane and wicked words and tricks before them, and these will easily stick in the flesh and minds of youth, to the corrupting of them.

4. If the Master have one guise for abroad, and another for home; that is, if his religion hangs by in his house as his cloak does, and he be seldom in it, except he be abroad; this young beginners will take notice of, and stumble at. We say, hedges have eyes, and little pitchers have ears; and, indeed, children make a greater inspection into the lives of fathers, masters, etc., than ofttimes they are aware of. And therefore should masters be careful, else they may soon destroy good beginnings in their servants.

5. If the master be unconscionable in his dealing, and trades with lying words; or if bad commodities be avouched to be good, or if he seeks after unreasonable gain, or the like; his servant sees it, and it is enough to undo him. Eli's sons being bad before the congregation, made men despise the sacrifices of the Lord (1 Sam. ii.).

But these things by the by, only they may serve for a hint to masters to take heed that they take not apprentices to destroy their souls. But young Badman had none of these hinderances; his father took care, and provided well for him, as to this. He had a good master, he wanted not good books, nor good instruction, nor good sermons, nor good examples, no nor good fellow-servants neither; but all would not do.

Atten. It is a wonder that in such a family, amidst so many spiritual helps, nothing should take hold of his heart! What! not good books, nor good instructions, nor good sermons, nor good examples, nor good fellow-servants, nor nothing do him good!

Wise. You talk, he minded none of these things; nay, all these were abominable to him. 1. For good books, they might lie in his master's house till they rotted for him, he would not regard to look into them; but contrariwise, would get all the bad and abominable books that he could, as beastly romances, and books full of ribaldry, even such as immediately tended to set all fleshly lusts on fire. True, he durst not be known to have any of these to his master; therefore would he never let them be seen by him, but would keep them in close places, and peruse them at such times as yielded him fit opportunities thereto.

2. For good instruction, he liked that much as he liked good books; his care was to hear but little thereof, and to forget what he heard as soon as it was spoken. Yea, I have heard some that knew him then say, that one might evidently discern by the show of his countenance and gestures that good counsel was to him like little ease, even a continual torment to him; nor did he ever count himself at liberty but when farthest off of wholesome words (Prov. xv. 12). He would hate them that rebuked him, and count them his deadly enemies (Prov. ix. 8).

3. For good example, which was frequently set him by his master, both in religious and civil matters, these young Badman would laugh at, and would also make a by-word of them when he came in place where he with safety could.

4. His master indeed would make him go with him to sermons, and that where he thought the best preachers were, but this ungodly young man, what shall I say, was, I think, a master of art in all mischief, he had these wicked ways to hinder himself of hearing, let the preacher thunder never so loud. (1) His way was, when come into the place of hearing, to sit down in some corner and then to fall fast asleep. (2) Or else to fix his adulterous eyes upon some beautiful object that was in the place, and so all sermon-

while therewith to be feeding of his fleshly lusts. (3) Or, if he could get near to some that he had observed would fit his humour, he would be whispering, giggling, and playing with them till such time as sermon was done.

Atten. Why! he was grown to a prodigious height of wickedness.

Wise. He was so, and that which aggravates all was, this was his practice as soon as he was come to his master—he was as ready at all these things as if he had, before he came to his master, served an apprenticeship to learn them.

Atten. There could not but be added, as you relate them, rebellion to his sin. Methinks it is as if he had said, I will not hear, I will not regard, I will not mind good, I will not mend, I will not turn, I will not be converted.

Wise. You say true, and I know not to whom more fitly to compare him than to that man who, when I myself rebuked him for his wickedness, in this great huff replied, What would the devil do for company if it was not for such as I?

Atten. Why, did you ever hear any man say so?

Wise. Yes, that I did, and this young Badman was as like him as an egg is like an egg. Alas! the Scripture makes mention of many that by their actions speak the same, "They say unto God, Depart from us, for we desire not the knowledge of thy ways" (Job xxi. 14). Again, "They refused to hearken, and pulled away the shoulder, and stopped their ears. Yea, they make their hearts" hard "as an adamant-stone, lest they should hear the law, and the words which the Lord of hosts hath sent" (Zech. vii. 11, 12). What are all these but such as Badman, and such as the young man but now mentioned? That young man was my play-fellow when I was solacing myself in my sins; I may make mention of him to my shame, but he has a great many fellows.

Atten. Young Badman was like him indeed, and he trod his steps as if his wickedness had been his very copy; I mean as to his desperateness, for had he not been a desperate one he would never have made you such a reply when you was rebuking of him for his sin. But when did you give him such a rebuke?

Wise. A while after God had parted him and I, by calling of me, as I hope, by his grace, still leaving him in his sins;

and so far as I could ever gather, as he lived, so he died, even as Mr. Badman did; but we will leave him and return again to our discourse.

Atten. Ha! poor obstinate sinners! Do they think that God cannot be even with them?

Wise. I do not know what they think, but I know that God hath said, "That *as* he cried, and they would not hear; so they cried and I would not hear, saith the Lord" (Zech. vii. 13). Doubtless there is a time coming when Mr. Badman will cry for this.

Atten. But I wonder that he should be so expert in wickedness so soon! Alas, he was but a stripling, I suppose he was as yet not twenty.

Wise. No, nor eighteen either; but, as with Ishmael, and with the children that mocked the prophet, the seeds of sin did put forth themselves betimes in him (Gen. xxi. 9, 10; 2 Kings ii. 23, 24).

Atten. Well, he was as wicked a young man as commonly one shall hear of.

Wise. You will say so when you know all.

Atten. All, I think, here is a great all; but if there is more behind, pray let us hear it.

Wise. Why then, I will tell you, that he had not been with his master much above a year and a half, but he came acquainted with three young villains, who here shall be nameless, that taught him to add to his sin much of like kind, and he as aptly received their instructions. One of them was chiefly given to uncleanness, another to drunkenness, and the third to purloining, or stealing from his master.

Atten. Alas! poor wretch, he was bad enough before, but these, I suppose, made him much worse.

Wise. That they made him worse you may be sure of, for they taught him to be an arch, a chief one in all their ways.

Atten. It was an ill hap that he ever came acquainted with them.

Wise. You must rather word it thus—it was the judgment of God that he did, that is, he came acquainted with them through the anger of God. He had a good master, and before him a good father; by these he had good counsel given him for months and years together, but his heart was set upon mischief, he loved wickedness more than to do good, even

until his iniquity came to be hateful, therefore, from the
anger of God it was that these companions of his and he
did at last so acquaint together. Says Paul, "They did not
like to retain God in *their* knowledge"; and what follows?
wherefore "God gave them over," or up to their own hearts'
lusts (Rom. i. 28). And again, "As for such as turn aside
unto *their* crooked ways, the Lord shall lead them forth
with the workers of iniquity" (Ps. cxxv. 5). This therefore
was God's hand upon him, that he might be destroyed, be
damned, "because he received not the love of the truth
that he might be saved" (2 Thess. ii. 10). He chose his
delusions and deluders for him, even the company of base
men, of fools, that he might be destroyed (Prov. xii. 20).

Atten. I cannot but think indeed that it is a great judgment of God for a man to be given up to the company of
vile men; for what are such but the devil's decoys, even those
by whom he draws the simple into his net? A whoremaster,
a drunkard, a thief, what are they but the devil's baits by
which he catcheth others?

Wise. You say right; but this young Badman was no
simple one, if by simple you mean one uninstructed; for he
had often good counsel given him; but, if by simple you
mean him that is a fool as to the true knowledge of, and faith
in Christ, then he was a simple one indeed; for he chose death
rather than life and to live in continual opposition to God
rather than to be reconciled unto him; according to that
saying of the wise man, "The fools *hated* knowledge, and did
not choose the fear of the Lord" (Prov. i. 29). And what
judgment more dreadful can a fool be given up to, than to
be delivered into the hands of such men, that have skill to
do nothing but to ripen sin, and hasten its finishing unto
damnation? And, therefore, men should be afraid of offending
God, because he can in this manner punish them for their
sins. I knew a man that once was, as I thought, hopefully
awakened about his condition; yea, I knew two that were
so awakened, but in time they began to draw back, and to
incline again to their lusts; wherefore, God gave them up
to the company of three or four men, that in less than three
years' time, brought them roundly to the gallows, where
they were hanged like dogs, because they refused to live
like honest men.

Atten. But such men do not believe that thus to be given up of God is in judgment and anger; they rather take it to be their liberty, and do count it their happiness; they are glad that their cord is loosed, and that the reins are on their neck; they are glad that they may sin without control, and that they may choose such company as can make them more expert in an evil way.

Wise. Their judgment is, therefore, so much the greater, because thereto is added blindness of mind, and hardness of heart in a wicked way. They are turned up to the way of death, but must not see to what place they are going. They must go as the ox to the slaughter, "and as a fool to the correction of the stocks, till a dart strike through his liver," not knowing "that it is for his life" (Prov. vii. 22, 23). This, I say, makes their judgment double; they are given up of God for a while, to sport themselves with that which will assuredly make them "mourn at the last, when their flesh and their body are consumed" (Prov. v. 11). These are those that Peter speaks, that shall utterly perish in their own corruptions; these, I say, who "count it pleasure to riot in the day-time," and that sport "themselves with their own deceivings," are "as natural brute beasts, made to be taken and destroyed" (2 Pet. ii. 12, 13).

Atten. Well, but I pray now concerning these three villains that were young Badman's companions; tell me more particularly how he carried it then.

Wise. How he carried it? why, he did as they. I intimated so much before, when I said they made him an arch, a chief one in their ways.

First, he became a frequenter of taverns and tippling-houses, and would stay there until he was even as drunk as a beast. And if it was so that he could not get out by day, he would, be sure, get out by night. Yea, he became so common a drunkard at last, that he was taken notice of to be a drunkard even by all.

Atten. This was swinish, for drunkenness is so beastly a sin, a sin so much against nature, that I wonder that any that have but the appearance of men can give up themselves to so beastly, yea, worse than beastly, a thing.

Wise. It is a swinish vanity indeed. I will tell you another story. There was a gentleman that had a drunkard to be his groom, and coming home one night very much abused with beer, his master saw it. Well, quoth his master within himself, I will let thee alone to-night, but to-morrow morning I will convince thee that thou art worse than a beast by the behaviour of my horse. So, when morning was come, he bids his man go and water his horse, and so he did; but, coming up to his master, he commands him to water him again; so the fellow rode into the water the second time, but his master's horse would now drink no more, so the fellow came up and told his master. Then, said his master, thou drunken sot, thou art far worse than my horse; he will drink but to satisfy nature, but thou wilt drink to the abuse of nature; he will drink but to refresh himself, but thou to thy hurt and damage; he will drink that he may be more serviceable to his master, but thou till thou art incapable of serving either God or man. O thou beast, how much art thou worse than the horse that thou ridest on!

Atten. Truly, I think that his master served him right; for, in doing as he did, he showed him plainly, as he said, that he had not so much government of himself as his horse had of himself; and, consequently, that his beast did live more according to the law of his nature by far than did his man. But, pray, go on with what you have further to say.

Wise. Why, I say, that there are four things, which, if they were well considered, would make drunkenness to be abhorred in the thoughts of the children of men. 1. It greatly tendeth to impoverish and beggar a man. "The drunkard," says Solomon, "shall come to poverty" (Prov. xxiii. 21). Many that have begun the world with plenty, have gone out of it in rags, through drunkenness. Yea, many children that have been born to good estates, have yet been brought to a flail and a rake, through this beastly sin of their parents. 2. This sin of drunkenness it bringeth upon the body many great and incurable diseases, by which men do, in little time, come to their end, and none can help them. So, because they are overmuch wicked, therefore they die before their time (Eccles. vii. 17). 3. Drunkenness is a sin that is oftentimes attended with abundance of other evils. "Who hath woe? Who hath sorrow? Who hath contentions? Who hath babbling? Who hath wounds without cause? Who hath redness of eyes? They that tarry long at the wine, they that go to seek mixed wine"; that is, the drunkard (Prov. xxiii. 29, 30). 4. By drunkenness, men do oftentimes shorten their days; go out of the ale-house drunk, and break their necks before they come home. Instances, not a few, might be given of this, but this is so manifest a man need say nothing.

Atten. But that which is worse than all is, it also prepares men for everlasting burnings (1 Cor. vi. 10).

Wise. Yea, and it so stupefies and besots the soul, that a man that is far gone in drunkenness is hardly ever recovered to God. Tell me, when did you see an old drunkard converted? No, no, such an one will sleep till he dies, though he sleeps on the top of a mast; let his dangers be never so great, and death and damnation never so near, he will not be awaked out of his sleep (Prov. xxiii. 34, 35). So that if a man have any respect either to credit, health, life, or salvation, he will not be a drunken man. But the truth is, where this sin gets the upper hand, men are, as I said before, so intoxicated and bewitched with the seeming pleasures and sweetness thereof, that they have neither heart nor mind to think of that which is better in itself, and would, if embraced, do them good.

Atten. You said that drunkenness tends to poverty, yet some make themselves rich by drunken bargains.

Wise. I said so, because the Word says so. And as to some men's getting thereby, that is indeed but rare and base; yea, and base will be the end of such gettings. The Word of God is against such ways, and the curse of God will be the end of such doings. An inheritance may sometimes thus be hastily gotten at the beginning, but the end thereof shall not be blessed. Hark what the prophet saith, "Woe to him that coveteth an evil covetousness, that he may set his nest on high" (Hab. ii. 5, 9–12, 15). Whether he makes drunkenness, or aught else, the engine and decoy to get it; for that man doth but consult the shame of his own house, the spoiling of his family, and the damnation of his soul; for that which he getteth by working of iniquity is but a getting by the devices of hell; therefore he can be no gainer neither for himself nor family, that gains by an evil course. But this was one of the sins that Mr. Badman was addicted to after he came acquainted with these three fellows, nor could all that his master could do break him off this beastly sin.

Atten. But where, since he was but an apprentice, could he get money to follow this practice? for drunkenness, as you have intimated, is a very costly sin.

Wise. His master paid for all. For, as I told you before, as he learned of these three villains to be a beastly drunkard, so he learned of them to pilfer and steal from his master. Sometimes he would sell off his master's goods, but keep the money, that is, when he could; also, sometimes he would beguile his master by taking out his cash-box; and when he could do neither of these, he would convey away of his master's wares, what he thought would be least missed, and send or carry them to such and such houses, where he knew they would be laid up to his use; and then appoint set times there, to meet and make merry with these fellows.

Atten. This was as bad, nay, I think, worse than the former; for by thus doing he did not only run himself under the wrath of God, but has endangered the undoing of his master and his family.

Wise. Sins go not alone, but follow one the other as do the links of a chain; he that will be a drunkard, must have money, either of his own or of some other man's; either of his father's, mother's, master's, or at the highway, or some way.

Atten. I fear that many an honest man is undone by such kind of servants.

Wise. I am of the same mind with you, but this should make the dealer the more wary what kind of servants he keeps, and what kind of apprentices he takes. It should also teach him to look well to his shop himself; also to take strict account of all things that are bought and sold by his servants. The master's neglect herein may embolden his servant to be bad, and may bring him too in short time to rags and a morsel of bread.

Atten. I am afraid that there is much of this kind of pilfering among servants in these bad days of ours.

Wise. Now while it is in my mind, I will tell you a story. When I was in prison, there came a woman to me that was under a great deal of trouble. So I asked her, she being a stranger to me, what she had to say to me. She said she was afraid she should be damned. I asked her the cause of those fears. She told me that she had, some time since, lived with a shopkeeper at Wellingborough, and had robbed his box in the shop several times of money, to the value of more than now I will say; and pray, says she, tell me what I shall do. I told her I would have her go to her master, and make him satisfaction. She said she was afraid; I asked her, why? She said, she doubted he would hang her. I told her that I would intercede for her life, and would make use of other friends too to do the like; but she told me she durst not venture that. Well, said I, shall I send to your master, while you abide out of sight, and make your peace with him, before he sees you? and with that I asked her her master's name. But all that she said, in answer to this, was, Pray let it alone till I come to you again. So away she went, and neither told me her master's name nor her own. This is about ten or twelve years since, and I never saw her again. I tell you this story for this cause; to confirm your fears that such kind of servants too many there be; and that God makes them sometimes like old Tod, of whom mention was made before, through the terrors that he lays upon them, to betray themselves.

I could tell you of another, that came to me with a like relation concerning herself, and the robbing of her mistress; but at this time let this suffice.

Atten. But what was that other villain addicted to? I mean young Badman's third companion.

Wise. Uncleanness; I told you before, but it seems you forgot.

Atten. Right, it was uncleanness. Uncleanness is also a filthy sin.

Wise. It is so; and yet it is one of the most reigning sins in our day.

Atten. So they say, and that too among those that one would think had more wit, even among the great ones.

Wise. The more is the pity; for usually examples that are set by them that are great and chief, spread sooner, and more universally, than do the sins of other men; yea, and when such men are at the head in transgressing, sin walks with a bold face through the land. As Jeremiah saith of the prophets, so may it be said of such, "From them is profaneness gone forth into all the land": that is, with bold and audacious face (Jer. xxiii. 15).

Atten. But pray let us return again to Mr. Badman and his companions. You say one of them was very vile in the commission of uncleanness.

Wise. Yes, so I say; not but that he was a drunkard and also thievish, but he was most arch in this sin of uncleanness; this roguery was his masterpiece, for he was a ringleader to them all in the beastly sin of whoredom. He was also best acquainted with such houses where they were, and so could readily lead the rest of his gang unto them. The strumpets also, because they knew this young villain, would at first discover themselves in all their whorish pranks to those that he brought with him.

Atten. That is a deadly sin: I mean, it is a deadly thing to young men, when such beastly queans shall, with words and carriages that are openly tempting, discover themselves unto them; it is hard for such to escape their snare.

Wise. That is true, therefore the wise man's counsel is the best: "Come not nigh the door of her house" (Prov. v. 8). For they are, as you say, very tempting, as is seen by her in the Proverbs. "I looked," says the wise man, "through my casement, and behold among the simple ones I discerned a young man void of understanding, passing through the street near her corner, and he went the way to her house, in the twilight, in the evening, in the black and dark night. And, behold, there met him a woman *with* the attire of an harlot, and subtle of heart; she is loud and stubborn; her feet abide not in her house; now is she without, now in the streets, and lieth in wait at every corner. So she caught him, and kissed him, *and*, with an impudent face, said unto him, I *have* peace-offerings with me; this day have I paid my vows. Therefore came I forth to meet thee diligently to seek thy face, and I have found thee. I have decked my bed with coverings of tapestry, with carved works, with fine linen of Egypt. I have perfumed my bed with myrrh, aloes, and cinnamon. Come, let us take our fill of love until the morning; let us solace ourselves with loves" (Prov. vii. 6–18). Here was a bold beast. And, indeed, the very eyes, hands, words, and ways of such, are all snares and bands to youthful, lustful fellows. And with these was young Badman greatly snared.

Atten. This sin of uncleanness is mightily cried out against both by Moses, the prophets, Christ, and his apostles; and yet, as we see, for all that, how men run headlong to it!

Wise. You have said the truth, and I will add, that God, to hold men back from so filthy a sin, has set such a stamp of his indignation upon it, and commanded such evil effects to follow it, that, were not they that use it bereft of all fear of God, and love to their own health, they could not but stop and be afraid to commit it. For besides the eternal damnation that doth attend such in the next world, for these have no "inheritance in the kingdom of Christ and of God" (Eph. v. 5), the evil effects thereof in this world are dreadful.

Atten. Pray show me some of them, that as occasion offereth itself, I may show them to others for their good.

Wise. So I will. (1) It bringeth a man, as was said of the sin before, to want and poverty; "For by means of a whorish woman, *a man is brought* to a piece of bread" (Prov. vi. 26). The reason is, for that a whore will not yield without hire; and men, when the devil and lust is in them, and God and his fear far away from them, will not stick, so they may accomplish their desire, to lay their signet, their bracelets, and their staff to pledge, rather than miss of the fulfilling of their lusts (Gen. xxxviii. 18). (2) Again, by this sin men diminish their strength, and bring upon themselves, even upon the body, a multitude of diseases. This King Lemuel's mother warned him of. "What, my son?" said she, "and what, the son of my womb? And what, the son of my vows? Give not thy strength unto women, nor thy ways to that which destroyeth kings" (Prov. xxxi. 2, 3). This sin is destructive to the body. Give me leave to tell you another story. I have heard of a great man that was a very unclean person, and he had lived so long in that sin that he had almost lost his sight. So his physicians were sent for, to whom he told his disease; but they told him that they could do him no good, unless he would forbear his women. Nay then, said he, farewell sweet sight. Whence observe, that this sin, as I said, is destructive to the body; and also, that some men be so in love therewith, that they will have it, though it destroy their body.

Atten. Paul says also, that he that sins this sin, sins against his own body. But what of that? He that will run the hazard of eternal damnation of his soul, but he will commit this sin, will for it run the hazard of destroying his body. If young Badman feared not the damnation of his soul, do you think that the consideration of impairing of his body would have deterred him therefrom?

Wise. You say true. But yet, methinks, there are still such bad effects follow, often upon the commission of it, that if men would consider them, it would put, at least, a stop to their career therein.

Atten. What other evil effects attend this sin?

Wise. Outward shame and disgrace, and that in these particulars:

First, There often follows this foul sin the foul disease, now called by us the pox. A disease so nauseous and stinking, so infectious to the whole body, and so entailed to this sin, that hardly are any common with unclean women, but they have more or less a touch of it to their shame.

Atten. That is a foul disease indeed! I knew a man once that rotted away with it; and another that had his nose eaten off, and his mouth almost quite sewed up thereby.

Wise. It is a disease, that where it is it commonly declares that the cause thereof is uncleanness. It declares to all that behold such a man, that he is an odious, a beastly, unclean person. This is that strange punishment that Job speaks of, that is appointed to seize on these workers of iniquity (Job xxxi. 1–3).

Atten. Then it seems you think, that the strange punishment that Job there speaks of should be the foul disease.

Wise. I have thought so indeed, and that for this reason. We see that this disease is entailed, as I may say, to this most beastly sin, nor is there any disease so entailed to any other sin as this to this. That this is the sin to which the strange punishment is entailed, you will easily perceive when you read the text. "I made a covenant with mine eyes," said Job, "why then should I think upon a maid? For what portion of God *is there*," for that sin, "from above, and *what* inheritance of the Almighty from on high?" And then he answers himself: "Is not destruction to the wicked, and a strange punishment to the workers of iniquity?" This strange punishment is the pox. Also, I think that this foul disease is that which Solomon intends when he saith, speaking of this unclean and beastly creature, "A wound and dishonour shall he get, and his reproach shall not be wiped away" (Prov. vi. 33). A punishment Job calls it; a wound and dishonour Solomon calls it; and they both do set it as a remark upon this sin; Job calling it a "strange punishment," and Solomon a "reproach that shall not be wiped away," from them that are common in it.

Atten. What other things follow upon the commission of this beastly sin?

Wise. Why, oftentimes it is attended with murder, with the murder of the babe begotten on the defiled bed. How common it is for the bastard-getter and bastard-bearer to consent together to murder their children, will be better known at the day of judgment, yet something is manifest now.

I will tell you another story. An ancient man, one of mine acquaintance, a man of good credit in our country, had a mother that was a midwife, who was mostly employed in laying great persons. To this woman's house, upon a time, comes a brave young gallant on horseback, to fetch her to lay a young lady. So she addresses herself to go with him, wherefore he takes her up behind him, and away they ride in the night. Now they had not rid far, but the gentleman lit off his horse, and, taking the old midwife in his arms from the horse, turned round with her several times, and then set her up again, then he got up and away they went till they came at a stately house, into which he had her, and so into a chamber where the young lady was in her pains. He then bid the midwife do her office, and she demanded help, but he drew out his sword, and told her if she did not make speed to do her office without, she must look for nothing but death. Well, to be short, this old midwife laid the young lady, and a fine sweet babe she had. Now there was made in a room hard by a very great fire; so the gentleman took up the babe, went and drew the coals from the stock, cast the child in and covered it up, and there was an end of that. So when the midwife had done her work he paid her well for her pains, but shut her up in a dark room all day, and when night came took her up behind him again, and carried her away till she came almost at home, then he turned her round and round as he did before, and had her to her house, set her down, bid her farewell, and away he went, and she could never tell who it was. This story the midwife's son, who was a minister, told me, and also protested that his mother told it him for a truth.

Atten. Murder doth often follow indeed, as that which is the fruit of this sin. But sometimes God brings even these adulterers and adulteresses to shameful ends. I heard of one, I think a doctor of physic, and his whore, who had three or four bastards betwixt them and had murdered them all, but at last themselves were hanged for it, in or near to Colchester. It came out after this manner,—the whore was so afflicted in her conscience about it that she could not be quiet until she had made it known. Thus God many times makes the actors of wickedness their own accusers, and brings them, by their own tongues, to condign punishment for their own sins.

Wise. There has been many such instances, but we will let that pass. I was once in the presence of a woman, a married woman, that lay sick of the sickness whereof she died, and being smitten in her conscience for the sin of uncleanness, which she had often committed with other men, I heard her, as she lay upon her bed, cry out thus, I am a whore, and all my children are bastards, and I must go to hell for my sin, and look, there stands the devil at my bed's feet to receive my soul when I die.

Atten. These are sad stories, tell no more of them now, but if you please show me yet some other of the evil effects of this beastly sin.

Wise. This sin is such a snare to the soul, that, unless a miracle of grace prevents, it unavoidably perishes in the enchanting and bewitching pleasures of it. This is manifest by these and such like texts—"The adulteress will hunt for the precious life" (Prov. vi. 26). "Whoso committeth adultery with a woman lacketh understanding. He *that* doeth it destroyeth his own soul" (Prov. vi. 32). "A whore *is* a deep ditch, and a strange woman *is* a narrow pit" (Prov. xxiii. 27). "Her house inclineth unto death, and her paths unto the dead. None that go unto her return again, neither take they hold of the paths of life" (Prov. ii. 18, 19). "She hath cast down many wounded; yea, many strong *men* have been slain by her. Her house *is* the way to hell, going down to the chambers of death" (Prov. vii. 26, 27).

Atten. These are dreadful sayings, and do show the dreadful state of those that are guilty of this sin.

Wise. Verily so they do. But yet that which makes the whole more dreadful is, that men are given up to this sin because they are abhorred of God, and because abhorred, therefore they shall fall into the commission of it, and shall live there. "The mouth," that is, the flattering lips, "of strange women *is* a deep pit, *he* that is abhorred of the Lord shall fall therein" (Prov. xxii. 14). Therefore it saith again of such, that they have none "inheritance in the kingdom of Christ and of God" (Ephes. v. 5).

Atten. Put all together, and it is a dreadful thing to live and die in this transgression.

Wise. True, but suppose that instead of all these judgments this sin had attending of it all the felicities of this life, and no bitterness, shame, or disgrace mixed with it, yet one hour in hell will spoil all. O! this hell, hell-fire, damnation in hell, it is such an inconceivable punishment that, were it but thoroughly believed, it would nip this sin, with others, in the head. But here is the mischief, those that give up themselves to these things do so harden themselves in unbelief and atheism about the things, the punishments that God hath threatened to inflict upon the committers of them, that at last they arrive to almost an absolute and firm belief that there is no judgment to come hereafter; else they would not, they could not, no not attempt to commit this sin by such abominable language as some do.

I heard of one that should say to his miss when he tempted her to the committing of this sin, If thou wilt venture thy body I will venture my soul. And I myself heard another say, when he was tempting of a maid to commit uncleanness with him—it was in Oliver's days—that if she did prove with child he would tell her how she might escape punishment—and that was then somewhat severe—Say, saith he, when you come before the judge, that you are with child by the Holy Ghost. I heard him say thus, and it greatly afflicted me; I had a mind to have accused him for it before some magistrate, but he was a great man, and I was poor and young, so I let it alone, but it troubled me very much.

Atten. It was the most horrible thing that ever I heard

in my life. But how far off are these men from that spirit and grace that dwelt in Joseph (Gen. xxxix. 10).

Wise. Right; when Joseph's mistress tempted him, yea, tempted him daily, yea, she laid hold on him and said, with her whore's forehead, Come, "*lie with me*," but he refused; he hearkened not to lie with her or to be with her. Mr. Badman would have taken the opportunity.

And a little to comment upon this of Joseph. 1. Here is a miss, a great miss, the wife of the captain of the guard, some beautiful dame I'll warrant you. 2. Here is a miss won, and in her whorish affections come over to Joseph without his speaking of a word. 3. Here is her unclean desire made known, Come, "lie with me," said she. 4. Here was a fit opportunity, there was none of the men of the house there within. 5. Joseph was a young man, full of strength, and therefore the more in danger to be taken. 6. This was to him a temptation from her that lasted days. 7. And yet Joseph refused, (1) Her daily temptation; (2) Her daily solicitation; (3) Her daily provocation, heartily, violently, and constantly. For when she got him by the garment, saying, "Lie with me," he left his garment in her hand and gat him out. Aye, and although contempt, treachery, slander, accusation, imprisonment, and danger of death followed— for a whore careth not what mischief she does when she cannot have her end—yet Joseph will not defile himself, sin against God, and hazard his own eternal salvation.

Atten. Blessed Joseph! I would thou hadst more fellows!

Wise. Mr. Badman has more fellows than Joseph, else there would not be so many whores as there are; for though I doubt not but that that sex is bad enough this way, yet I verily believe that many of them are made whores at first by the flatteries of Badman's fellows. Alas! there is many a woman plunged into this sin at first even by promises of marriage. I say by these promises they are flattered, yea, forced into a consenting to these villainies, and so being in, and growing hardened in their hearts, they at last give themselves up, even as wicked men do, to act this kind of wickedness with greediness. But Joseph, you see, was of another mind, for the fear of God was in him.

I will, before I leave this, tell you here two notable stories; and I wish Mr. Badman's companions may hear of them

They are found in Clark's *Looking-glass for Sinners*; and are these: Mr. Cleaver, says Mr. Clark, reports of one whom he knew that had committed the act of uncleanness, whereupon he fell into such horror of conscience that he hanged himself, leaving it thus written in a paper: "Indeed," saith he, "I do acknowledge it to be utterly unlawful for a man to kill himself, but I am bound to act the magistrate's part because the punishment of this sin is death."

Clark doth also, in the same page, make mention of two more, who, as they were committing adultery in London, were immediately struck dead with fire from heaven, in the very act. Their bodies were so found, half burned up, and sending out a most loathsome savour.

Atten. These are notable stories indeed.

Wise. So they are, and I suppose they are as true as notable.

Atten. Well, but I wonder if young Badman's master knew him to be such a wretch, that he would suffer him in his house.

Wise. They liked one another even as fire and water do. Young Badman's ways were odious to his master, and his master's ways were such as young Badman could not endure. Thus, in these two, were fulfilled that saying of the Holy Ghost: "An unjust man *is* an abomination to the just; and *he that is* upright in the way *is* an abomination to the wicked" (Prov. xxix. 27). The good man's ways, Mr. Badman could not abide, nor could the good man abide the bad ways of his base apprentice. Yet would his master, if he could, have kept him, and also have learned him his trade.

Atten. If he could! Why, he might, if he would, might he not?

Wise. Alas, Badman ran away from him once and twice, and would not at all be ruled. So the next time he did run away from him, he did let him go indeed. For he gave him no occasion to run away, except it was by holding of him as much as he could, and that he could do but little, to good and honest rules of life. And had it been one's own case, one should have let him go. For what should a man do that had either regard to his own peace, his children's good, or the preservation of the rest of his servants from evil, but let him go? Had he staid, the house of correction had been most fit for him, but thither his master was loth to send him, because of the love that he bore to his father. A house of correction, I say, had been the fittest place for him, but his master let him go.

Atten. He ran away, you say, but whither did he run?

Wise. Why, to one of his own trade, and also like himself. Thus the wicked joined hand in hand, and there he served out his time.

Atten. Then, sure, he had his heart's desire when he was with one so like himself.

Wise. Yes, so he had, but God gave it him in his anger.

Atten. How do you mean?

Wise. I mean as before, that for a wicked man to be by the providence of God turned out of a good man's doors, into a wicked man's house to dwell, is a sign of the anger of God. For God by this, and such judgments, says thus to such an one, Thou wicked one, thou lovest not me, my ways, nor my people; thou castest my law and good counsel behind thy back. Come, I will dispose of thee in my wrath; thou shalt be turned over to the ungodly, thou shalt be put to school to the devil, I will leave thee to sink and swim in sin, till I shall visit thee with death and judgment. This was, therefore, another judgment that did come upon this young Badman.

Atten. You have said the truth, for God by such a judgment as this, in effect says so indeed; for he takes them out of the hand of the just, and binds them up in the hand of the wicked, and whither they then shall be carried a man may easily imagine.

Wise. It is one of the saddest tokens of God's anger that happens to such kind of persons: and that for several reasons. 1. Such a one, by this judgment, is put out of the way, and from under the means which ordinarily are made use of to do good to the soul. For a family, where godliness is professed and practised, is God's ordinance, the place which he has appointed to teach young ones the way and fear of God (Gen. xviii. 18, 19). Now, to be put out of such a family, into a bad, a wicked one, as Mr. Badman was, must needs be in judgment, and a sign of the anger of God. For in ungodly families men learn to forget God, to hate goodness, and to estrange themselves from the ways of those that are good. 2. In bad families they have continually fresh examples, and also incitements to evil, and fresh encouragements to it too. Yea, moreover, in such places evil is commended, praised, well-spoken of, and they that do it are applauded; and this, to be sure, is a drowning judgment. 3. Such places are the very haunts and walks of the infernal spirits, who are continually poisoning the cogitations and minds of one or other in such families, that they may be able to poison others. Therefore observe it, usually in wicked families, some one or two are more arch for wickedness than are any other that are there. Now such are Satan's conduit pipes, for by them he conveys of the spawn of hell, through their being crafty in wickedness, into the ears and souls of their companions. Yea, and when they have once conceived wickedness, they travail with it, as doth a woman with child, till they have brought it forth; "Behold, he travaileth with iniquity, and hath conceived mischief, and brought forth falsehood" (Ps. vii. 14). Some men, as here is intimated in the text, and as was hinted also before, have a kind of mystical but hellish copulation with the devil, who is the father, and their soul the mother of sin and wickedness; and they, so soon as they have conceived by him, finish, by bringing forth sin, both it and their own damnation (Jas. i. 15).

Atten. How much then doth it concern those parents that love their children, to see, that if they go from them, they be put into such families as be good, that they may learn there betimes to eschew evil, and to follow that which is good!

Wise. It doth concern them indeed; and it doth also concern them that take children into their families, to take heed what children they receive. For a man may soon, by a bad boy, be damaged both in his name, estate, and family, and also hindered in his peace and peaceable pursuit after God and godliness; I say, by one such vermin as a wicked and filthy apprentice.

Atten. True, for one sinner destroyeth much good, and a poor man is better than a liar. But many times a man cannot help it; for such as at the beginning promise very fair are by a little time proved to be very rogues, like young Badman.

Wise. That is true also; but when a man has done the best he can to help it, he may with the more confidence expect

the blessing of God to follow, or he shall have the more peace
if things go contrary to his desire.

Atten. Well, but did Mr. Badman and his master agree so
well? I mean his last master, since they were birds of a
feather, I mean since they were so well met for wickedness.

Wise. This second master was, as before I told you, bad
enough; but yet he would often fall out with young Badman,
his servant, and chide, yea and sometimes beat him too,
for his naughty doings.

Atten. What! for all he was so bad himself! This is like
the proverb, The devil corrects vice.

Wise. I will assure you it is as I say. For you must know
that Badman's ways suited not with his master's gains.
Could he have done as the damsel that we read of (Acts
xvi. 16) did, to wit, fill his master's purse with his badness,
he had certainly been his white-boy, but it was not so with
young Badman; and, therefore, though his master and he
did suit well enough in the main, yet in this and that point
they differed. Young Badman was for neglecting of his
master's business, for going to the whore-house, for beguiling
of his master, for attempting to debauch his daughters, and
the like. No marvel then if they disagreed in these points.
Not so much for that his master had an antipathy against
the fact itself, for he could do so when he was an apprentice;
but for that his servant by his sin made spoil of his commodities, etc., and so damnified his master.

Had, as I said before, young Badman's wickedness had
only a tendency to his master's advantage, as could he have
sworn, lied, cozened, cheated, and defrauded customers for
his master—and indeed sometimes he did so—but had that
been all that he had done, he had not had, no, not a wry
word from his master; but this was not always Mr. Badman's way.

Atten. That was well brought in, even the maid that we
read of in the Acts, and the distinction was as clear betwixt
the wickedness and wickedness of servants.

Wise. Alas! men that are wicked themselves, yet greatly
hate it in others, not simply because it is wickedness, but
because it opposeth their interest. Do you think that that
maid's master would have been troubled at the loss of her,
if he had not lost, with her, his gain? No, I'll warrant you;

she might have gone to the devil for him; but "when her masters saw that the hope of their gains was gone," then, then he fell to persecuting Paul (Acts xvi. 17–20). But Mr. Badman's master did sometimes lose by Mr. Badman's sins, and then Badman and his master were at odds.

Atten. Alas, poor Badman! Then it seems thou couldest not at all times please thy like.

Wise. No, he could not, and the reason I have told you.

Atten. But do not bad masters condemn themselves in condemning the badness of their servants?

Wise. Yes; in that they condemn that in another which they either have, or do allow in themselves (Rom. xiv. 22). And the time will come when that very sentence that hath gone out of their own mouths against the sins of others, themselves living and taking pleasure in the same, shall return with violence upon their own pates. The Lord pronounced judgment against Baasha, as for all his evils in general, so for this in special, because he was "like the house of Jeroboam and" yet "killed him" (1 Kings xvi. 7). This is Mr. Badman's master's case; he is like his man, and yet he beats him. He is like his man, and yet he rails at him for being bad.

Atten. But why did not young Badman run away from this master, as he ran away from the other?

Wise. He did not. And if I be not mistaken, the reason why was this. There was godliness in the house of the first, and that young Badman could not endure. For fare, for lodging, for work, and time, he had better and more by this master's allowance, than ever he had by his last; but all this would not content, because godliness was promoted there. He could not abide this praying, this reading of Scriptures, and hearing and repeating of sermons; he could not abide to be told of his transgressions in a sober and godly manner.

Atten. There is a great deal in the manner of reproof; wicked men both can and cannot abide to hear their transgressions spoken against.

Wise. There is a great deal of difference indeed. This last master of Mr. Badman's would tell Mr. Badman of his sins in Mr. Badman's own dialect; he would swear, and curse, and damn, when he told him of his sins, and this he could bear better, than to be told of them after a godly sort. Besides, that last master would, when his passions and rage were over, laugh at and make merry with the sins of his servant Badman; and that would please young Badman well. Nothing offended Badman but blows, and those he had but few of now, because he was pretty well grown up. For the most part when his master did rage and swear, he would give him oath for oath, and curse for curse, at least secretly, let him go on as long as he would.

Atten. This was hellish living.

Wise. It was hellish living indeed; and a man might say, that with this master, young Badman completed himself yet more and more in wickedness, as well as in his trade: for by that he came out of his time, what with his own inclination to sin, what with his acquaintance with his three companions, and what with this last master, and the wickedness he saw in him, he became a sinner in grain. I think he had a bastard laid to his charge before he came out of his time.

Atten. Well, but it seems he did live to come out of his time, but what did he then?

Wise. Why, he went home to his father, and he, like a loving and tender-hearted father, received him into his house.

Atten. And how did he carry it there?

Wise. Why, the reason why he went home, was, for money to set up for himself; he stayed but a little at home, but that little while that he did stay, he refrained himself as well as he could, and did not so much discover himself to be base, for fear his father should take distaste, and so should refuse, or for a while forbear to give him money. Yet even then he would have his times, and companions, and the fill of his lusts with him, but he used to blind all with this, he was glad to see his old acquaintances, and they as glad to see him, and he could not in civility but accommodate them with a bottle or two of wine, or a dozen or two of drink.

Atten. And did the old man give him money to set up with?

Wise. Yes, above two hundred pounds.

Atten. Therein, I think, the old man was out. Had I been his father, I would have held him a little at staves-end, till I had had far better proof of his manners to be good; for

I perceive that his father did know what a naughty boy he had been, both by what he used to do at home, and because he changed a good master for a bad, etc. He should not therefore have given him money so soon. What if he had pinched a little, and gone to journey-work for a time, that he might have known what a penny was, by his earning of it? Then, in all probability, he had known better how to have spent it: yea, and by that time perhaps, have better considered with himself, how to have lived in the world. Aye, and who knows but he might have come to himself with the prodigal, and have asked God and his father forgiveness for the villainies that he had committed against them.

Wise. If his father could also have blessed this manner of dealing to him, and have made it effectual for the ends that you have propounded, then I should have thought as you. But alas, alas, you talk as if you never knew, or had at this present forgot what the bowels and compassions of a father are. Why, did you not serve your own son so? But it is evident enough that we are better at giving good counsel to others, than we are at taking good counsel ourselves. But, mine honest neighbour, suppose that Mr. Badman's father had done as you say, and by so doing had driven his son to ill courses, what had he bettered either himself or his son in so doing?

Atten. That is true, but it doth not follow that if the father had done as I said, the son would have done as you suppose. But if he had done as you have supposed, what had he done worse than what he hath done already?

Wise. He had done bad enough, that is true. But suppose his father had given him no money, and suppose that young Badman had taken a pet thereat, and in an anger had gone beyond sea, and his father had neither seen him nor heard of him more. Or suppose that of a mad and headstrong stomach, he had gone to the highway for money, and so had brought himself to the gallows, and his father and family to great contempt, or if by so doing he had not brought himself to that end, yet he had added to all his wickedness such and such evils besides; and what comfort could his father have had in this? Besides, when his father had done for him what he could, with desire to make him an honest man, he would then, whether his son had proved honest or no, have laid down his head with far more peace than if he had taken your counsel.

Atten. Nay, I think I should not have been forward to have given advice in the cause; but truly you have given me such an account of his villainies, that the hearing thereof has made me angry with him.

Wise. In an angry mood we may soon outshoot ourselves, but poor wretch as he is, he is gone to his place. But, as I said, when a good father hath done what he can for a bad child, and that child shall prove never the better, he will lie down with far more peace, than if through severity he had driven him to inconveniences.

I remember that I have heard of a good woman, that had, as this old man, a bad and ungodly son, and she prayed for him, counselled him, and carried it motherly to him for several years together; but still he remained bad. At last, upon a time, after she had been at prayer, as she was wont, for his conversion, she comes to him, and thus, or to this effect, begins again to admonish him. Son, said she, thou hast been and art a wicked child, thou hast cost me many a prayer and tear, and yet thou remainest wicked. Well, I have done my duty, I have done what I can to save thee; now I am satisfied, that if I shall see thee damned at the day of judgment, I shall be so far off from being grieved for thee, that I shall rejoice to hear the sentence of thy damnation at that day; and it converted him.

I tell you that if parents carry it lovingly towards their children, mixing their mercies with loving rebukes, and their loving rebukes with fatherly and motherly compassions, they are more likely to save their children, than by being churlish and severe towards them: but if they do not save them, if their mercy do them no good, yet it will greatly ease them at the day of death, to consider: I have done by love as much as I could, to save and deliver my child from hell.

Atten. Well, I yield. But pray let us return again to Mr. Badman. You say, that his father gave him a piece of money that he might set up for himself.

Wise. Yes, his father did give him a piece of money, and he did set up, and almost as soon set down again: for he was not long set up, but by his ill managing of his matters at home, together with his extravagant expenses abroad, he was got so far into debt, and had so little in his shop to pay, that he was hard put to it to keep himself out of prison. But when his creditors understood that he was about to marry, and in a fair way to get a rich wife, they said among themselves, We will not be hasty with him; if he gets a rich wife he will pay us all.

Atten. But how could he so quickly run out, for I perceive it was in little time, by what you say?

Wise. It was in little time indeed, I think he was not above two years and a half in doing of it; but the reason is apparent, for he being a wild young man, and now having the bridle loose before him, and being wholly subjected to his lusts and vices, he gave himself up to the way of his heart, and to the sight of his eye, forgetting that for all these things God would bring him to judgment (Eccles. xi. 9). And he that doth thus, you may be sure, shall not be able long to stand on his legs. Besides he had now an addition of new companions; companions you must think most like himself in manners, and so such that cared not who sunk, if they themselves might swim. These would often be haunting of him, and of his shop too when he was absent. They would commonly egg him to the ale-house, but yet make him jack-pay-for-all; they would also be borrowing money of him, but take no care to pay again, except it was with more of their company, which also he liked very well; and so his poverty came like "one that travelleth, and his want as an armed man" (Prov. vi. 11). But all the while they studied his temper; he loved to be flattered, praised, and commended for wit, manhood, and personage; and this was like stroking him over the face. Thus they colleagued with him, and got yet more and more into him, and so, like horse leeches, they drew away that little that his father had given him, and brought him quickly down, almost to dwell next door to the beggar.

Atten. Then was the saying of the wise man fulfilled, "He that keepeth company with harlots," and "a companion of fools, shall be destroyed" (Prov. xxix. 3; xiii. 20).

Wise. Aye, and that too, "A companion of riotous *persons* shameth his father" (Prov. xxviii. 7). For he, poor man, had both grief and shame, to see how his son, now at his own hand, behaved himself in the enjoyment of those good things, in and under the lawful use of which he might have lived to God's glory, his own comfort, and credit among his neighbours. "But he that followeth after vain *persons*, shall have poverty enough" (Prov. xxviii. 19). The way that he took, led him directly into this condition; for who can expect other things of one that follows such courses? Besides, when he was in his shop, he could not abide to be doing; he was naturally given to idleness. He loved to live high, but his hands refused to labour; and what else can the end of such an one be but that which the wise man saith? "The drunkard and the glutton shall come to poverty, and drowsiness shall clothe *a man* with rags" (Prov. xxiii. 21).

Atten. But now, methinks, when he was brought thus low, he should have considered the hand of God that was gone out against him, and should have smote upon the breast, and have returned.

Wise. Consideration, good consideration, was far from him, he was as stout and proud now as ever in all his life, and was as high too in the pursuit of his sin, as when he was in the midst of his fulness; only he went now like a tired jade, the devil had rid him almost off of his legs.

Atten. Well, but what did he do when all was almost gone?

Wise. Two things were now his play. 1. He bore all in hand by swearing, and cracking, and lying, that he was as well to pass as he was the first day he set up for himself, yea, that he had rather got than lost; and he had at his beck some of his companions that would swear to confirm it as fast as he.

Atten. This was double wickedness, it was a sin to say it, and another to swear it.

Wise. That is true, but what evil is that that he will not do, that is left of God, as I believe Mr. Badman was?

Atten. And what was the other thing?

Wise. Why that which I hinted before, he was for looking out for a rich wife: and now I am come to some more of his invented, devised, designed, and abominable roguery, such that will yet declare him to be a most desperate sinner.

The thing was this: a wife he wanted, or rather money; for as for a woman, he could have whores enow at his whistle. But, as I said, he wanted money, and that must be got by a wife or no way; nor could he so easily get a wife neither, except he became an artist at the way of dissembling; nor would dissembling do among that people that could dissemble as well as he. But there dwelt a maid not far from him, that was both godly, and one that had a good portion, but how to get her, there lay all the craft. Well, he calls a council of some of his most trusty and cunning companions, and breaks his mind to them; to wit, that he had a mind to marry: and he also told them to whom; but, said he, how shall I accomplish my end; she is religious, and I am not? Then one of them made reply, saying, Since she is religious, you must pretend to be so likewise, and that for some time before you go to her. Mark therefore whither she goes daily to hear, and do you go thither also; but there you must be sure to behave yourself soberly, and make as if you liked the Word wonderful well; stand also where she may see you, and when you come home, be sure that you walk the street very soberly, and go within sight of her. This done for a while, then go to her, and first talk of how sorry you are for your sins, and show great love to the religion that she is of, still speaking well of her preachers and of her godly acquaintance, bewailing your hard hap that it was not your lot to be acquainted with her and her fellow-professors sooner; and this is the way to get her. Also you must write down sermons, talk of scriptures, and protest that you came a-wooing to her, only because she is godly, and because you should count it your greatest happiness if you might but have such a one. As for her money, slight it, it will be never the farther off, that is the way to come soonest at it, for she will be jealous at first that you come for her money; you know what she has, but make not a word about it. Do this, and you shall see if you do not entangle the lass. Thus was the snare laid for this poor honest maid, and she was quickly catched in his pit.

Atten. Why, did he take this counsel?

Wise. Did he! yes, and after a while, went as boldly to her, and that under a vizard of religion, as if he had been for honesty and godliness one of the most sincere and up-right-hearted in England. He observed all his points, and followed the advice of his counsellors, and quickly obtained her too; for natural parts he had; he was tall, and fair, and had plain, but very good clothes on his back; and his religion was the more easily attained; for he had seen something in the house of his father, and first master, and so could the more readily put himself into the form and show thereof.

So he appointed his day, and went to her, as that he might easily do, for she had neither father nor mother to oppose. Well, when he was come, and had given her a civil compliment, to let her understand why he was come, then he began and told her that he had found in his heart a great deal of love to her person; and that of all the damsels in the world he had pitched upon her, if she thought fit, to make her his beloved wife. The reasons, as he told her, why he had pitched upon her were her religious and personal excellencies; and therefore entreated her to take his condition into her tender and loving consideration. As for the world, quoth he, I have a very good trade, and can maintain myself and family well, while my wife sits still on her seat; I have got thus and thus much already, and feel money come in every day, but that is not the thing that I aim at; it is an honest and godly wife. Then he would present her with a good book or two, pretending how much good he had got by them himself. He would also be often speaking well of godly ministers, especially of those that he perceived she liked, and loved most. Besides he would be often telling of her what a godly father he had, and what a new man he was also become himself; and thus did this treacherous dealer deal with this honest and good girl, to her great grief and sorrow, as afterward you shall hear.

Atten. But had the maid no friend to look after her?

Wise. Her father and mother were dead, and that he knew well enough, and so she was the more easily overcome by his naughty lying tongue. But if she had never so many friends, she might have been beguiled by him. It is too much the custom of young people now, to think themselves wise enough to make their own choice; and that they need not ask counsel of those that are older, and also wiser than they; but this is a great fault in them, and many of them have paid dear for it. Well, to be short, in little time Mr. Badman obtains his desire, gets this honest girl, and her money, is married to her, brings her home, makes a feast, entertains her royally, but her portion must pay for all.

Atten. This was wonderful deceitful doings, a man shall seldom hear of the like.

Wise. By this his doing, he showed how little he feared God, and what little dread he had of his judgments. For all this carriage and all these words were by him premeditated evil; he knew he lied, he knew he dissembled; yea, he knew that he made use of the name of God, of religion, good men, and good books, but as a stalking-horse, thereby the better to catch his game. In all this his glorious pretence of religion, he was but a glorious painted hypocrite, and hypocrisy is the highest sin that a poor carnal wretch can attain unto; it is also a sin that most dareth God, and that also bringeth the greater damnation. Now was he a whited wall, now was he a painted sepulchre (Matt. xxiii. 27). Now was he a grave that appeared not (Luke xi. 44). For this poor, honest, godly damsel little thought that both her peace and comfort, and estate, and liberty, and person, and all, were going to her burial, when she was going to be married to Mr. Badman; and yet so it was, she enjoyed herself but little afterwards; she was as if she was dead and buried to what she enjoyed before.

Atten. Certainly some wonderful judgment of God must attend and overtake such wicked men as these.

Wise. You may be sure that they shall have judgment to the full, for all these things, when the day of judgment is come. But as for judgment upon them in this life, it doth not always come, no not upon those that are worthy thereof. "They that tempt God are delivered, and they that work wickedness are set up" (Mal. iii. 15). But they are reserved to the day of wrath; and then, for their wickedness, God will repay them to their faces. "The wicked is reserved to the day of destruction; they shall be brought forth to the day of wrath. Who shall declare his way to his face? and who shall repay him what he hath done? Yet shall he be brought to the grave, and shall remain in the tomb" (Job xxi. 30–2). That is, ordinarily they escape God's hand in this life, save only a few examples are made, that others may be cautioned, and take warning thereby. But at the day of judgment they must be rebuked for their evil with the lashes of devouring fire.

Atten. Can you give me no examples of God's wrath

upon men that have acted this tragical wicked deed of Mr. Badman?

Wise. Yes; Hamor and Shechem, and all the men of their city, for attempting to make God and religion the stalking-horse to get Jacob's daughters to wife, were together slain with the edge of the sword. A judgment of God upon them, no doubt, for their dissembling in that matter (Gen. xxxiv. 1). All manner of lying and dissembling is dreadful, but to make God and religion a disguise, therewith to blind thy dissimulation from others' eyes, is highly provoking to the Divine majesty. I knew one that dwelt not far off from our town, that got him a wife as Mr. Badman got his; but he did not enjoy her long; for one night as he was riding home from his companions, where he had been at a neighbouring town, his horse threw him to the ground, where he was found dead at break of day; frightfully and lamentably mangled with his fall, and besmeared with his own blood.

Atten. Well, but pray return again to Mr. Badman; how did he carry it to his wife, after he was married to her?

Wise. Nay, let us take things along as we go. He had not been married but a little while, but his creditors came upon him for their money. He deferred them a little while, but at last things were come to that point that pay he must, or must do worse; so he appointed them a time, and they came for their money, and he payed them down with her money, before her eyes, for those goods that he had profusely spent among his whores long before, besides the portion that his father gave him, to the value of two hundred pounds.

Atten. This beginning was bad, but what shall I say? It was like Mr. Badman himself. Poor woman! this was but a bad beginning for her; I fear it filled her with trouble enough, as I think such a beginning would have done one perhaps much stronger than she.

Wise. Trouble, aye, you may be sure of it, but now it was too late to repent; she should have looked better to herself when being wary would have done her good; her harms may be an advantage to others that will learn to take heed thereby, but for herself, she must take what follows, even such a life now as Mr. Badman her husband will lead her, and that will be bad enough.

Atten. This beginning was bad, and yet I fear it was but the beginning of bad.

Wise. You may be sure that it was but the beginning of badness, for other evils came on apace; as, for instance, it was but a little while after he was married, but he hangs his religion upon the hedge, or rather dealt with it as men deal with their old clothes, who cast them off, or leave them to others to wear; for his part he would be religious no longer.

Now therefore he had pulled off his vizard, and began to show himself in his old shape, a base, wicked, debauched fellow; and now the poor woman saw that she was betrayed indeed, now also his old companions begin to flock about him, and to haunt his house and shop as formerly. And who with them but Mr. Badman? And who with him again but they?

Now those good people that used to company with his wife began to be amazed and discouraged, also he would frown and glout upon them as if he abhorred the appearance of them, so that in little time he drove all good company from her, and made her sit solitary by herself. He also began now to go out a-nights to those drabs who were his familiars before, with whom he would stay sometimes till midnight, and sometimes till almost morning, and then would come home as drunk as a swine: and this was the course of Mr. Badman.

Now when he came home in this case, if his wife did but speak a word to him about where he had been and why he had so abused himself, though her words were spoken in never so much meekness and love, then she was whore, and bitch, and jade! and it was well if she missed his fingers and heels. Sometimes also he would bring his punks home to his house, and woe be to his wife when they were gone if she did not entertain them with all varieties possible, and also carry it lovingly to them. Thus this good woman was made by Badman, her husband, to possess nothing but disappointments as to all that he had promised her, or that she hoped to have at his hands.

But that that added pressing weight to all her sorrow was that, as he had cast away all religion himself, so he attempted, if possible, to make her do so too. He would not suffer her to go out to the preaching of the Word of Christ, nor to the rest of his appointments, for the health and salvation of her soul. He would now taunt at and reflectingly speak of her preachers, and would receive, yea, raise scandals of them, to her very great grief and affliction.

Now she scarce durst go to an honest neighbour's house, or have a good book in her hand, especially when he had his companions in his house, or had got a little drink in his head. He would also, when he perceived that she was dejected, speak tauntingly and mockingly to her in the presence of his companions, calling of her his religious wife, his demure dame, and the like, also he would make a sport of her among his wanton ones abroad.

If she did ask him, as sometimes she would, to let her go out to a sermon, he would in a churlish manner reply, Keep at home, keep at home and look to your business, we cannot live by hearing of sermons. If she still urged that he would let her go, then he would say to her, Go if you dare. He would also charge her with giving of what he had to her ministers, when, vile wretch, he had spent it on his vain companions before. This was the life that Mr. Badman's good wife lived, within few months after he had married her.

Atten. This was a disappointment indeed.

Wise. A disappointment indeed, as ever I think poor woman had. One would think that the knave might a little let her have had her will since it was nothing but to be honest, and since she brought him so sweet, so lumping a portion—for she brought hundreds into his house—I say, one would think he should have let her had her own will a little, since she desired it only in the service and worship of God; but could she win him to grant her that? No, not a bit, if it would have saved her life. True, sometimes she would steal out when he was from home, or on a journey, or among his drunken companions, but with all privacy imaginable; and, poor woman, this advantage she had she carried it so to all her neighbours that, though many of them were but carnal, yet they would not betray her, or tell of her going out to the Word if they saw it, but would rather endeavour to hide it from Mr. Badman himself.

Atten. This carriage of his to her was enough to break her heart.

Wise. It was enough to do it indeed, yea, it did effectually do it. It killed her in time, yea, it was all the time a-killing of her. She would oftentimes, when she sat by herself, thus mournfully bewail her condition: "Woe is me that I sojourn in Meshech," and "*that* I dwell in the tents of Kedar! My soul hath long dwelt with him that hateth peace." O "what shall be given unto thee," thou "deceitful tongue?" "or what shall be done unto thee, thou false tongue?" (Ps. cxx.). I am a woman grieved in spirit, my husband has bought me and sold me for his lusts. It was not me, but my money that he wanted; O that he had had it, so I had had my liberty! This she said, not of contempt of his person, but of his conditions, and because she saw that, by his hypocritical tongue, he had brought her not only almost to beggary, but robbed her of the Word of God.

Atten. It is a deadly thing, I see, to be unequally yoked with unbelievers. If this woman had had a good husband, how happily might they have lived together! Such an one would have prayed for her, taught her, and also would have encouraged her in the faith and ways of God; but now, poor creature, instead of this there is nothing but the quite contrary.

Wise. It is a deadly thing indeed, and therefore, by the Word of God, his people are forbid to be joined in marriage with them. "Be ye not," saith it, "unequally yoked together with unbelievers: for what fellowship hath righteousness with unrighteousness? and what communion hath light with darkness? And what concord hath Christ with Belial? or what part hath he that believeth with an infidel? and what agreement hath the temple of God with idols?" (2 Cor. vi. 14–16). There can be no agreement where such matches are made; even God himself hath declared the contrary from the beginning of the world. "I," says he, "will put enmity between thee and the woman, and between thy seed and her seed" (Gen. iii. 15). Therefore he saith in another place they can mix no better than iron and clay (Dan. ii. 43). I say they cannot agree, they cannot be one, and therefore they should be aware at first, and not lightly receive such into their affections. God has often made such matches bitter, especially to his own. Such matches are, as God said of Eli's sons that were spared, to consume the eyes and to grieve the heart. O! the wailing and lamentation that they have made that have been thus yoked, especially if they were such as would be so yoked against their light and good counsel to the contrary.

Atten. Alas! he deluded her with his tongue, and feigned reformation.

Wise. Well, well, she should have gone more warily to work. What if she had acquainted some of her best, most knowing, and godly friends therewith? What if she had engaged a godly minister or two to have talked with Mr. Badman? Also, what if she had laid wait round about him, to espy if he was not otherwise behind her back than he was before her face? And besides I verily think—since in the multitude of counsellors there is safety—that if she had acquainted the congregation with it, and desired them to spend some time in prayer to God about it, and if she must have had him, to have received him as to his godliness upon the judgment of others, rather than her own—she knowing them to be godly and judicious and unbiassed men—she had had more peace all her life after, than to trust to her own poor, raw, womanish judgment as she did. Love is blind, and will see nothing amiss where others may see a hundred faults. Therefore I say she should not have trusted to her own thoughts in the matter of his goodness.

As to his person, there she was fittest to judge, because she was to be the person pleased, but as to his godliness, there the Word was the fittest judge, and they that could best understand it, because God was therein to be pleased. I wish that all young maidens will take heed of being beguiled with flattering words, with feigning and lying speeches, and take the best way to preserve themselves from being bought and sold by wicked men as she was, lest they repent with her, when, as to this, repentance will do them no good, but for their unadvisedness go sorrowing to their graves.

Atten. Well, things are past with this poor woman and cannot be called back, let others beware by her misfortunes, lest they also fall into her distress.

Wise. That is the thing that I say, let them take heed, lest for their unadvisedness they smart, as this poor woman has done. And ah! methinks, that they that yet are single persons, and that are tempted to marry to such as Mr. Badman, would, to inform and warn themselves in this matter before they entangle themselves, but go to some that already are in the snare, and ask them how it is with them, as to the suitable or unsuitableness of their marriage, and desire their advice. Surely they would ring such a peal in their ears about the unequality, unsuitableness, disadvantages, and disquietments, and sins that attend such marriages, that would make them beware as long as they live. But the bird in the air knows not the notes of the bird in the snare until she comes thither herself. Besides, to make up such marriages, Satan and carnal reason, and lust, or at least inconsiderateness, has the chiefest hand; and where these things bear sway, designs, though never so destructive, will go headlong on; and therefore I fear that but little warning will be taken by young girls at Mr. Badman's wife's affliction.

Atten. But are there no dissuasive arguments to lay before such, to prevent their future misery?

Wise. Yes: there is the law of God, that forbiddeth marriage with unbelievers. These kind of marriages also are condemned even by irrational creatures. 1. It is forbidden by the law of God, both in the Old Testament and in the New. (1) In the Old. Thou shalt not "make marriages with them; thy daughter thou shalt not give unto his son, nor his daughter shalt thou take unto thy son" (Deut. vii. 3). (2) In the New Testament it is forbidden. "Be ye not unequally yoked together with unbelievers," let them marry to whom they will, "only in the Lord" (2 Cor. vi. 14-16; 1 Cor. vii. 39).

Here now is a prohibition, plainly forbidding the believer to marry with the unbeliever, therefore they should not do it. Again, these unwarrantable marriages are, as I may so say, condemned by irrational creatures, who will not couple but with their own sort. Will the sheep couple with a dog, the partridge with a crow, or the pheasant with an owl? No, they will strictly tie up themselves to those of their own sort only. Yea, it sets all the world a-wondering, when they see or hear the contrary. Man only is most subject to wink at, and allow of these unlawful mixtures of men and women; because man only is a sinful beast, a sinful bird, therefore he, above all, will take upon him, by rebellious actions, to answer, or rather to oppose and violate the law of his God

H 815

and Creator; nor shall these or other interrogatories, What fellowship? what concord? what agreement? what communion can there be in such marriages? be counted of weight or thought worth the answering by him.

But further, the dangers that such do commonly run themselves into, should be to others a dissuasive argument to stop them from doing the like: for besides the distresses of Mr. Badman's wife, many that have had very hopeful beginnings for heaven, have, by virtue of the mischiefs that have attended these unlawful marriages, miserably and fearfully miscarried. Soon after such marriages, conviction, the first step towards heaven, hath ceased; prayer, the next step towards heaven, hath ceased; hungerings and thirstings after salvation, another step towards the kingdom of heaven, hath ceased. In a word, such marriages have estranged them from the Word, from their godly and faithful friends, and have brought them again into carnal company, among carnal friends, and also into carnal delights, where, and with whom, they have in conclusion both sinfully abode, and miserably perished.

And this is one reason why God hath forbidden this kind of unequal marriages. "For they," saith he, meaning the ungodly, "will turn away thy son from following me, that they may serve other gods; so will the anger of the Lord be kindled against you, and destroy thee suddenly" (Deut. vii. 4). Now mark, there were some in Israel, that would notwithstanding this prohibition, venture to marry to the heathens and unbelievers. But what followed? "They served their idols, they sacrificed their sons and their daughters unto devils. Thus were they defiled with their own works, and went a-whoring with their own inventions; therefore was the wrath of the Lord kindled against his people, insomuch that he abhorred his own inheritance" (Ps. cvi. 36–40).

Atten. But let us return again to Mr. Badman; had he any children by his wife?

Wise. Yes, seven.

Atten. I doubt they were but badly brought up.

Wise. One of them loved its mother dearly, and would constantly hearken to her voice. Now that child she had the opportunity to instruct in the principles of Christian religion, and it became a very gracious child. But that child Mr.

Badman could not abide, he would seldom afford it a pleasant word, but would scowl and frown upon it, speak churlishly and doggedly to it, and though, as to nature, it was the most feeble of the seven, yet it oftenest felt the weight of its father's fingers. Three of his children did directly follow his steps, and began to be as vile as, in his youth, he was himself. The other that remained became a kind of mongrel professors, not so bad as their father, nor so good as their mother, but were betwixt them both. They had their mother's notions, and their father's actions, and were much like those that you read of in the book of Nehemiah; these children were half of Ashdod, "and could not speak in the Jews' language, but according to the language of each people" (Neh. xiii. 24).

Atten. What you say in this matter is observable, and if I take not my mark amiss, it often happeneth after this manner where such unlawful marriages are contracted.

Wise. It sometimes doth so, and the reason, with respect to their parents, is this. Where the one of the parents is godly, and the other ungodly and vile, though they can agree in begetting of children, yet they strive for their children when they are born. The godly parent strives for the child, and by prayers, counsel, and good examples, labours to make it holy in body and soul, and so fit for the kingdom of heaven; but the ungodly would have it like himself, wicked, and base, and sinful; and so they both give instructions accordingly. Instructions did I say? yea, and examples too according to their minds. Thus the godly, as Hannah, is presenting her Samuel unto the Lord: but the ungodly, like them that went before them, are for offering their children to Moloch, to an idol, to sin, to the devil, and to hell. Thus one hearkeneth to the law of their mother and is preserved from destruction, but as for the other, as their fathers did, so do they. Thus did Mr. Badman and his wife part some of their children betwixt them; but as for the other three that were, as it were, mongrels, betwixt both, they were like unto those that you read of in Kings, they feared the Lord, but served their own idols (2 Kings xvii.). They had, as I said, their mother's notions, and I will add, profession too; but their father's lusts, and something of his life. Now their father did not like them, because they had their mother's tongue; and the mother did not like them because they had still their father's heart and life; nor were they indeed fit company for good or bad. The good would not trust them because they were bad, the bad would not trust them because they were good; namely, the good would not trust them because they were bad in their lives, and the bad would not trust them because they were good in their words. So they were forced with Esau to join in affinity with Ishmael; to wit, to look out a people that were hypocrites like themselves, and with them they matched, and lived, and died.

Atten. Poor woman, she could not but have much perplexity.

Wise. Yea, and poor children, that ever they were sent into the world as the fruit of the loins, and under the government of such a father as Mr. Badman.

Atten. You say right, for such children lie almost under all manner of disadvantages: but we must say nothing, because this also is the sovereign will of God.

Wise. We may not by any means object against God; yet we may talk of the advantages and disadvantages that children have by having for their parents such as are either godly or the contrary.

Atten. You say right, we may so, and pray now, since we are about it, speak something in brief unto it, that is, unto this: what advantage those children have above others, that have for their parents such as indeed are godly?

Wise. So I will, only I must first premise these two or three things. 1. They have not the advantage of election for their fathers' sakes. 2. They are born as others, the children of wrath, though they come of godly parents. 3. Grace comes not unto them as an inheritance, because they have godly parents. These things premised I shall now proceed.

1. The children of godly parents are the children of many prayers. They are prayed for before, and prayed for after they are born; and the prayer of a godly father and godly mother doth much. 2. They have the advantage of what restraint is possible, from what evils their parents see them inclinable to, and that is a second mercy. 3. They have the advantage of godly instruction, and of being told which be and which be not the right ways of the Lord. 4. They

have also those ways commended unto them, and spoken well of in their hearing, that are good. 5. Such are also, what may be kept out of evil company, from evil books, and from being taught the way of swearing, lying, and the like, as sabbath-breaking, and mocking at good men and good things, and this is a very great mercy. 6. They have also the benefit of a godly life set before them doctrinally by their parents, and that doctrine backed with a godly and holy example. And all these are very great advantages.

Now all these advantages the children of ungodly parents want; and so are more in danger of being carried away with the error of the wicked. For ungodly parents neither pray for their children, nor do nor can they heartily instruct them; they do not after a godly manner restrain them from evil, nor do they keep them from evil company. They are not grieved at, nor yet do they forewarn their children to beware of such evil actions that are abomination to God and to all good men. They let their children break the sabbath, swear, lie, be wicked and vain. They commend not to their children a holy life, nor set a good example before their eyes. No, they do in all things contrary: estranging of their children what they can, from the love of God and all good men, so soon as they are born. Therefore it is a very great judgment of God upon children, to be the offspring of base and ungodly men (Job xxx. 8).

Atten. Well, but before we leave Mr. Badman's wife and children, I have a mind, if you please, to inquire a little more after one thing, the which I am sure you can satisfy me in.

Wise. What is that?

Atten. You said a while ago that this Mr. Badman would not suffer his wife to go out to hear such godly ministers as she liked, but said, if she did, she had as good never come home any more. Did he often carry it thus to her?

Wise. He did say so, he did often say so. This I told you then, and had also then told you more, but that other things put me out.

Atten. Well said; pray, therefore, now go on.

Wise. So I will. Upon a time, she was, on a Lord's day, for going to hear a sermon, and Mr. Badman was unwilling she should; but she at that time, as it seems, did put on more courage than she was wont; and, therefore, after she had spent upon him a great many fair words and entreaties, if perhaps she might have prevailed by them, but all to no purpose at all, at last she said she would go, and rendered this reason for it: I have a husband, but also a God; my God has commanded me, and that upon pain of damnation, to be a continual worshipper of him, and that in the way of his own appointments. I have a husband, but also a soul, and my soul ought to be more unto me than all the world besides. This soul of mine I will look after, care for, and, if I can, provide it a heaven for its habitation. You are commanded to love me, as you love your own body, and so do I love you; but I tell you true, I prefer my soul before all the world, and its salvation I will seek (Eph. v. 28).

At this, first he gave her an ugly wish, and then fell into a fearful rage, and sware moreover that if she did go, he would make both her and all her damnable brotherhood, for so he was pleased to call them, to repent their coming thither.

Atten. But what should he mean by that?

Wise. You may easily guess what he meant. He meant he would turn informer, and so either weary out those that she loved from meeting together to worship God, or make them pay dearly for their so doing, the which, if he did, he knew it would vex every vein of her tender heart.

Atten. But do you think Mr. Badman would have been so base?

Wise. Truly he had malice and enmity enough in his heart to do it, only he was a tradesman; also he knew that he must live by his neighbours, and so he had that little wit in his anger, that he refrained himself and did it not. But, as I said, he had malice and envy enough in his heart to have made him to do it, only he thought it would worst him in his trade; yet these three things he would be doing: 1. He would be putting of others on to molest and abuse her friends. 2. He would be glad when he heard that any mischief befel them. 3. And would laugh at her when he saw her troubled for them. And now I have told you Mr. Badman's way as to this.

Atten. But was he not afraid of the judgments of God that did fly about at that time?

Wise. He regarded not the judgment nor mercy of God,

for had he at all done that he could not have done as he did. But what judgments do you mean?

Atten. Such judgments, that if Mr. Badman himself had taken but sober notice of, they might have made him a hung down his ears.

Wise. Why, have you heard of any such persons that the judgments of God have overtaken?

Atten. Yes, and so, I believe, have you too, though you make so strange about it.

Wise. I have so indeed, to my astonishment and wonder.

Atten. Pray, therefore, if you please, tell me what it is, as to this, that you know; and then, perhaps, I may also say something to you of the same.

Wise. In our town there was one W. S., a man of a very wicked life; and he, when there seemed to be countenance given to it, would needs turn informer. Well, so he did, and was as diligent in his business as most of them could be; he would watch of nights, climb trees, and range the woods of days, if possible, to find out the meeters, for then they were forced to meet in the fields; yea, he would curse them bitterly, and swear most fearfully what he would do to them when he found them. Well, after he had gone on like a bedlam in his course awhile, and had done some mischiefs to the people, he was stricken by the hand of God, and that in this manner: 1. Although he had his tongue naturally at will, now he was taken with a faltering in his speech, and could not for weeks together speak otherwise than just like a man that was drunk. 2. Then he was taken with a drauling, or slabbering at his mouth, which slabber sometimes would hang at his mouth well nigh half-way down to the ground. 3. Then he had such a weakness in the back sinews of his neck, that ofttimes he could not look up before him, unless he clapped his hand hard upon his forehead, and held up his head that way, by strength of hand. 4. After this his speech went quite away, and he could speak no more than a swine or a bear. Therefore, like one of them, he would gruntle and make an ugly noise, according as he was offended, or pleased, or would have anything done, etc.

In this posture he continued for the space of half a year or thereabouts, all the while otherwise well, and could go about his business, save once that he had a fall from the bell as it hangs in our steeple, which it was a wonder it did not kill him. But after that he also walked about, until God had made a sufficient spectacle of his judgment for his sin, and then on a sudden he was stricken, and died miserably; and so there was an end of him and his doings.

I will tell you of another. About four miles from St. Neots, there was a gentleman had a man, and he would needs be an informer, and a lusty young man he was. Well, an informer he was, and did much distress some people, and had perfected his informations so effectually against some, that there was nothing further to do but for the constables to make distress on the people, that he might have the money or goods; and, as I heard, he hastened them much to do it. Now, while he was in the heat of his work, as he stood one day by the fire-side, he had, it should seem, a mind to a sop in the pan, for the spit was then at the fire, so he went to make him one; but behold, a dog, some say his own dog, took distaste at something, and bit his master by the leg; the which bite, notwithstanding all the means that was used to cure him, turned, as was said, to a gangrene; however, that wound was his death, and that a dreadful one too. For my relator said that he lay in such a condition by this bite, as the beginning, until his flesh rotted from off him before he went out of the world. But what need I instance in particular persons, when the judgment of God against this kind of people was made manifest, I think I may say, if not in all, yet in most of the counties in England where such poor creatures were? But I would, if it had been the will of God, that neither I nor anybody else, could tell you more of these stories; true stories, that are neither lie nor romance.

Atten. Well, I also heard of both these myself, and of more too, as remarkable in their kind as these, if I had any list to tell them; but let us leave those that are behind to others, or to the coming of Christ, who then will justify or condemn them, as the merit of their work shall require; or if they repented, and found mercy, I shall be glad when I know it, for I wish not a curse to the soul of mine enemy.

Wise. There can be no pleasure in the telling of such stories, though to hear of them may do us a pleasure. They may put us in mind that there is a God that judgeth in the earth, and that doth not always forget nor defer to hear the cry of the destitute; they also carry along with them both caution and counsel to those that are the survivors of such. Let us tremble at the judgments of God, and be afraid of sinning against him, and it shall be our protection. It shall go well with them that fear God, that fear before him.

Atten. Well, sir, as you have intimated, so I think we have, in this place, spoken enough about these kind of men; if you please, let us return again to Mr. Badman himself, if you have any more to say of him.

Wise. More! we have yet scarce thoroughly begun with anything that we have said. All the particulars are in themselves so full of badness, that we have rather only looked in them, than indeed said anything to them; but we will pass them and proceed. You have heard of the sins of his youth, of his apprenticeship, and how he set up, and married, and what a life he hath led his wife; and now I will tell you some more of his pranks. He had the very knack of knavery; had he, as I said before, been bound to serve an apprenticeship to all these things, he could not have been more cunning, he could not have been more artificial at it.

Atten. Nor perhaps so artificially neither. For as none can teach goodness like to God himself, so, concerning sin and knavery, none can teach a man it like the devil, to whom, as I perceive, Mr. Badman went to school from his childhood to the end of his life. But, pray, sir, make a beginning.

Wise. Well, so I will. You may remember that I told you what a condition he was in for money before he did marry, and how he got a rich wife, with whose money he paid his debts. Now, when he had paid his debts, he having some money left, he sets up again as briskly as ever, keeps a great shop, drives a great trade, and runs again a great way into debt; but now not into the debt of one or two, but into the debt of many, so that at last he came to owe some thousands, and thus he went on a good while. And, to pursue his ends the better, he begun now to study to please all men, and to suit himself to any company; he could now be as they, say as they, that is, if he listed; and then he would list, when he perceived that by so doing he might either make them his customers or creditors for his commodities. If he dealt with honest men, as with some honest men he did, then he would

* H 815

be as they, talk as they, seem to be sober as they, talk of justice and religion as they, and against debauchery as they; yea, and would too seem to show a dislike of them that said, did, or were otherwise than honest.

Again, when he did light among those that were bad, then he would be as they, but yet more close and cautiously, except he were sure of his company. Then he would carry it openly, be as they, say, damn them and sink them as they. If they railed on good men, so could he; if they railed on religion, so could he; if they talked beastly, vainly, idly, so would he; if they were for drinking, swearing, whoring, or any the like villainies, so was he. This was now the path he trod in, and could do all artificially as any man alive. And now he thought himself a perfect man, he thought he was always a boy till now. What think you now of Mr. Badman?

Atten. Think! why I think he was an atheist; for no man but an atheist can do this. I say it cannot be but that the man that is such as this Mr. Badman must be a rank and stinking atheist, for he that believes that there is either God or devil, heaven or hell, or death and judgment after, cannot do as Mr. Badman did; I mean if he could do these things without reluctancy and check of conscience, yea, if he had not sorrow and remorse for such abominable sins as these.

Wise. Nay, he was so far off from reluctances and remorse of conscience for these things, that he counted them the excellency of his attainments, the quintessence of his wit, his rare and singular virtues, such as but few besides himself could be the masters of. Therefore, as for those that made boggle and stop at things, and that could not in conscience, and for fear of death and judgment, do such things as he, he would call them fools and noddies, and charge them for being frighted with the talk of unseen bugbears, and would encourage them, if they would be men indeed, to labour after the attainment of this his excellent art. He would oftentimes please himself with the thoughts of what he could do in this matter, saying within himself, I can be religious and irreligious, I can be anything or nothing; I can swear, and speak against swearing; I can lie, and speak against lying; I can drink, wench, be unclean, and defraud, and not be troubled for it. Now I enjoy myself, and am master of mine own ways, and not they of me. This I have attained with much study, great care, and more pains. But this his talk should be only with himself, to his wife, who he knew durst not divulge it, or among his intimates, to whom he knew he might say anything.

Atten. Did I call him before an atheist? I may call him now a devil, or a man possessed with one, if not with many. I think that there cannot be found in every corner such a one as this. True, it is said of king Ahaz that he sinned more and more (2. Chron. xxviii. 22). And of Ahab, that he sold "himself to work wickedness" (1 Kings xxi. 25). And of the men of Sodom, that they "were sinners before the Lord exceedingly" (Gen. xiii. 13).

Wise. An atheist he was no doubt, if there be such a thing as an atheist in the world; but for all his brags of perfection and security in his wickedness, I believe that at times God did let down fire from heaven into his conscience (Job xxi. 17). True, I believe he would quickly put it out again, and grow more wicked and desperate afterward, but this also turned to his destruction, as afterward you may hear.

But I am not of your mind to think that there are but few such in the world, except you mean as to the degree of wickedness unto which he had attained. For otherwise, no doubt, there is abundance of such as he; men of the same mind, of the same principles, and of the same conscience too, to put them into practice. Yea, I believe that there are many that are endeavouring to attain to the same pitch of wickedness, and all them are such as he in the judgment of the law, nor will their want of hellish wit to attain thereto excuse them at the day of judgment. You know that in all science some are more arch than some, and so it is in the art as well as in the practice of wickedness, some are two-fold and some seven-fold more the children of hell than others—and yet all the children of hell—else they would all be masters, and none scholars in the school of wickedness. But there must be masters, and there must be learners; Mr. Badman was a master in this art, and therefore it follows that he must be an arch and chief one in that mystery.

Atten. You are in the right, for I perceive that some men, though they desire it, are not so arch in the practice thereof as others, but are, as I suppose they call them, fools and dunces to the rest, their heads and capacities will not serve them to act and do so wickedly. But Mr. Badman wanted not a wicked head to contrive, as well as a wicked heart to do his wickedness.

Wise. True, but yet I say such men shall at the day of judgment be judged, not only for what they are, but also for what they would be. For if "the thought of foolishness *is* sin," doubtless the desire of foolishness is more sin; and if the desire be more, the endeavour after it must needs be more and more (Ps. xxiv. 9). He then that is not an artificial atheist and transgressor, yet if he desires to be so, if he endeavoureth to be so, he shall be judged and condemned to hell for such a one. For the law judgeth men, as I said, according to what they would be. He that "looketh on a woman to lust after her, hath committed adultery with her already in his heart" (Matt. v. 28). By the same rule, he that would steal, doth steal; he that would cheat, doth cheat; he that would swear, doth swear; and he that would commit adultery, doth do so. For God judgeth men according to the working of their minds, and saith, "As he thinketh, so *is* he" (Prov. xxiii. 7). That is, so is he in his heart, in his intentions, in his desires, in his endeavours; and God's law, I say, lays hold of the desires, intentions, and endeavours, even as it lays hold of the act of wickedness itself (Matt. v.; Rom. vii. 7). A man then that desires to be as bad as Mr. Badman, and desires to be so wicked have many in their hearts, though he never attains to that proficiency in wickedness as he, shall be judged for as bad a man as he, because it was in his desires to be such a wicked one.

Atten. But this height of wickedness in Mr. Badman will not yet out of my mind. This hard, desperate, or, what shall I call it, diabolical frame of heart, was in him a foundation, a ground-work to all acts and deeds that were evil.

Wise. The heart, and the desperate wickedness of it, is the foundation and ground-work of all. Atheism, professed and practical, spring both out of the heart, yea, and all manner of evil besides. For they be not bad deeds that make a bad man, but he is already a bad man that doth bad deeds. A man must be wicked before he can do wickedness. "Wickedness proceedeth from the wicked" (1 Sam. xxiv. 13). It is an evil tree that bears evil fruit. Men gather

no grapes of thorns; the heart therefore must be evil before the man can do evil, and good before the man doth good (Matt. vii. 16–18).

Atten. Now I see the reason why Mr. Badman was so base as to get a wife by dissimulation, and to abuse her so like a villain when he had got her; it was because he was before, by a wicked heart, prepared to act wickedness.

Wise. You may be sure of it, "For from within, out of the heart of men, proceed evil thoughts, adulteries, fornications, murders, thefts, covetousness, wickedness, deceit, lasciviousness, an evil eye, blasphemy, pride, foolishness: all these things come from within and defile the man" (Mark vii. 20–23). And a man, as his naughty mind inclines him, makes use of these, or any of these, to gratify his lust, to promote his designs, to revenge his malice, to enrich, or to wallow himself in the foolish pleasures and pastimes of this life. And all these did Mr. Badman do, even to the utmost, if either opportunity, or purse, or perfidiousness, would help him to the obtaining of his purpose.

Atten. Purse! why he could not but have purse to do almost what he would, having married a wife with so much money.

Wise. Hold you there; some of Mr. Badman's sins were costly, as his drinking, and whoring, and keeping other bad company; though he was a man that had ways too many to get money, as well as ways too many to spend it.

Atten. Had he then such a good trade, for all he was such a bad man? Or was his calling so gainful to him as always to keep his purse's belly full, though he was himself a great spender?

Wise. No, it was not his trade that did it, though he had a pretty trade too. He had another way to get money, and that by hatfuls and pocketfuls at a time

Atten. Why I trow he was no highwayman, was he?

Wise. I will be sparing in my speech as to that, though some have muttered as if he could ride out now and then, about nobody but himself knew what, over-night, and come home all dirty and weary next morning. But that is not the thing I aim at.

Atten. Pray let me know it, if you think it convenient that I should.

Wise. I will tell you; it was this, he had an art to break, and get hatfuls of money by breaking.

Atten. But what do you mean by Mr. Badman's breaking? You speak mystically, do you not?

Wise. No, no, I speak plainly. Or, if you will have it in plainer language, it is this: When Mr. Badman had swaggered and whored away most of his wife's portion, he began to feel that he could not much longer stand upon his legs in this course of life and keep up his trade and repute— such as he had—in the world, but by the new engine of breaking. Wherefore upon a time he gives a great and sudden rush into several men's debts, to the value of about four or five thousand pounds, driving at the same time a very great trade, by selling many things for less than they cost him, to get him custom, therewith to blind his creditors' eyes. His creditors therefore seeing that he had a great employ, and dreaming that it must needs at length turn to a very good account to them, trusted him freely without mistrust, and so did others too, to the value of what was mentioned before. Well, when Mr. Badman had well feathered his nest with other men's goods and money, after a little time he breaks. And by and by it was noised abroad that Mr. Badman had shut up shop, was gone, and could trade no longer. Now by that time his breaking was come to his creditors' ears, he had by craft and knavery made so sure of what he had, that his creditors could not touch a penny. Well, when he had done, he sends his mournful sugared letters to his creditors, to let them understand what had happened unto him, and desired them not to be severe with him, for he bore towards all men an honest mind, and would pay so far as he was able. Now he sends his letters by a man confederate with him, who could make both the worst and best of Mr. Badman's case; the best for Mr. Badman and the worst for his creditors. So when he comes to them he both bemoans them and condoles Mr. Badman's condition, telling of them that, without a speedy bringing of things to a conclusion, Mr. Badman would be able to make them no satisfaction, but at present he both could and would, and that to the utmost of his power, and to that end he desired that they would come over to him. Well, his creditors appoint him a time and come over, and he, meanwhile, authorises another

to treat with them, but will not be seen himself, unless it
was on a Sunday, lest they should snap him with a writ.
So his deputed friend treats with them about their concern
with Mr. Badman, first telling them of the great care that
Mr. Badman took to satisfy them and all men for whatsoever he owed, as far as in him lay, and how little he thought
a while since to be in this low condition. He pleaded also
the greatness of his charge, the greatness of taxes, the badness of the times, and the great losses that he had by many
of his customers; some of which died in his debt, others
were run away, and for many that were alive he never
expected a farthing from them. Yet nevertheless he would
show himself an honest man, and would pay as far as he
was able; and if they were willing to come to terms, he would
make a composition with them, for he was not able to pay
them all. The creditors asked what he would give? It was
replied, Half a crown in the pound. At this they began to
huff, and he to renew his complaint and entreaty, but the
creditors would not hear, and so for that time their meeting
without success broke up. But after his creditors were in
cool blood, and admitting of second thoughts, and fearing
lest delays should make them lose all, they admit of a
second debate, come together again, and, by many words
and great ado, they obtained five shillings in the pound. So
the money was produced, releases and discharges drawn,
signed, and sealed, books crossed, and all things confirmed;
and then Mr. Badman can put his head out a doors again,
and be a better man than when he shut up shop, by several
thousands of pounds.

Atten. And did he do thus indeed?

Wise. Yes, once and again. I think he brake twice or
thrice.

Atten. And did he do it before he had need to do it?

Wise. Need! What do you mean by need? There is no
need at any time for a man to play the knave. He did it of
a wicked mind, to defraud and beguile his creditors. He had
wherewithal of his father, and also by his wife, to have
lived upon, with lawful labour, like an honest man. He had
also, when he made this wicked break, though he had been
a profuse and prodigal spender, to have paid his creditors
their own to a farthing. But had he done so, he had not

done like himself, like Mr. Badman; had he, I say, dealt like an honest man, he had then gone out of Mr. Badman's road. He did it therefore of a dishonest mind, and to a wicked end; to wit, that he might have wherewithal, howsoever unlawfully gotten, to follow his cups and queans, and to live in the full swing of his lusts, even as he did before.

Atten. Why this was a mere cheat.

Wise. It was a cheat indeed. This way of breaking, it is nothing else but a more neat way of thieving, of picking of pockets, of breaking open of shops, and of taking from men what one has nothing to do with. But though it seem easy, it is hard to learn; no man that has conscience to God or man, can ever be his crafts-master in this hellish art.

Atten. O! sir! what a wicked man was this!

Wise. A wicked man indeed. By this art he could tell how to make men send their goods to his shop, and then be glad to take a penny for that which he had promised, before it came thither, to give them a groat: I say, he could make them glad to take a crown for a pound's worth, and a thousand for that for which he had promised before to give them four thousand pounds.

Atten. This argueth that Mr. Badman had but little conscience.

Wise. This argued that Mr. Badman had no conscience at all; for conscience, the least spark of a good conscience, cannot endure this.

Atten. Before we go any farther in Mr. Badman's matters, let me desire you, if you please, to give me an answer to these two questions. (1) What do you find in the Word of God against such a practice as this of Mr. Badman's is? (2) What would you have a man do that is in his creditor's debt, and can neither pay him what he owes him, nor go on in a trade any longer?

Wise. I will answer you as well as I can. And first, to the first of your questions; to wit, What I find in the Word of God against such a practice as this of Mr. Badman's is.

The Word of God doth forbid this wickedness; and to make it the more odious in our eyes, it joins it with theft and robbery. "Thou shalt not," says God, "defraud thy neighbour, neither rob him" (Lev. xix. 13). Thou shalt not defraud, that is, deceive or beguile. Now thus to break, is

to defraud, deceive and beguile; which is, as you see, forbidden by the God of heaven: "Thou shalt not defraud thy neighbour, neither rob him." It is a kind of theft and robbery, thus to defraud and beguile. It is a vilely robbing of his shop, and picking of his pocket; a thing odious to reason and conscience, and contrary to the law of nature. It is a designed piece of wickedness, and therefore a double sin. A man cannot do this great wickedness on a sudden, and through a violent assault of Satan. He that will commit this sin, must have time to deliberate, that by invention he may make it formidable, and that with lies and high dissimulations. He that commits this wickedness, must first hatch it upon his bed, beat his head about it, and lay his plot strong. So that to the completing of such a wickedness, there must be adjoined many sins, and they too must go hand in hand until it be completed. But what saith the scripture? "Let no *man* go beyond and defraud his brother in *any* matter: because *that* the Lord *is* the avenger of all such" (1 Thess. iv. 6). But this kind of breaking is a going beyond my brother; this is a compassing of him about, that I may catch him in my net; and as I said, an art to rob my brother, and to pick his pocket, and that with his consent. Which doth not therefore mitigate, but so much the more greaten, and make odious the offence. For men that are thus wilily abused, cannot help themselves; they are taken in a deceitful net. But God will here concern himself, he will be the avenger, he will be the avenger of all such either here, or in another world.

And this, the apostle testifies again, where he saith, "But he that doeth wrong, shall receive for the wrong which he hath done; and there is no respect of persons" (Col. iii. 25). That is, there is no man, be he what he will, if he will be guilty of this sin, of going beyond, of beguiling of, and doing wrong to his brother, but God will call him to an account for it, and will pay him with vengeance for it too; for "there is no respect of persons."

I might add, that this sin of wronging, of going beyond, and defrauding of my neighbour, it is like that first prank that the devil played with our first parents, as the altar that Uriah built for Ahaz, was taken from the fashion of that that stood at Damascus, to be the very pattern of it. The serpent beguiled me, says Eve; Mr. Badman beguiles his creditors. The serpent beguiled Eve with lying promises of gain; and so did Mr. Badman beguile his creditors. The serpent said one thing and meant another, when he beguiled Eve; and so did Mr. Badman when he beguiled his creditors.

That man therefore that doth thus deceive and beguile his neighbour, imitateth the devil; he taketh his examples from him, and not from God, the Word, or good men; and this did Mr. Badman.

And now to your second question; to wit, What I would have a man do, that is in his creditor's debt, and that can neither pay him, nor go on in a trade any longer?

Answ. First of all, If this be his case, and he knows it, let him not run one penny farther in his creditors' debt, for that cannot be done with good conscience. He that knows he cannot pay, and yet will run into debt, does knowingly wrong and defraud his neighbour, and falls under that sentence of the Word of God, "The wicked borroweth, and payeth not again" (Ps. xxxvii. 21). Yea, worse, he borrows, though at the very same time he knows that he cannot pay again. He doth also craftily take away what is his neighbour's. That is therefore the first thing that I would propound to such; let him not run any farther into his creditors' debt.

Secondly, After this, let him consider, how, and by what means he was brought into such a condition that he could not pay his just debts. To wit, whether it was by his own remissness in his calling, by living too high in diet or apparel, by lending too lavishingly that which was none of his own, to his loss; or whether by the immediate hand and judgment of God.

If by searching he finds that this is come upon him through remissness in his calling, extravagancies in his family, or the like; let him labour for a sense of his sin and wickedness, for he has sinned against the Lord. First, in his being slothful in business, and in not providing, to wit, of his own, by the sweat of his brow, or other honest ways, for those of his own house (Rom. xii. 11; 1 Tim. v. 8). And, secondly, in being lavishing in diet and apparel in the family, or in lending to others that which was none of his own. This cannot be done with good conscience. It is both against reason and nature, and therefore must be a sin against God. I say therefore, if thus this debtor hath done, if ever he would live quietly in conscience, and comfortably in his condition for the future, let him humble himself before God, and repent of this his wickedness. For "he that is slothful in his work, is brother to him that is a great waster" (Prov. xviii. 9). To be slothful and a waster too, is to be as it were a double sinner.

But again, as this man should inquire into these things, so he should also into this, How came I into this way of dealing in which I have now miscarried? Is it a way that my parents brought me up in, put me apprentice to, or that by providence I was first thrust into? Or is it a way into which I have twisted myself, as not being contented with my first lot, that by God and my parents I was cast into? This ought duly to be considered, and if upon search a man shall find that he is out of the place and calling into which he was put by his parents, or the providence of God, and has miscarried in a new way, that through pride and dislike of his first state he has chose rather to embrace; his miscarriage is his sin, the fruit of his pride, and a token of the judgment of God upon him for his leaving of his first state. And for this he ought, as for the former, to be humble and penitent before the Lord.

But if by search he finds that his poverty came by none of these; if by honest search he finds it so, and can say with good conscience, I went not out of my place and state in which God by his providence had put me; but have abode with God in the calling wherein I was called, and have wrought hard, and fared meanly, been civilly apparelled, and have not directly nor indirectly made away with my creditors' goods; then has his fall come upon him by the immediate hand of God, whether by visible or invisible ways. For sometimes it comes by visible ways, to wit, by fire, by thieves, by loss of cattle, or the wickedness of sinful dealers, etc. And sometimes by means invisible, and then no man knows how; we only see things are going, but cannot see by what way they go. Well, now suppose that a man, by an immediate hand of God, is brought to a morsel of bread, what must he do now?

I answer: His surest way is still to think, that this is the fruit of some sin, though possibly not sin in the management

of his calling, yet of some other sin. "God casteth away
the substance of the wicked" (Prov. x. 3). Therefore let
him still humble himself before his God, because his hand
is upon him, and say, What sin is this, for which this hand
of God is upon me? (1 Pet. v. 6). And let him be diligent to
find it out, for some sin is the cause of this judgment; for
God "doth not afflict willingly nor grieve the children of
men" (Lam. iii. 33). Either the heart is too much set upon
the world, or religion is too much neglected in thy family,
or something. There is a snake in the grass, a worm in the
gourd; some sin in thy bosom, for the sake of which God
doth thus deal with thee.

Thirdly, This thus done, let that man again consider thus
with himself: Perhaps God is now changing of my condition
and state in the world; he has let me live in fashion, in fullness,
and abundance of worldly glory; and I did not to his glory
improve, as I should, that his good dispensation to me. But
when I lived in full and fat pasture, I did there lift up the
heel (Deut. xxxii. 15). Therefore he will now turn me into
hard commons, that with leanness, and hunger, and meanness,
and want, I may spend the rest of my days. But let him do
this without murmuring and repining; let him do it in a godly
manner, submitting himself to the judgment of God. "Let
the rich rejoice in that he is made low" (Jas. i. 9, 10).

This is duty, and it may be privilege to those that are
under this hand of God. And for thy encouragement to this
hard work, for this is a hard work, consider of these four
things. (1) This is right lying down under God's hand, and
the way to be exalted in God's time. When God would have
Job embrace the dunghill, he embraces it, and says, "The
Lord gave, and the Lord hath taken away, blessed be the
name of the Lord" (Job i. 21). (2) Consider, that there are
blessings also that attend a low condition, more than all
the world are aware of. A poor condition has preventing
mercy attending of it. The poor, because they are poor, are
not capable of sinning against God as the rich man does
(Ps. xlix. 6). (3) The poor can more clearly see himself preserved by the providence of God than the rich, for he trusteth
in the abundance of his riches. (4) It may be God has made
thee poor, because he would make thee rich. "Hearken, my
beloved brethren, hath not God chosen the poor of this

world, rich in faith, and heirs of the kingdom which God hath promised to them that love him?" (Jas. ii. 5).

I am persuaded if men upon whom this hand of God is, would thus quietly lie down and humble themselves under it, they would find more peace, yea more blessing of God attending them in it, than the most of men are aware of But this is a hard chapter, and therefore I do not expect that many should either read it with pleasure, or desire to take my counsel.

Having thus spoken to the broken man, with reference to his own self, I will now speak to him as he stands related to his creditors. In the next place therefore, let him fall upon the most honest way of dealing with his creditors, and that I think must be this:

First, Let him timely make them acquainted with his condition, and also do to them these three things. (1) Let him heartily and unfeignedly ask them forgiveness for the wrong that he has done them. (2) Let him proffer them ALL, and the whole ALL that ever he has in the world; let him hide nothing, let him strip himself to his raiment for them; let him not keep a ring, a spoon, or anything from them. (3) If none of these two will satisfy them, let him proffer them his body, to be at their dispose, to wit, either to abide imprisonment at their pleasure, or to be at their service, till by labour and travail he hath made them such amends as they in reason think fit, only reserving something for the succour of his poor and distressed family out of his labour, which in reason, and conscience, and nature, he is bound also to take care of. Thus shall he make them what amends he is able, for the wrong that he hath done them in wasting and spending of their estates.

By thus doing, he submits himself to God's rod, commits himself to the dispose of his providence; yea, by thus doing, he casteth the lot of his present and future condition into the lap of his creditors, and leaves the whole dispose thereof to the Lord, even as he shall order and incline their hearts to do with him (Prov. xvi. 33). And let that be either to forgive him, or to take that which he hath for satisfaction, or to lay his body under affliction, this way or that, according to law; can he, I say, thus leave the whole dispose to God, let the issue be what it will, that man shall have peace

in his mind afterward. And the comforts of that state, which
will be comforts that attend equity, justice, and duty, will
be more unto him, because more according to godliness, than
can be the comforts that are the fruits of injustice, fraudu-
lency, and deceit. Besides, this is the way to engage God to
favour him by the sentence of his creditors; for HE can
entreat them to use him kindly, and he will do it when his
ways are pleasing in his sight (Jer. xv. 10, 11). When a
man's ways please the Lord, he maketh even his enemies
to be at peace with him (Prov. xxi. 7). And surely, for a
man to seek to make restitution for wrongs done to the
utmost of his power, by what he is, has, and enjoys in
this world, is the best way, in that capacity, and with
reference to that thing, that a man can at this time be
found active in.

But he that doth otherwise, abides in his sin, refuses to
be disposed of by the providence of God, chooseth an high
estate, though not attained in God's way; when God's will
is that he should descend into a low one. Yea, he desperately
saith in his heart and actions, I will be mine own chooser,
and that in mine own way, whatever happens or follows
thereupon.

Atten. You have said well, in my mind. But suppose now
that Mr. Badman was here, could he not object as to what
you have said, saying, Go and teach your brethren, that
are professors, this lesson, for they as I am are guilty of
breaking; yea, I am apt to think, of that which you call
my knavish way of breaking, to wit, of breaking before they
have need to break. But if not so, yet they are guilty of
neglect in their calling, of living higher, both in fare and
apparel, than their trade or income will maintain. Besides
that they do break all the world very well knows, and that
they have the art to plead for a composition, is very well
known to men; and that it is usual with them to hide their
linen, their plate, their jewels, and it is to be thought, sometimes money and goods besides, is as common as four eggs
a penny. And thus they beguile men, debauch their consciences, sin against their profession, and make, it is to be
feared, their lusts in all this, and the fulfilling of them their
end. I say, if Mr. Badman was here to object thus unto you,
what would be your reply?

Wise. What? Why I would say, I hope no good man, no man of good conscience, no man that either feareth God, regardeth the credit of religion, the peace of God's people, or the salvation of his own soul, will do thus. Professors such, perhaps, there may be, and who upon earth can help it? Jades there be of all colours. If men will profess, and make their profession a stalking-horse to beguile their neighbours of their estates, as Mr. Badman himself did, when he beguiled her that now is with sorrow his wife, who can help it? The churches of old were pestered with such, and therefore no marvel if these perilous difficult times be so. But mark how the apostle words it: "Nay, ye do wrong, and defraud, and that *your* brethren. Know ye not that the unrighteous shall not inherit the kingdom of God? Be not deceived, neither fornicators, nor idolaters, nor adulterers, nor effeminate, nor abusers of themselves with mankind, nor thieves, nor covetous, nor drunkards, nor revilers, nor extortioners, shall inherit the kingdom of God" (1 Cor. vi. 8–10; 2 Tim. iii. 1–5).

None of these shall be saved in this state, nor shall profession deliver them from the censure of the godly, when they shall be manifest such to be. But their profession we cannot help. How can we help it, if men should ascribe to themselves the title of holy ones, godly ones, zealous ones, self-denying ones, or any other such glorious title? and while they thus call themselves, they should be the veriest rogues for all evil, sin, and villainy imaginable, who could help it? True, they are a scandal to religion, a grief to the honest-hearted, an offence to the world, and a stumbling-stone to the weak, and these offences have come, do come, and will come, do what all the world can; but woe be to them through whom they come (Matt. xviii. 6–8). Let such professors therefore be disowned by all true Christians, and let them be reckoned among those base men of the world, which, by such actions, they most resemble. They are Mr. Badman's kindred. For they are a shame to religion, I say, these slithy, rob-shop, pick-pocket men, they are a shame to religion, and religious men should be ashamed of them. God puts such an one among the fools of the world, therefore let not Christians put them among those that are wise for heaven. "As the partridge sitteth *on eggs,* and hatcheth *them* not, *so* he that getteth riches, and not by right, shall leave them in the midst of his days, and at his end shall be a fool" (Jer. xvii. 11). And the man under consideration is one of these, and therefore must look to fall by this judgment.

A professor! and practise such villainies as these! such a one is not worthy to bear that name any longer. We may say to such as the prophet spake to their like, to wit, to the rebellious that were in the house of Israel: "Go ye, serve ye every one his idols" (Ezek. xx. 39), if ye will not hearken to the law and testament of God, to lead your lives hereafter: "but pollute God's holy name no more with your gifts, and with your idols."

Go, professors, go; leave off profession, unless you will lead your lives according to your profession. Better never profess, than to make profession a stalking-horse to sin, deceit, to the devil, and hell. The ground and rules of religion allow not any such thing: "Receive us," says the apostle; "we have wronged no man, we have corrupted no man, we have defrauded no man" (2 Cor. vii. 2). Intimating that those that are guilty of wronging, corrupting, or defrauding of any, should not be admitted to the fellowship of saints, no, nor into the common catalogue of brethren with them. Nor can men with all their rhetoric, and eloquent speaking, prove themselves fit for the kingdom of heaven, or men of good conscience on earth. O that godly plea of Samuel: "Behold, here I am," says he; "witness against me, before the Lord, and before his anointed; whose ox have I taken? or whose ass have I taken? or whom have I defrauded? whom have I oppressed?" etc. (1 Sam. xii. 3). This was to do like a man of good conscience indeed (Matt. x. 19). And in this his appeal, he was so justified in the consciences of the whole congregation, that they could not but with one voice, as with one mouth, break out jointly, and say, "Thou hast not defrauded us, nor oppressed us" (Matt. x. 4).

A professor, and defraud, away with him! A professor should not owe any man anything but love. A professor should provide things, not of other men's but of his own, of his own honest getting, and that not only in the sight of God, but of all men; that he may adorn the doctrine of God our Saviour in all things.

Atten. But suppose God should blow upon a professor in his estate and calling, and he should be run out before he is aware, must he be accounted to be like Mr. Badman, and lie under the same reproach as he?

Wise. No: if he hath dutifully done what he could to avoid it. It is possible for a ship to sink at sea, notwithstanding the most faithful endeavour of the most skilful pilot under heaven. And thus, as I suppose, it was with the prophet, that left his wife in debt, to the hazarding the slavery of her children by the creditors (2 Kings iv. 1, 2). He was no profuse man, nor one that was given to defraud, for the text says he feared God; yet, as I said, he was run out more than she could pay.

If God would blow upon a man, who can help it? (Hag. i. 9). And he will do so sometimes, because he will change dispensations with men, and because he will try their graces Yea, also, because he will overthrow the wicked with his judgments; and all these things are seen in Job. But then the consideration of this should bid men have a care that they be honest, lest this comes upon them for their sin. It should also bid them beware of launching farther into the world, than in an honest way, by ordinary means, they can godlily make their retreat; for the farther in the greater fall. It should also teach them to beg of God his blessing upon their endeavours, their honest and lawful endeavours. And it should put them upon a diligent looking to their steps, that if in their going they should hear the ice crack, they may timely go back again. These things considered, and duly put in practice, if God will blow upon a man, then let him be content, and with Job embrace the dunghill. Let him give unto all their dues, and not fight against the providence of God, but humble himself rather under his mighty hand, which comes to strip him naked and bare: for he that doth otherwise fights against God; and declares that he is a stranger to that of Paul; "I know both how to be abased, and I know how to abound; everywhere and in all things I am instructed both to be full and to be hungry, both to abound and to suffer need" (Phil. iv. 12).

Atten. But Mr. Badman would not, I believe, have put this difference betwixt things feigned and those that fall of necessity.

Wise. If he will not, God will, conscience will; and that not thine own only, but the consciences of all those that have seen the way, and that have known the truth of the condition of such a one.

Atten. Well: let us at this time leave this matter, and return again to Mr. Badman.

Wise. With all my heart will I proceed to give you a relation of what is yet behind of his life, in order to our discourse of his death.

Atten. But pray, do it with as much brevity as you can.

Wise. Why, are you weary of my relating of things?

Atten. No: but it pleases me to hear a great deal in few words.

Wise. I profess myself not an artist that way, but yet, as briefly as I can, I will pass through what of his life is behind; and again I shall begin with his fraudulent dealing, as before I have showed with his creditors, so now with his customers, and those that he had otherwise to deal withal.

He dealt by deceitful weights and measures. He kept weights to buy by, and weights to sell by; measures to buy by, and measures to sell by: those he bought by were too big, those he sold by were too little.

Besides, he could use a thing called sleight of hand, if he had to do with other men's weights and measures, and by that means make them, whether he did buy or sell, yea though his customer or chapman looked on, turn to his own advantage.

Moreover, he had the art to misreckon men in their accounts, whether by weight, or measure, or money, and would often do it to his worldly advantage, and their loss. What say you to Mr. Badman now? And if a question was made of his faithful dealing, he had his servants ready, that to his purpose he had brought up, that would avouch and swear to his book or word. This was Mr. Badman's practice. What think you of Mr. Badman now?

Atten. Think! Why I can think no other but that he was a man left to himself, a naughty man: for these, as his other, were naughty things; if the tree, as indeed it may, ought to be judged, what it is, by its fruits, then Mr. Badman must needs be a bad tree. But pray, for my further satisfaction, show me now, by the Word of God, the evil of this his practice; and first of his using false weights and measures.

Wise. The evil of that! Why the evil of that appears to every eye. The heathens, that live like beasts and brutes in many things, do abominate and abhor such wickedness as this. Let a man but look upon these things as he goes by, and he shall see enough in them from the light of nature to make him loathe so base a practice, although Mr. Badman loved it.

Atten. But show me something out of the Word against it, will you?

Wise. I will willingly do it. And first, look into the Old Testament: "Ye shall," saith God there, "do no unrighteousness in judgment, in mete-yard, in weight, or in measure; just balances, just weights, a just ephah and a just hin shall you have" (Lev. xix. 35, 36). This is the law of God, and that which all men, according to the law of the land, ought to obey. So again: "Ye shall have just balances, and a just ephah," etc. (Ezek. xlv. 10).

Now having showed you the law, I will also show you how God takes swerving therefrom. "A false balance is not good" (Prov. xx. 23). "A false balance is abomination to the Lord" (Prov. xi. 1). Some have just weights, but false balances; and by virtue of these false balances, by their just weights, they deceive the country. Wherefore God first of all commands that the balance be made just. A just balance shalt thou have; else they may be, yea are, deceivers, notwithstanding their just weights.

Now, having commanded that men have a just balance, and testifying that a false one is an abomination to the Lord, he proceedeth also unto weight and measure. Thou shalt not have in thy bag divers weights, a great and a small; that is, one to buy by, and another to sell by, as Mr. Badman had. "Thou shalt not have in thine house divers measures, a great and a small. (And these had Mr. Badman also.) *But* thou shalt have a perfect and just weight; a perfect and just measure shalt thou have, that thy days may be lengthened in the land which the Lord thy God giveth thee. For all that do such things (that is, that use false weights and measures), and all that do unrighteously, *are an* abomination unto the Lord" (Deut. xxv. 13-16). See now both how plentiful and how punctual the Scripture is in this matter. But perhaps it may be objected, that all this is old law, and therefore hath nothing to do with us under the New Testament. Not that I think you, neighbour, will object thus. Well, to this foolish objection, let us make an answer. First, he that makes this objection, if he doth it to overthrow the authority of those texts, discovereth that himself is first cousin to Mr. Badman. For a just man is willing to speak reverently of those commands. That man therefore hath, I doubt, but little conscience, if any at all that is good, that thus objecteth against the text. But let us look into the New Testament, and there we shall see how Christ confirmeth the same; where he commandeth that men make to others good measure, including also that they make good weight; telling such that do thus, or those that do it not, that they may be encouraged to do it: "Good measure, pressed down, and shaken together, and running over, shall men give into your bosom. For with the same measure that ye mete withal, it shall be measured to you again" (Luke vi. 38). To wit, both from God and man. For as God will show his indignation against the false man, by taking away even that he hath, so he will deliver up the false man to the oppressor, and the extortioner shall catch from him, as well as he hath catched from his neighbour; therefore, another scripture saith, "When thou shalt make an end to deal treacherously, they shall deal treacherously with thee" (Is. xxxiii. 1). That the New Testament also hath an inspection into men's trading, yea, even with their weights and measures, is evident from these general exhortations: "Defraud not"; "lie not one to another." "Let no man go beyond his brother in *any* matter, for the Lord is the avenger of all such." "Whatsoever ye do, do *it* heartily, as to the Lord," "doing all in his name," "to his glory"; and the like. All these injunctions and commandments do respect our life and conversation among men, with reference to our dealing, trading, and so, consequently, they forbid false, deceitful, yea, all doings that are corrupt.

Having thus in a word or two showed you that these things are bad, I will next, for the conviction of those that use them, show you where God saith they are to be found.

1. They are not to be found in the house of the good and

godly man, for he, as his God, abhors them; but they are to be found in the house of evil-doers, such as Mr. Badman's is. "Are there," saith the prophet, "yet the treasures of wickedness in the house of the wicked, and the scant measure *that is* abominable?" (Mic. vi. 10). Are they there yet, notwithstanding God's forbidding, notwithstanding God's tokens of anger against those that do such things? O how loth is a wicked man to let go a sweet, a gainful sin, when he hath hold of it! They hold fast deceit, they refuse to let it go.

2. These deceitful weights and measures are not to be found in the house of the merciful, but in the house of the cruel; in the house of them that love to oppress. "The balances of deceit *are* in his hand; he loveth to oppress" (Hos. xii. 7). He is given to oppression and cruelty, therefore he useth such wicked things in his calling. Yea, he is a very cheat, and, as was hinted before concerning Mr. Badman's breaking, so I say now, concerning his using these deceitful weights and measures, it is as bad, as base, as to take a purse, or pick a pocket; for it is a plain robbery; it takes away from a man that which is his own, even the price of his money.

3. The deceitful weights and measures are not to be found in the house of such as relieve the belly, and that cover the loins of the poor, but of such as indeed would swallow them up. "Hear this, O ye that swallow up the needy, even to make the poor of the land to fail, saying, When will the new moon be gone, that we may sell corn? and the Sabbath, that we may set forth wheat, making the ephah small, and the shekel great (making the measure small, and the price great), and falsifying the balances by deceit? That we may buy the poor for silver, and the needy for a pair of shoes, and sell the refuse of the wheat? The Lord hath sworn by the excellency of Jacob, Surely I will never forget any of their works" (Amos viii. 4–8). So detestable and vile a thing is this in the sight of God.

4. God abominates the thoughts of calling of those that use false weights and measures, by any other term than that they be impure ones, or the like: "Shall I count *them* pure," saith he, "with the bag of deceitful weights?" (Mic. vi. 11). No, by no means, they are impure ones; their

hands are defiled, deceitful gain is in their houses, they have gotten what they have by coveting an evil covetousness, and therefore must and shall be counted among the impure, among the wicked of the world.

Thus you see how full and plain the Word of God is against this sin, and them that use it. And therefore Mr. Badman, for that he used by these things thus to rook and cheat his neighbours, is rightly rejected from having his name in and among the catalogue of the godly.

Atten. But I am persuaded that the using of these things, and the doing by them thus deceitfully, is not counted so great an evil by some.

Wise. Whether it be counted an evil or a virtue by men, it mattereth not; you see by the Scriptures the judgment of God upon it. It was not counted an evil by Mr. Badman, nor is it by any that still are treading in his steps. But, I say, it is no matter how men esteem of things, let us adhere to the judgment of God. And the rather, because when we ourselves have done weighing and measuring to others, then God will weigh and measure both us and our actions. And when he doth so, as he will do shortly, then woe be to him to whom, and of whose actions it shall be thus said by him, "TEKEL, thou art weighed in the balances, and are found wanting" (Dan. v. 27). God will then recompense their evil of deceiving upon their own head, when he shall shut them out of his presence, favour, and kingdom, for ever and ever.

Atten. But it is a wonder, that since Mr. Badman's common practice was to do thus, that some one or more did not find him out, and blame him for this his wickedness.

Wise. For the generality of people he went away clever with his knavery. For what with his balance, his false balance, and good weight, and what with his sleight of hand to boot, he beguiled sometimes a little, and sometimes more, most that he had to deal with; besides, those that use this naughty trade are either such as blind men with a show of religion, or by hectoring the buyer out by words. I must confess Mr. Badman was not so arch at the first; that is, to do it by show of religion; for now he began to grow threadbare, though some of his brethren are arch enough this way, yea, and of his sisters too, for I told you at first that there were a great many of them, and never a one of them good; but for hectoring, for swearing, for lying, if these things would make weight and measure, they should not be wanting to Mr. Badman's customers.

Atten. Then it seems he kept good weights and a bad balance; well that was better than that both should be bad.

Wise. Not at all. There lay the depth of his deceit; for if any at any time found fault that he used them hardly, and that they wanted their weight of things, he would reply, Why, did you not see them weighed? will you not believe your own eyes? if you question my weights, pray carry them whither you will, I will maintain them to be good and just. The same he would say of his scales, so he blinded all by his balance.

Atten. This is cunning indeed; but as you say, there must be also something done or said to blind therewith, and this I perceive Mr. Badman had.

Wise. Yes, he had many ways to blind, but he was never clever at it by making a show of religion, though he cheated his wife therewith; for he was, especially by those that dwelt near him, too well known to do that, though he would bungle at it as well as he could. But there are some that are arch villains this way; they shall to view live a whole life religiously, and yet shall be guilty of these most horrible sins. And yet religion in itself is never the worse, nor yet the true professors of it. But, as Luther says, in the name of God begins all mischief. For hypocrites have no other way to bring their evils to maturity but by using and mixing the name of God and religion therewith. Thus they become whited walls; for by this white, the white of religion, the dirt of their actions is hid. Thus also they become graves that appear not, and they that go over them, that have to do with them, are not aware of them, but suffer themselves to be deluded by them. Yea, if there shall, as there will sometimes, rise a doubt in the heart of the buyer about the weight and measure he should have, why, he suffereth his very senses to be also deluded, by recalling of his chapman's religion to mind, and thinks verily that not his good chapman but himself is out; for he dreams not that his chapman can deceive. But if the buyer shall find it out, and shall make it apparent, that he is beguiled, then shall he be healed by having amends made, and perhaps fault shall be laid upon servants, etc. And so Mr. Cheat shall stand for a right honest man in the eye of his customer, though the next time he shall pick his pocket again.

Some plead custom for their cheat, as if that could acquit them before the tribunal of God. And others say it came to them for so much, and, therefore, another must take it for so much, though there is wanting both as to weight and measure; but in all these things there are juggles; or if not, such must know that "that which is altogether just," they must do (Deut. xvi. 20). Suppose that I be cheated myself with a brass half-crown, must I therefore cheat another therewith? if this be bad in the whole, it is also bad in the parts. Therefore, however thou art dealt withal in thy buying, yet thou must deal justly in selling, or thou sinnest against thy soul, and art become as Mr. Badman. And know, that a pretence to custom is nothing worth. It is not custom, but good conscience that will help at God's tribunal.

Atten. But I am persuaded that that which is gotten by men this way doth them but little good.

Wise. I am of your mind for that, but this is not considered by those thus minded. For if they can get it, though they get, as we say, the devil and all, by their getting, yet they are content, and count that their getting is much.

Little good! why do you think they consider that? No; no more than they consider what they shall do in the judgment, at the day of God Almighty, for their wrong getting of what they get, and that is just nothing at all.

But to give you a more direct answer. This kind of getting is so far off from doing them little good, that it doth them no good at all; because thereby they lose their own souls: "What shall it profit a man if he shall gain the whole world, and lose his own soul?" (Mark viii. 36). He loseth then, he loseth greatly that getteth after this fashion. This is the man that is penny-wise and pound-foolish; this is he that loseth his good sheep for a halfpenny-worth of tar; that loseth a soul for a little of the world. And then what doth he get thereby but loss and damage? Thus he getteth or rather loseth about the world to come. But what doth he get in this world, more than travail and sorrow, vexation of spirit, and disappointment? Men aim at blessedness in getting, I mean, at temporal blessedness; but the man that thus getteth, shall not have that. For though an inheritance after this manner may be hastily gotten at the beginning, yet the end thereof shall not be blessed. They gather it indeed, and think to keep it too, but what says Solomon? God casteth it away. "The Lord will not suffer the soul of the righteous to famish; but he casteth away the substance of the wicked" (Prov. x. 3; Jer. xv. 13; xvii. 3).

The time, as I said, that they do enjoy it, it shall do them no good at all; but long, to be sure, they must not have it. For God will either take it away in their lifetime, or else in the generation following, according to that of Job: "He," the wicked, "may prepare *it*, but the just shall put *it* on, and the innocent shall divide the silver" (Job xxvii. 17).

Consider that also that it is written in the Proverbs: "A good *man* leaveth an inheritance to his children's children, and the wealth of the sinner *is* laid up for the just" (Prov. xiii. 22). What then doth he get thereby, that getteth by dishonest means? Why he getteth sin and wrath, hell and damnation, and now tell me how much he doth get.

This, I say, is his getting; so that as David says, we may be bold to say too: I beheld the wicked in great prosperity, and presently I cursed his habitation; for it cannot prosper with him (Ps. lxxiii.). Fluster and huff, and make ado for a while he may, but God hath determined that both he and it shall melt like grease, and any observing man may see it so. Behold the unrighteous man, in a way of injustice, getteth much, and loadeth himself with thick clay, but anon it withereth, it decayeth, and even he, or the generation following, decline, and return to beggary. And this Mr. Badman, notwithstanding his cunning and crafty tricks to get money, did die, nobody can tell whether worth a farthing or no.

Atten. He had all the bad tricks, I think, that it was possible for a man to have, to get money; one would think that he should have been rich.

Wise. You reckon too fast, if you count these all his bad tricks to get money; for he had more besides. If his customers were in his books, as it should go hard but he would have them there; at least, if he thought he could make any advantage of them, then, then would he be sure to impose upon them his worst, even very bad commodity, yet set down for it the price that the best was sold at; like those that sold the refuse wheat; or the worst of the wheat; making the shekel great, yet hoisting up the price (Amos viii.). This was Mr. Badman's way. He would sell goods that cost him not the best price by far, for as much as he sold his best of all for. He had also a trick to mingle his commodity, that that which was bad might go off with the least mistrust. Besides, if his customers at any time paid him money, let them look to themselves, and to their acquaintances, for he would usually attempt to call for that payment again, especially if he thought that there were hopes of making a prize thereby, and then to be sure if they could not produce good and sufficient ground of the payment, a hundred to one but they paid it again. Sometimes the honest chapman would appeal to his servants for proof of the payment of money, but they were trained up by him to say after his mind, right or wrong; so that relief that way he could get none.

Atten. It is a bad, yea, an abominable thing for a man to have such servants. For by such means a poor customer may be undone, and not know how to help himself. Alas! if the master be so unconscionable, as I perceive Mr. Badman was to call for his money twice, and if his servant will swear that it is a due debt, where is any help for such a man? He must sink, there is no remedy.

Wise. This is very bad, but this has been a practice, and that hundreds of years ago. But what saith the Word of God? "I will punish all those that leap on the threshold, which fill their masters' houses with violence and deceit" (Zeph. i. 9).

Mr. Badman also had this art; could he get a man at advantage, that is, if his chapman durst not go from him, or if the commodity he wanted could not for the present be conveniently had elsewhere, then let him look to himself, he would surely make his purse-strings crack; he would exact upon him without any pity or conscience.

Atten. That was extortion, was it not? I pray let me hear your judgment of extortion, what it is, and when committed?

Wise. Extortion is a screwing from men more than by the law of God or men is right; and it is committed sometimes by them in office, about fees, rewards, and the like: but it is most commonly committed by men of trade, who without all conscience, when they have the advantage, will make a prey of their neighbour. And thus was Mr. Badman an extortioner; for although he did not exact, and force away, as bailiffs and clerks have used to do, yet he had his opportunities, and such cruelty to make use of them, that he would often, in his way, be extorting and forcing of money out of his neighbour's pocket. For every man that makes a prey of his advantage upon his neighbour's necessities, to force from him more than in reason and conscience, according to the present prices of things such commodity is worth, may very well be called an extortioner, and judged for one that hath no inheritance in the kingdom of God (1 Cor. vi. 9, 10).

Atten. Well, this Badman was a sad wretch.

Wise. Thus you have often said before. But now we are in discourse of this, give me leave a little to go on. We have a great many people in the country too that live all their days in the practice, and so under the guilt of extortion; people, alas! that think scorn to be so accounted.

As for example: There is a poor body that dwells, we will suppose, so many miles from the market; and this man wants a bushel of grist, a pound of butter, or a cheese for himself, his wife, and poor children; but dwelling so far from the market, if he goes thither, he shall lose his day's work, which will be eightpence or tenpence damage to him, and that is something to a poor man. So he goeth to one of his masters or dames for what he wanteth, and asks them to help him with such a thing; yes, say they, you may have it; but withal they will give him a gripe, perhaps make him pay as much or more for it at home, as they can get when they have carried it five miles to a market, yea, and that too for the refuse of their commodity. But in this the women are especially faulty, in the sale of their butter and cheese, etc. Now this is a kind of extortion, it is a making a prey of the necessity of the poor, it is a grinding of their faces, a buying and selling of them.

But above all, your hucksters, that buy up the poor man's victuals by wholesale, and sell it to him again for unreasonable gains, by retail, and as we call it by piecemeal; they are got into a way, after a stinging rate, to play their game upon such by extortion: I mean such who buy up butter, cheese, eggs, bacon, etc., by wholesale, and sell it again, as they call it, by pennyworths, two pennyworths, a halfpenny-worth, or the like, to the poor, all the week after the market is past.

These, though I will not condemn them all, do, many of them, bite and pinch the poor by this kind of evil dealing. These destroy the poor because he is poor, and that is a grievous sin. "He that oppresseth the poor to increase his *riches, and* he that giveth to the rich, *shall* surely *come* to want." Therefore he saith again, "Rob not the poor because he *is* poor, neither oppress the afflicted in the gate: for the Lord will plead their cause, and spoil the soul of them that spoiled them" (Prov. xxii. 16, 22, 23).

O that he that gripeth and grindeth the face of the poor, would take notice of these two scriptures! Here is threatened the destruction of the estate, yea and of the soul too, of them that oppress the poor. Their soul we shall better see where, and in what condition that is in, when the day of doom is come; but for the estates of such, they usually quickly moulder; and that sometimes all men, and sometimes no man knows how.

Besides, these are usurers, yea, they take usury for victuals, which thing the Lord has forbidden (Deut. xxiii. 19). And because they cannot so well do it on the market-day, there-fore they do it, as I said, when the market is over; for then the poor fall into their mouths, and are necessitated to have, as they can, for their need, and they are resolved they shall pay soundly for it. Perhaps some will find fault for my meddling thus with other folks' matters, and for my thus prying into the secrets of their iniquity. But to such I would say, since such actions are evil, it is time they were hissed out of the world. For all that do such things offend against God, wrong their neighbour, and like Mr. Badman do pro-voke God to judgment.

Atten. God knows there is abundance of deceit in the world!

Wise. Deceit! Aye, but I have not told you the thousandth part of it; nor is it my business now to rake to the bottom of that dunghill. What would you say, if I should anatomise some of those vile wretches called pawnbrokers, that lend money and goods to poor people, who are by necessity forced to such an inconvenience; and will make, by one trick or other, the interest of what they so lend amount to thirty, forty, yea sometimes fifty pound by the year; notwithstanding the principal is secured by a sufficient pawn; which they will keep too at last, if they can find any shift to cheat the wretched borrower.

Atten. Say! Why such miscreants are the pest and vermin of the commonwealth, not fit for the society of men; but methinks by some of those things you discoursed before, you seem to import that it is not lawful for a man to make the best of his own.

Wise. If by making the best, you mean to sell for as much as by hook or crook he can get for his commodity; then I say it is not lawful. And if I should say the contrary, I should justify Mr. Badman and all the rest of that gang; but that I never shall do, for the Word of God condemns them. But that it is not lawful for a man at all times to sell his commodity for as much as he can, I prove by these reasons:

First, If it be lawful for me alway to sell my commodity as dear, or for as much as I can, then it is lawful for me to lay aside in my dealing with others good conscience to them and to God; but it is not lawful for me, in my dealing with others, to lay aside good conscience, etc. Therefore it is not lawful for me always to sell my commodity as dear, or for as much as I can. That it is not lawful to lay aside good conscience in our dealings has already been proved in the former part of our discourse; but that a man must lay it aside that will sell his commodity always as dear, or for as much as he can, is plainly manifest thus.

1. He that will, as is mentioned afore, sell his commodity as dear as he can, must sometimes make a prey of the ignorance of his chapman. But that he cannot do with a good conscience, for that is to overreach, and to go beyond my chapman, and is forbidden (1 Thess. iv. 6). Therefore he that will sell his commodity as afore, as dear, or for as much as he can, must of necessity lay aside good conscience.

2. He that will sell his commodity always as dear as he can, must needs sometimes make a prey of his neighbour's necessity; but that he cannot do with a good conscience, for that is to go beyond and defraud his neighbour, contrary to 1 Thess. iv. 6. Therefore he that will sell his commodity,

as afore, as dear, or for as much as he can, must needs cast off and lay aside a good conscience.

3. He that will, as afore, sell his commodity as dear, or for as much as he can, must, if need be, make a prey of his neighbour's fondness; but that a man cannot do with a good conscience, for that is still a going beyond him, contrary to 1 Thess. iv. 6. Therefore, he that will sell his commodity as dear, or for as much as he can, must needs cast off and lay aside good conscience.

The same also may be said for buying; no man may always buy as cheap as he can, but must also use good conscience in buying; the which he can by no means use and keep, if he buys always as cheap as he can, and that for the reasons urged before. For such will make a prey of the ignorance, necessity, and fondness of their chapman, the which they cannot do with a good conscience. When Abraham would buy a burying-place of the sons of Heth, thus he said unto them: "Intreat for me to Ephron the son of Zohar, that he may give me the cave of Machpelah, which he hath . . . in the end of his field; for as much . . . as it is worth" shall he give it me (Gen. xxiii. 8, 9). He would not have it under foot, he scorned it, he abhorred it; it stood not with his religion, credit, nor conscience. So also, when David would buy a field of Ornan the Jebusite, thus he said unto him: "Grant me the place of *this* threshing-floor, that I may build an altar therein unto the Lord; thou shalt grant it me for the full price" (1 Chron. xxi. 22). He also, as Abraham, made conscience of this kind of dealing. He would not lie at catch to go beyond, no, not the Jebusite, but will give him his full price for his field. For he knew that there was wickedness, as in selling too dear, so in buying too cheap, therefore he would not do it.

There ought therefore to be good conscience used, as in selling so in buying; for it is also unlawful for a man to go beyond or to defraud his neighbour in buying; yea, it is unlawful to do it in any matter, and God will plentifully avenge that wrong, as I also before have forewarned and testified. See also the text, Lev. xxv. 14. But,

Secondly, If it be lawful for me always to sell my commodity as dear, or for as much as I can, then it is lawful for me to deal with my neighbour without the use of charity.

But it is not lawful for me to lay aside, or to deal with my neighbour without the use of charity, therefore it is not lawful for me always to sell my commodity to my neighbour for as much as I can. A man in dealing should as really design his neighbour's good, profit, and advantage, as his own, for this is to exercise charity in his dealing.

That I should thus use, or exercise charity towards my neighbour in my buying and selling, etc., with him, is evident from the general command: "Let all your things be done with charity" (1 Cor. xvi. 14). But that a man cannot live in the exercise of charity that selleth as afore, as dear, or that buyeth as cheap as he can, is evident by these reasons:

1. He that sells his commodity as dear, or for as much money always as he can, seeks himself, and himself only. But charity seeketh not her own, not her own only (1 Cor. xiii.). So then he that seeks himself, and himself only, as he that sells, as afore, as dear as he can, does, maketh not use of, nor doth he exercise charity in his so dealing.

2. He that selleth his commodity always for as much as he can get, hardeneth his heart against all reasonable entreaties of the buyer. But he that doth so cannot exercise charity in his dealing; therefore it is not lawful for a man to sell his commodity, as afore, as dear as he can.

3. If it be lawful for me to sell my commodity, as afore, as dear as I can, then there can be no sin in my trading, how unreasonably soever I manage my calling, whether by lying, swearing, cursing, cheating, for all this is but to sell my commodity as dear as I can (Eph. iv. 25). But that there is sin in these is evident, therefore I may not sell my commodity always as dear as I can.

4. He that sells, as afore, as dear as he can, offereth violence to the law of nature, for that saith, Do unto all men even as ye would that they should do unto you (Matt. vii. 12). Now, was the seller a buyer, he would not that he of whom he buys should sell him always as dear as he can, therefore he should not sell so himself when it is his lot to sell and others to buy of him.

5. He that selleth, as afore, as dear as he can, makes use of that instruction that God hath not given to others, but sealed up in his hand, to abuse his law, and to wrong his neighbour withal, which indeed is contrary to God (Job

xxxvii. 7). God hath given thee more skill, more knowledge and understanding in thy commodity, than he hath given to him that would buy of thee. But what! canst thou think that God hath given thee this that thou mightest thereby make a prey of thy neighbour? that thou mightest thereby go beyond and beguile thy neighbour? No, verily, but he hath given thee it for his help, that thou mightest in this be eyes to the blind, and save thy neighbour from that damage that this ignorance, or necessity, or fondness would betray him into the hands of (1 Cor. x. 13).

6. In all that a man does he should have an eye to the glory of God, but that he cannot have that sells his commodity always for as much as he can, for the reasons urged before.

7. All that a man does he should do "in the name of the Lord Jesus" Christ, that is, as being commanded and authorised to do it by him (Col. iii. 17). But he that selleth always as dear as he can, cannot so much as pretend to this without horrid blaspheming of that name, because commanded by him to do otherwise.

8. And lastly, in all that a man does he should have an eye to the day of judgment, and to the consideration of how his actions will be esteemed of in that day (Acts xxiv. 15, 16). Therefore there is not any man can, or ought to sell always as dear as he can, unless he will, yea, he must say in so doing, I will run the hazard of the trial of that day. "If thou sell aught unto thy neighbour, or buyest *aught* of thy neighbour's hand, ye shall not oppress one another" (Lev. xxv. 14).

Atten. But why do you put in these cautionary words, They must not sell always as dear, nor buy always as cheap as they can? Do you not thereby intimate that a man may sometimes do so?

Wise. I do indeed intimate that sometimes the seller may sell as dear, and the buyer buy as cheap as he can; but this is allowable only in these cases: when he that sells is a knave, and lays aside all good conscience in selling, or when the buyer is a knave, and lays aside all good conscience in buying. If the buyer therefore lights of a knave, or if the seller lights of a knave, then let them look to themselves; but yet so as not to lay aside conscience, because he that thou dealest with doth so, but how vile or base soever the chapman is, do thou keep thy commodity at a reasonable price; or, if thou buyest, offer reasonable gain for the thing thou wouldst have, and if this will not do with the buyer or seller, then seek thee a more honest chapman. If thou objectest, But I have not skill to know when a pennyworth is before me, get some that have more skill than thyself in that affair, and let them in that matter dispose of thy money. But if there were no knaves in the world these objections need not be made.

And thus, my very good neighbour, have I given you a few of my reasons why a man that hath it should not always sell too dear nor buy as cheap as he can, but should use good conscience to God and charity to his neighbour in both.

Atten. But were some men here to hear you, I believe they would laugh you to scorn.

Wise. I question not that at all, for so Mr. Badman used to do when any man told him of his faults; he used to think himself wiser than any, and would count, as I have hinted before, that he was not arrived to a manly spirit that did stick or boggle at any wickedness. But let Mr. Badman and his fellows laugh, I will bear it, and still give them good counsel (Luke xvi. 13–15). But I will remember also, for my further relief and comfort, that thus they that were covetous of old served the Son of God himself. It is their time to laugh now, that they may mourn in time to come (Luke vi. 25). And I say again, when they have laughed out their laugh, he that useth not good conscience to God and charity to his neighbour in buying and selling, dwells next door to an infidel, and is near of kin to Mr. Badman.

Atten. Well, but what will you say to this question? You know that there is no settled price set by God upon any commodity that is bought or sold under the sun, but all things that we buy and sell do ebb and flow, as to price, like the tide; how then shall a man of a tender conscience do, neither to wrong the seller, buyer, nor himself, in buying and selling of commodities?

Wise. This question is thought to be frivolous by all that are of Mr. Badman's way, it is also difficult in itself, yet I will endeavour to shape you an answer, and that first to the matter of the question, to wit, how a tradesman should, in trading, keep a good conscience; a buyer or seller either.

Secondly, how he should prepare himself to this work and live in the practice of it. For the first, he must observe what hath been said before, to wit, he must have conscience to God, charity to his neighbour, and, I will add, much moderation in dealing. Let him therefore keep within the bounds of the affirmative of those eight reasons that before were urged to prove that men ought not, in their dealing, but to do justly and mercifully betwixt man and man, and then there will be no great fear of wronging the seller, buyer, or himself. But particularly to prepare or instruct a man to this work:

1. Let the tradesman or others consider that there is not that in great getting and in abundance which the most of men do suppose; for all that a man has over and above what serves for his present necessity and supply, serves only to feed the lusts of the eye. For "what good *is there* to the owners thereof, saving the beholding *of them* with their eyes?" (Eccles. v. 11). Men also, many times, in getting of riches, get therewith a snare to their soul (1 Tim. vi. 7-9). But few get good by getting of them. But this consideration Mr. Badman could not abide.

2. Consider that the getting of wealth dishonestly—as he does that getteth it without good conscience and charity to his neighbour—is a great offender against God. Hence he says, "I have smitten mine hand at thy dishonest gain which thou hast made" (Ezek. xxii. 13). It is a manner of speech that shows anger in the very making of mention of the crime. Therefore,

3. Consider that a little, honestly gotten, though it may yield thee but a dinner of herbs at a time, will yield more peace therewith than will a stalled ox ill gotten (Prov. xv. 17). "Better *is* a little with righteousness, than great revenues without right" (Prov. xvi. 8; 1 Sam. ii. 5).

4. Be thou confident that God's eyes are upon all thy ways, and "that he pondereth all thy goings," and also that he marks them, writes them down, and seals them up in a bag against the time to come (Prov. v. 21; Job xiv. 17).

5. Be thou sure that thou rememberest that thou knowest not the day of thy death. Remember also that when death comes God will give thy substance, for the which thou hast laboured, and for the which perhaps thou hast hazarded

thy soul, to one thou knowest not who, nor whether he shall be a wise man or a fool. And then, "what profit hath he that hath laboured for the wind?" (Eccles. v. 16).

Besides, thou shalt have nothing that thou mayest so much as carry away in thine hand. Guilt shall go with thee if thou hast got it [thy substance] dishonestly, and they also to whom thou shalt leave it shall receive it to their hurt. These things duly considered and made use of by thee to the preparing of thy heart to thy calling of buying and selling, I come, in the next place, to show thee how thou shouldst live in the practick part of this art. Art thou to buy or sell?

1. If thou sellest, do not commend; if thou buyest, do not dispraise, any otherwise but to give the thing that thou hast to do with its just value and worth; for thou canst not do otherwise, knowingly, but of a covetous and wicked mind. Wherefore else are commodities overvalued by the seller, and also undervalued by the buyer. "*It is* naught, *it is* naught, saith the buyer*," but when he hath got his bargain he boasteth thereof (Prov. xx. 14). What hath this man done now, but lied in the dispraising of his bargain? and why did he dispraise it, but of a covetous mind to wrong and beguile the seller?

2. Art thou a seller, and do things grow dear? set not thy hand to help or hold them up higher; this cannot be done without wickedness neither, for this is a making of the shekel great (Amos viii. 5). Art thou a buyer, and do things grow dear? use no cunning or deceitful language to pull them down, for that cannot be done but wickedly too. What then shall we do, will you say? Why I answer, leave things to the providence of God, and do thou with moderation submit to his hand. But since, when they are growing dear, the hand that upholds the price is, for the time, more strong than that which would pull it down; that being the hand of the seller, who loveth to have it dear, especially if it shall rise in his hand. Therefore I say, do thou take heed and have not a hand in it, the which thou mayest have to thine own and thy neighbour's hurt, these three ways:

1. By crying out scarcity, scarcity, beyond the truth and state of things; especially take heed of doing of this by way

of a prognostic for time to come. It was for this for which he was trodden to death in the gate of Samaria, that you read of in the second book of Kings (2 Kings vii. 17). This sin hath a double evil in it. (1) It belieth the present blessing of God among us; and (2) It undervalueth the riches of his goodness, which can make all good things to abound towards us.

2. This wicked thing may be done by hoarding up when the hunger and necessity of the poor calls for it. Now, that God may show his dislike against this, he doth, as it were, license the people to curse such a hoarder up—"He that withholdeth corn, the people shall curse him, but blessing *shall be* upon the head of him that selleth *it*" (Prov. xi. 26).

3. But if things will rise, do thou be grieved, be also moderate in all thy sellings, and be sure let the poor have a pennyworth, and sell thy corn to those in necessity. Which then thou wilt do when thou showest mercy to the poor in thy selling to him, and when thou, for his sake because he is poor, undersellest the market. This is to buy and sell with good conscience; thy buyer thou wrongest not, thy conscience thou wrongest not, thyself thou wrongest not, for God will surely recompense thee (Is. lviii. 6–8). I have spoken concerning corn, but thy duty is to "let your moderation" in all things "be known unto all men. The Lord *is* at hand" (Phil. iv. 5).

Atten. Well, sir, now I have heard enough of Mr. Badman's naughtiness, pray now proceed to his death.

Wise. Why, sir, the sun is not so low, we have yet three hours to night.

Atten. Nay, I am not in any great haste, but I thought you had even now done with his life.

Wise. Done! no, I have yet much more to say.

Atten. Then he has much more wickedness than I thought he had.

Wise. That may be. But let us proceed. This Mr. Badman added to all his wickedness this, he was a very proud man, a very proud man. He was exceeding proud and haughty in mind; he looked that what he said ought not, must not be contradicted or opposed. He counted himself as wise as the wisest in the country, as good as the best, and as beautiful as he that had most of it. He took great delight in praising of himself, and as much in the praises that others gave him. He could not abide that any should think themselves above him, or that their wit or personage should by others be set before his. He had scarce a fellowly carriage for his equals. But for those that were of an inferior rank, he would look over them in great contempt. And if at any time he had any remote occasion of having to do with them, he would show great height and a very domineering spirit. So that in this it may be said that Solomon gave a characteristical note of him when he said, "Proud *and* haughty scorner *is* his name, who dealeth in proud wrath" (Prov. xxi. 24). He never thought his diet well enough dressed, his clothes fine enough made, or his praise enough refined.

Atten. This pride is a sin that sticks as close to nature, I think, as most sins. There is uncleanness and pride, I know not of any two gross sins that stick closer to men than they. They have, as I may call it, an interest in nature; it likes them because they most suit its lusts and fancies; and therefore no marvel though Mr. Badman was tainted with pride, since he had so wickedly given up himself to work all iniquity with greediness.

Wise. You say right; pride is a sin that sticks close to nature, and is one of the first follies wherein it shows itself to be polluted. For even in childhood, even in little children, pride will first of all show itself; it is a hasty, an early appearance of the sin of the soul. It, as I may say, is that corruption that strives for predominancy in the heart, and therefore usually comes out first. But though children are so incident to it, yet methinks those of more years should be ashamed thereof. I might at the first have begun with Mr. Badman's pride, only I think it is not the pride in infancy that begins to make a difference betwixt one and another, as did, and do those wherewith I began my relation of his life, therefore I passed it over, but now, since he had no more consideration of himself, and of his vile and sinful state, but to be proud when come to years, I have taken the occasion in this place to make mention of his pride.

Atten. But pray, if you can remember them, tell me of some places of Scripture that speak against pride. I the rather desire this because that pride is now a reigning sin, and I happen sometimes to fall into the company of them that in my conscience are proud, very much, and I have a mind also to tell them of their sin, now when I tell them of it, unless I bring God's Word too, I doubt they will laugh me to scorn.

Wise. Laugh you to scorn! the proud man will laugh you to scorn bring to him what text you can, except God shall smite him in his conscience by the Word. Mr. Badman did use to serve them so that did use to tell him of his; and besides, when you have said what you can, they will tell you they are not proud, and that you are rather the proud man, else you would not judge, nor so malapertly meddle with other men's matters as you do. Nevertheless, since you desire it, I will mention two or three texts; they are these: "Pride and arrogancy . . . do I hate" (Prov. viii. 13). "A man's pride shall bring him low" (Prov. xxix. 23). "And he shall bring down their pride" (Is. xxv. 11). "And all the proud, yea, and all that do wickedly, shall be stubble, and the day that cometh shall burn them up" (Mal. iv. 1). This last is a dreadful text, it is enough to make a proud man shake. God, saith he, will make the proud ones as stubble; that is, as fuel for the fire, and the day that cometh shall be like a burning oven, and that day shall burn them up, saith the Lord. But Mr. Badman could never abide to hear pride spoken against, nor that any should say of him, He is a proud man.

Atten. What should be the reason of that?

Wise. He did not tell me the reason; but I suppose it to be that which is common to all vile persons. They love this vice, but care not to bear its name. The drunkard loves the sin, but loves not to be called a drunkard. The thief loveth to steal, but cannot abide to be called a thief; the whore loveth to commit uncleanness, but loveth not to be called a whore. And so Mr. Badman loved to be proud, but could not abide to be called a proud man. The sweet of sin is desirable to polluted and corrupted man, but the name thereof is a blot in his escutcheon.

Atten. It is true that you have said; but pray how many sorts of pride are there?

Wise. There are two sorts of pride; pride of spirit, and pride of body. The first of these is thus made mention of in the Scriptures: "Every one *that is* proud in heart *is* an abomination to the Lord" (Prov. xvi. 5). "A high look, and a proud heart, *and* the ploughing of the wicked, *is* sin" (Prov. xxi. 4). "The patient in spirit is better than the proud in spirit" (Eccles. vii. 8). Bodily pride the Scriptures mention. "In that day the Lord will take away the bravery of *their* tinkling ornaments *about their feet*, and *their* cauls, and *their* round tires like the moon, the chains, and the bracelets, and the mufflers, the bonnets, and the ornaments of the legs, and the headbands, and the tablets, and the earrings, the rings, and nose jewels, the changeable suits of apparel, and the mantles, and the wimples, and the crisping pins, the glasses, and the fine linen, and the hoods, and the vails" (Is. iii. 18–23). By these expressions it is evident that there is pride of body, as well as pride of spirit, and that both are sin, and so abominable to the Lord. But these texts Mr. Badman could never abide to read; they were to him as Micaiah was to Ahab, they never spake good of him, but evil.

Atten. I suppose that it was not Mr. Badman's case alone even to malign those texts that speak against their vices; for I believe that most ungodly men, where the Scriptures are, have a secret antipathy against those words of God that do most plainly and fully rebuke them for their sins.

Wise. That is out of doubt; and by that antipathy they show that sin and Satan are more welcome to them than are wholesome instructions of life and godliness.

Atten. Well, but not to go off from our discourse of Mr. Badman. You say he was proud; but will you show me now some symptoms of one that is proud?

Wise. Yes, that I will; and first I will show you some symptoms of pride of heart. Pride of heart is seen by outward things, as pride of body in general is a sign of pride of heart; for all proud gestures of the body flow from pride of heart; therefore Solomon saith, "*There is* a generation, O how lofty are their eyes, and their eye-lids are lifted up" (Prov. xxx. 13). And again there is "that exalteth his gait," his going (Prov. xvii. 19). Now, these lofty eyes, and this exalting of the gait, is a sign of a proud heart; for both these actions come from the heart. For out of the heart comes pride, in all the visible appearances of it (Mark vii.). But more particularly—

(1) Heart pride is discovered by a stretched-out neck, and by mincing as they go. For the wicked, the proud, have a proud neck, a proud foot, a proud tongue, by which this their going is exalted. This is that which makes them look scornfully, speak ruggedly, and carry it huffingly among their neighbours. (2) A proud heart is a persecuting one. "The wicked in *his* pride doth persecute the poor" (Ps. x. 2). (3) A prayerless man is a proud man (Ps. x. 4). (4) A contentious man is a proud man (Prov. xiii. 10). (5) The disdainful man is a proud man (Ps. cxix. 51). (6) The man that oppresses his neighbour is a proud man (Ps. cxix. 122). (7) He that hearkeneth not to God's word with reverence and fear is a proud man (Jer. xiii. 15, 17). (8) And he that calls the proud happy is, be sure, a proud man. All these are proud in heart, and this their pride of heart doth thus discover itself (Jer. xliii. 2; Mal. iii. 15).

As to bodily pride, it is discovered that is something of it, by all the particulars mentioned before; for though they are said to be symptoms of pride of heart, yet they are symptoms of that pride, by their showing of themselves in the body. You know diseases that are within are seen ofttimes by outward and visible signs, yet by these very signs even the outside is defiled also. So all those visible signs of heart pride are signs of bodily pride also. But to come to more outward signs. The putting on of gold, and pearls, and costly array; the plaiting of the hair, the following of fashions, the seeking by gestures to imitate the proud, either by speech, looks, dresses, goings, or other fools' baubles, of which at this time the world is full, all these, and many more, are signs, as of a proud heart, so of bodily pride also (1 Tim. ii. 9; 1 Pet. iii. 3–5).

But Mr. Badman would not allow, by any means, that this should be called pride, but rather neatness, handsomeness, comeliness, cleanliness, etc., neither would he allow that following of fashions was anything else, but because he would not be proud, singular, and esteemed fantastical by his neighbours.

Atten. But I have been told that when some have been rebuked for their pride, they have turned it again upon the brotherhood of those by whom they have been rebuked, saying Physician, heal thy friends, look at home among your brotherhood, even among the wisest of you, and see if you yourselves be clear, even you professors. For who is prouder than you professors? scarcely the devil himself.

Wise. My heart aches at this answer, because there is too much cause for it. This very answer would Mr. Badman give his wife when she, as she would sometimes, reproved him for his pride. We shall have, says he, great amendments in living now, for the devil is turned a corrector of vice; for no sin reigneth more in the world, quoth he, than pride among professors. And who can contradict him? Let us give the devil his due, the thing is too apparent for any man to deny. And I doubt not but the same answer is ready in the mouths of Mr. Badman's friends; for they may and do see pride display itself in the apparel and carriages of professors, one may say, almost as much, as among any people in the land, the more is the pity. Aye, and I fear that even their extravagancies in this hath hardened the heart of many a one, as I perceive it did somewhat the heart of Mr. Badman himself. For my own part, I have seen many myself, and those church members too, so decked and be-daubed with their fangles and toys, and that when they have been at the solemn appointments of God in the way of his worship, that I have wondered with what face such painted persons could sit in the place where they were without swoon-ing. But certainly the holiness of God, and also the pollu-tion of themselves by sin, must need be very far out of the minds of such people, what profession soever they make.

I have read of a whore's forehead, and I have read of Christian shamefacedness (Jer. iii. 3; 1 Tim. ii. 9). I have read of costly array, and of that which becometh women professing godliness, with good works (1 Pet. iii. 1–3). But if I might speak, I know what I know, and could say, and yet do no wrong, that which would make some professors stink in their places; but now I forbear (Jer. xxiii. 15).

Atten. Sir, you seem greatly concerned at this, but what if I shall say more? It is whispered that some good ministers have countenanced their people in their light and wanton apparel, yea, have pleaded for their gold and pearls, and costly array, etc.

Wise. I know not what they have pleaded for, but it is easily seen that they tolerate, or at leastwise, wink and connive at such things, both in their wives and children. And so "from the prophets of Jerusalem is profaneness gone forth into all the land" (Jer. xxiii. 15). And when the hand of the rulers are chief in a trespass, who can keep their people from being drowned in that trespass? (Ezra ix. 2).

Atten. This is a lamentation, and must stand for a lamentation.

Wise. So it is, and so it must. And I will add, it is a shame, it is a reproach, it is a stumbling-block to the blind; for though men be as blind as Mr. Badman himself, yet they can see the foolish lightness that must needs be the bottom of all these apish and wanton extravagancies. But many have their excuses ready; to wit, their parents, their husbands, and their breeding calls for it, and the like; yea, the examples of good people prompt them to it; but all these will be but the spider's web, when the thunder of the word of the great God shall rattle from heaven against them, as it will at death or judgment; but I wish it might do it before. But alas! these excuses are but bare pretences, these proud ones love to have it so. I once talked with a maid by way of reproof for her fond and gaudy garment. But she told me, The tailor would make it so; when alas! poor proud girl, she gave order to the tailor so to make it. Many make parents, and husbands, and tailors, etc., the blind to others; but their naughty hearts, and their giving of way thereto, that is the original cause of all these evils.

Atten. Now you are speaking of the cause of pride, pray show me yet further why pride is now so much in request.

Wise. I will show you what I think are the reasons of it.

1. The first is, because, such persons are led by their own hearts, rather than by the Word of God (Mark vii. 21–23). I told you before that the original fountain of pride is the heart. For out of the heart comes pride; it is, therefore, because they are led by their hearts, which naturally tend to lift them up in pride. This pride of heart tempts them, and by its deceits overcometh them; yea, it doth put a bewitching virtue into their peacock's feathers, and then they are swallowed up with the vanity of them (Obad. 3).

2. Another reason why professors are so proud for those we are talking of now, is because they are more apt to take example by those that are of the world, than they are to

take example of those that are saints indeed. Pride is of the world. "For all that *is* in the world, the lust of the flesh, and the lust of the eyes, and the pride of life, is not of the Father but of the world" (1 John ii. 16). Of the world, therefore, professors learn to be proud. But they should not take them for example. It will be objected, No, nor your saints neither, for you are as proud as others; well, let them take shame that are guilty. But when I say professors should take example for their life by those that are saints indeed, I mean as Peter says; they should take example of those that were in old time the saints; for saints of old time were the best, therefore to these he directed us for our pattern. Let the wives' conversation be chaste and also coupled with fear. "Whose adorning," saith Peter, "let it not be that outward *adorning* of plaiting the hair, and of wearing of gold, or of putting on of apparel; but *let it be* the hidden man of the heart, in that which is not corruptible, *even the ornament* of a meek and quiet spirit, which is in the sight of God of great price. For after this manner, in the old time, the holy women also, who trusted in God, adorned themselves, being in subjection to their own husbands" (1 Pet. iii. 1–5).

3. Another reason is, because they have forgotten the pollution of their nature. For the remembrance of that must needs keep us humble, and being kept humble, we shall be at a distance from pride. The proud and the humble are set in opposition; "God resisteth the proud, but giveth grace unto the humble." And can it be imagined that a sensible Christian should be a proud one; sense of baseness tends to lay us low, not to lift us up with pride; not with pride of heart, nor pride of life. But when a man begins to forget what he is, then he, if ever, begins to be proud. Methinks it is one of the most senseless and ridiculous things in the world that a man should be proud of that which is given him on purpose to cover the shame of his nakedness with.

4. Persons that are proud have gotten God and his holiness out of their sight. If God was before them, as he is behind their back. And if they saw him in his holiness, as he sees them in their sins and shame, they would take but little pleasure in their apish knacks. The holiness of God makes the angels cover their faces, crumbles Christians, when

they behold it, into dust and ashes. And as his majesty is, such is his Word (Is. vi.). Therefore they abuse it that bring it to countenance pride.

Lastly, But what can be the end of those that are proud in the decking of themselves after their antic manner? Why are they for going with their bull's foretops, with their naked shoulders, and paps hanging out like a cow's bag? Why are they for painting their faces, for stretching out their neck, and for putting of themselves unto all the formalities which proud fancy leads them to? Is it because they would honour God? because they would adorn the gospel? because they would beautify religion, and make sinners to fall in love with their own salvation? No, no, it is rather to please their lusts, to satisfy their wild and extravagant fancies; and I wish none doth it to stir up lust in others, to the end they may commit uncleanness with them. I believe, whatever is their end, this is one of the great designs of the devil; and I believe also that Satan has drawn more into the sin of uncleanness by the spangling show of fine cloths, than he could possibly have drawn unto it without them. I wonder what it was that of old was called the attire of a harlot; certainly it could not be more bewitching and tempting than are the garments of many professors this day.

Atten. I like what you say very well, and I wish that all the proud dames in England that profess were within the reach and sound of your words.

Wise. What I have said I believe is true; but as for the proud dames in England that profess, they have Moses and the prophets, and if they will not hear them, how then can we hope that they should receive good by such a dull-sounding ram's-horn as I am? However, I have said my mind, and now, if you will, we will proceed to some other of Mr. Badman's doings.

Atten. No; pray, before you show me anything else of Mr. Badman, show me yet more particularly the evil effects of this sin of pride.

Wise. With all my heart I will answer your request.

1. Then: It is pride that makes poor man so like the devil in hell, that he cannot in it be known to be the image and similitude of God. The angels, when they became devils, it was through their being lifted or puffed up with pride

(1 Tim. iii. 6). It is pride also that lifteth or puffeth up the heart of the sinner, and so makes him to bear the very image of the devil.

2. Pride makes a man so odious in the sight of God, that he shall not, must not, come nigh his majesty. "Though the Lord *be* high, yet hath he respect unto the lowly; but the proud he knoweth afar off" (Ps. cxxxviii. 6). Pride sets God and the soul at a distance; pride will not let a man come nigh God, nor God will not let a proud man come nigh unto him. Now this is a dreadful thing.

3. As pride sets, so it keeps God and the soul at a distance "God resisteth the proud" (Jas. iv. 6). Resists, that is, he opposes him, he thrusts him from him, he contemneth his person and all his performances. Come unto God's ordinances the proud man may; but come into his presence, have communion with him, or blessing from him, he shall not. For the high God doth resist him.

4. The Word saith that "The Lord will destroy the house of the proud" (Prov. xv. 25). He will destroy his house; it may be understood he will destroy him and his. So he destroyed proud Pharaoh, so he destroyed proud Korah, and many others.

5. Pride, where it comes, and is entertained, is a certain forerunner of some judgment that is not far behind. When pride goes before, shame and destruction will follow after. "*When* pride cometh, then cometh shame" (Prov. xi. 2). "Pride *goeth* before destruction, and a haughty spirit before a fall" (Prov. xvi. 18).

6. Persisting in pride makes the condition of a poor man as remediless as is that of the devils themselves (1 Tim. iii. 6). And this, I fear, was Mr. Badman's condition, and that was the reason that he died so as he did; as I shall show you anon.

But what need I thus talk of the particular actions, or rather the prodigious sins of Mr. Badman, when his whole life, and all his actions, went, as it were, to the making up one massy body of sin? Instead of believing that there was a God, his mouth, his life and actions, declared that he believed no such thing. His "transgression saith within my heart, *that there was* no fear of God before his eyes" (Ps. xxxvi. 1). Instead of honouring of God, and of giving glory to him for any of his mercies, or under any of his good providences towards him, for God is good to all, and lets his sun shine, and his rain fall upon the unthankful and unholy, he would ascribe the glory to other causes. If they were mercies, he would ascribe them, if the open face of the providence did not give him the lie, to his own wit, labour, care, industry, cunning, or the like. If they were crosses, he would ascribe them, or count them the offspring of fortune, ill luck, chance, the ill management of matters, the ill will of neighbours, or to his wife's being religious, and spending, as he called it, too much time in reading, praying, or the like. It was not in his way to acknowledge God, that is, graciously, or his hand in things. But, as the prophet saith, "Let favour be showed to the wicked, *yet* will he not learn righteousness" (Is. xxvi. 10). And again, They returned not to him that smote them, nor did they seek the Lord of hosts (Is. ix. 13). This was Mr. Badman's temper, neither mercies nor judgment would make him seek the Lord. Nay, as another scripture says, "He would not see the works of God, nor regard the operations of his hands either in mercies or in judgments" (Is. xxvi. 11; Ps. xxix. 5). But further, when by providence he has been cast under the best means for his soul—for, as was showed before, he having had a good master, and before him a good father, and after all a good wife, and being sometimes upon a journey, and cast under the hearing of a good sermon, as he would sometimes for novelty's sake go to hear a good preacher—he was always without heart to make use thereof (Prov. xvii. 6). In this land of righteousness he would deal unjustly, and would not behold the majesty of the Lord (Is. xxvi. 10).

Instead of reverencing the Word, when he heard it preached, read, or discoursed of, he would sleep, talk of other business, or else object against the authority, harmony, and wisdom of the Scriptures; saying, How do you know them to be the Word of God? How do you know that these sayings are true? The Scriptures, he would say, were as a nose of wax, and a man may turn them whithersoever he lists. One scripture says one thing, and another says the quite contrary; besides, they make mention of a thousand impossibilities; they are the cause of all dissensions and discords that are in the land. Therefore you may, would he say, still think what you will, but in my mind they are best at ease that have least to do with them.

Instead of loving and honouring of them that did bear in their foreheads the name, and in their lives the image of Christ, they should be his song, the matter of his jests, and the objects of his slanders. He would either make a mock at their sober deportment, their gracious language, quiet behaviour, or else desperately swear that they did all in deceit and hypocrisy. He would endeavour to render godly men as odious and contemptible as he could; any lies that were made by any, to their disgrace, those he would avouch for truth, and would not endure to be controlled. He was much like those that the prophet speaks of, that would sit and slander his mother's son (Ps. l. 19, 20). Yea, he would speak reproachfully of his wife, though his conscience told him, and many would testify, that she was a very virtuous woman. He would also raise slanders of his wife's friends himself, affirming that their doctrine tended to lasciviousness, and that in their assemblies they acted and did unbeseeming men and women, that they committed uncleanness, etc. He was much like those that affirmed the apostle should say, "Let us do evil that good may come" (Rom. iii. 7, 8). Or, like those of whom it is thus written: "Report, *say they*, and we will report it" (Jer. xx. 10). And if he could get anything by the end that had scandal in it, if it did but touch professors, how falsely soever reported, O! then he would glory, laugh, and be glad, and lay it upon the whole party; saying, Hang them rogues, there is not a barrel better herring of all the holy brotherhood of them. Like to like, quoth the devil to the collier, this is your precise crew. And then he would send all home with a curse.

Atten. If those that make profession of religion be wise, Mr. Badman's watchings and words will make them the more wary, and careful in all things.

Wise. You say true. For when we see men do watch for our halting, and rejoice to see us stumble and fall, it should make us so much abundantly the more careful.

I do think it was as delightful to Mr. Badman to hear, raise, and tell lies, and lying stories of them that fear the Lord, as it was for him to go to bed when a-weary. But we will at this time let these things pass. For as he was in these things bad enough, so he added to these many more the like.

He was an angry, wrathful, envious man, a man that knew not what meekness or gentleness meant, nor did he desire to learn. His natural temper was to be surly, huffy, and rugged, and worse; and he so gave way to his temper, as to this, that it brought him to be furious and outrageous in all things, especially against goodness itself, and against other things too, when he was displeased.

Atten. Solomon saith, He is a fool that rageth (Prov. xiv. 16).

Wise. He doth so; and says moreover, that "Anger resteth in the bosom of fools" (Eccles. vii. 9). And truly, if it be a sign of a fool to have anger rest in his bosom, then was Mr. Badman, notwithstanding the conceit that he had of his own abilities, a fool of no small size.

Atten. Fools are mostly most wise in their own eyes.

Wise. True; but I was a-saying, that if it be a sign that a man is a fool, when anger rests in his bosom; then what is it a sign of, think you, when malice and envy rests there? For, to my knowledge, Mr. Badman was as malicious and as envious a man as commonly you can hear of.

Atten. Certainly, malice and envy flow from pride and arrogancy, and they again from ignorance, and ignorance from the devil. And I thought, that since you spake of the pride of Mr. Badman before, we should have something of these before we had done.

Wise. Envy flows from ignorance indeed. And this Mr. Badman was so envious an one, where he set against, that he would swell with it as a toad, as we say, swells with poison. He whom he maligned, might at any time even read envy in his face wherever he met with him, or in whatever he had to do with him. His envy was so rank and strong, that if it at any time turned its head against a man, it would hardly ever be pulled in again; he would watch over that man to do him mischief, as the cat watches over the mouse to destroy it; yea, he would wait seven years, but he would have an opportunity to hurt him, and when he had it, he would make him feel the weight of his envy.

Envy is a devilish thing, the scripture intimates that none can stand before it: "A stone *is* heavy, and the sand weighty;

but a fool's wrath *is* heavier than them both. Wrath *is* cruel, and anger *is* outrageous; but who *is* able to stand before envy?" (Prov. xxvii. 3, 4).

This envy, for the foulness of it, is reckoned among the foulest villainies that are, as adultery, murder, drunkenness, revellings, witchcrafts, heresies, seditions, etc. (Gal. v. 19, 20). Yea, it is so malignant a corruption, that it rots the very bones of him in whom it dwells. "A sound heart *is* the life of the flesh; but envy the rottenness of the bones" (Prov. xiv. 30).

Atten. This envy is the very father and mother of a great many hideous and prodigious wickednesses. I say, it is the very father and mother of them; it both begets them, and also nourishes them up, till they come to their cursed maturity in the bosom of him that entertains them.

Wise. You have given it a very right description, in calling of it the father and mother of a great many other prodigious wickednesses; for it is so venomous and vile a thing that it puts the whole course of nature out of order, and makes it fit for nothing but confusion, and a hold for every evil thing: "For where envying and strife *is*, there *is* confusion, and every evil work" (Jas. iii. 16). Wherefore, I say, you have rightly called it the very father and mother of a great many other sins. And now for our further edification, I will reckon up of some of the births of envy. (1) Envy, as I told you before, it rotteth the very bones of him that entertains it. And, (2) As you have also hinted, it is heavier than a stone, than sand; yea, and I will add, it falls like a millstone upon the head. Therefore, (3) It kills him that throws it, and him at whom it is thrown. "Envy slayeth the silly one" (Job v. 2), that is, him in whom it resides, and him who is its object. (4) It was that also that slew Jesus Christ himself; for his adversaries persecuted him through their envy (Matt. xxvii. 18; Mark xv. 10). (5) Envy was that by virtue of which Joseph was sold by his brethren into Egypt (Acts vii. 9). (6) It is envy that hath the hand in making of variance among God's saints (Is. xi. 13). (7) It is envy in the hearts of sinners, that stirs them up to thrust God's ministers out of their coasts (Acts xiii. 50; xiv. 6). (8) What shall I say? It is envy that is the very nursery of whisperings, debates, backbitings, slanders, reproaches, murders, &c.

It is not possible to repeat all the particular fruits of this sinful root. Therefore, it is no marvel that Mr. Badman was such an ill-natured man, for the great roots of all manner of wickedness were in him unmortified, unmaimed, untouched.

Atten. But it is a rare case, even this of Mr. Badman, that he should never in all his life be touched with remorse for his ill-spent life.

Wise. Remorse, I cannot say he ever had, if by remorse you mean repentance for his evils. Yet twice I remember he was under some trouble of mind about his condition. Once when he broke his leg as he came home drunk from the ale-house; and another time when he fell sick, and thought he should die. Besides these two times, I do not remember any more.

Atten. Did he break his leg then?

Wise. Yes; once as he came home drunk from the ale-house.

Atten. Pray how did he break it?

Wise. Why upon a time he was at an ale-house, that wicked house about two or three miles from home, and having there drank hard the greatest part of the day, when night was come, he would stay no longer, but calls for his horse, gets up and like a madman, as drunken persons usually ride, away he goes, as hard as horse could lay legs to the ground. Thus he rid, till coming to a dirty place, where his horse flouncing in, fell, threw his master, and with his fall broke his leg. So there he lay. But you would not think how he swore at first. But after a while, he coming to himself, and feeling by his pain, and the uselessness of his leg, what case he was in, and also fearing that this bout might be his death; he began to cry out after the manner of such, Lord help me, Lord have mercy upon me, good God deliver me, and the like. So there he lay, till some came by, who took him up, carried him home, where he lay for some time, before he could go abroad again.

Atten. And then you say he called upon God.

Wise. He cried out in his pain, and would say, O God, and, O Lord, help me. But whether it was that his sin might be pardoned, and his soul saved, or whether to be rid of his pain, I will not positively determine; though I fear it was but for the last; because when his pain was gone, and he had got hopes of mending, even before he could go abroad, he cast off prayer, and began his old game; to wit, to be as bad as he was before. He then would send for his old companions; his sluts also would come to his house to see him, and with them he would be, as well as he could for his lame leg, as vicious as they could be for their hearts.

Atten. It was a wonder he did not break his neck.

Wise. His neck had gone instead of his leg, but that God was long-suffering towards him; he had deserved it ten thousand times over. There have been many, as I have heard, and as I have hinted to you before, that have taken their horses when drunk as he; but they have gone from the pot to the grave; for they have broken their necks betwixt the ale-house and home. One hard by us also drunk himself dead; he drank, and died in his drink.

Atten. It is a sad thing to die drunk.

Wise. So it is; but yet I wonder that no more do so. For considering the heinousness of that sin, and with how many other sins it is accompanied, as with oaths, blasphemies, lies, revellings, whorings, brawlings, etc., it is a wonder to me that any that live in that sin should escape such a blow from Heaven, that should tumble them into their graves. Besides, when I consider also how, when they are as drunk as beasts, they, without all fear of danger, will ride like bedlams and madmen, even as if they did dare God to meddle with them if he durst, for their being drunk. I say, I wonder that he doth not withdraw his protecting providences from them, and leave them to those dangers and destructions that by their sin they have deserved, and that by their bedlam madness they would rush themselves into. Only I consider again, that he has appointed a day wherein he will reckon with them, and doth also commonly make examples of some, to show that he takes notice of their sin, abhors their way, and will count with them for it at the set time (Acts xvii. 30, 31).

Atten. It is worthy of our remark, to take notice how God, to show his dislike of the sins of men, strikes some of them down with a blow; as the breaking of Mr. Badman's leg, for doubtless that was a stroke from heaven.

Wise. It is worth our remark, indeed. It was an open stroke, it fell upon him while he was in the height of his sin; and it looks much like to that in Job: "Therefore he knoweth their works, and overturneth *them* in the night, so that they are destroyed. He striketh them as wicked men in the open sight of others." Or, as the margin reads it, "in the place of beholders" (Job xxxiv. 25, 26). He lays them, with his stroke, in the place of beholders. There was Mr. Badman laid; his stroke was taken notice of by every one, his broken leg was at this time the town talk. Mr. Badman has broken his leg, says one. How did he break it? says another. As he came home drunk from such an ale-house, said a third. A judgment of God upon him, said a fourth. This his sin, his shame and punishment, are all made conspicuous to all that are about him. I will here tell you another story or two.

I have read, in Mr. Clark's *Looking-glass for Sinners*, that upon a time a certain drunken fellow boasted in his cups that there was neither heaven nor hell; also he said he believed that man had no soul, and that, for his own part, he would sell his soul to any that would buy it. Then did one of his companions buy it of him for a cup of wine, and presently the devil, in man's shape, bought it of that man again at the same price; and so, in the presence of them all, laid hold on the soul-seller, and carried him away through the air, so that he was never more heard of.

He tells us also, that there was one at Salisbury, in the midst of his health, drinking and carousing in a tavern; and he drank a health to the devil, saying that if the devil would not come and pledge him, he would not believe that there was either God or devil. Whereupon his companions, stricken with fear, hastened out of the room; and presently after, hearing a hideous noise, and smelling a stinking savour, the vintner ran up into the chamber; and coming in he missed his guest, and found the window broken, the iron bar in it bowed, and all bloody. But the man was never heard of afterwards.

Again, he tells us of a bailiff of Hedley, who, upon a Lord's day, being drunk at Melford, got upon his horse, to ride through the streets, saying that his horse would carry him to the devil. And presently his horse threw him, and broke his neck. These things are worse than the breaking of Mr. Badman's leg; and should be a caution to all of his friends that are living, lest they also fall by their sin into these sad judgments of God.

But, as I said, Mr. Badman quickly forgot all; his conscience was choked before his leg was healed. And, therefore, before he was well of the fruit of one sin, he tempts God to send another judgment to seize upon him. And so he did quickly after. For not many months after his leg was well, he had a very dangerous fit of sickness, insomuch that now he began to think he must die in very deed.

Atten. Well, and what did he think and do then?

Wise. He thought he must go to hell; this I know, for he could not forbear but say so. To my best remembrance, he lay crying out all one night for fear; and at times he would so tremble that he would make the very bed shake under him. But O! how the thoughts of death, of hell-fire, and of eternal judgment, did then wrack his conscience. Fear might be seen in his face, and in his tossings to and fro; it might also be heard in his words, and be understood by his heavy groans. He would often cry, I am undone, I am undone; my vile life has undone me!

Atten. Then his former atheistical thoughts and principles were too weak now to support him from the fears of eternal damnation.

Wise. Aye! they were too weak indeed. They may serve to stifle conscience, when a man is in the midst of his prosperity; and to harden the heart against all good counsel, when a man is left of God, and given up to his reprobate mind. But, alas, atheistical thoughts, notions, and opinions must shrink and melt away, when God sends, yea, comes with sickness to visit the soul of such a sinner for his sin. There was a man dwelt about twelve miles off from us, that had so trained up himself in his atheistical notions, that at last he attempted to write a book against Jesus Christ, and against the Divine authority of the Scriptures. But I think it was not printed. Well, after many days, God struck him with sickness, whereof he died. So, being sick, and musing upon his former doings, the book that he had written came into his mind, and with it such a sense of his evil in writing of it, that it tore his conscience as a lion would tear a kid. He lay, therefore, upon his death-bed in sad case, and much affliction of conscience; some of my friends also went to see him; and as they were in his chamber one day, he hastily called for pen, ink, and paper; which when it was given him, he took it and writ to this purpose: I, such a one, in such a town, must go to hell-fire, for writing a book against Jesus Christ, and against the Holy Scriptures. And would also have leaped out of the window of his house, to have killed himself, but was by them prevented of that; so he died in his bed, such a death as it was. It will be well if others take warning by him.

Atten. This is a remarkable story.

Wise. It is as true as remarkable. I had it from them that I dare believe, who also themselves were eye and ear witnesses; and also that catched him in their arms, and saved him, when he would have leaped out of his chamber window, to have destroyed himself!

Atten. Well, you have told me what were Mr. Badman's thoughts now, being sick, of his condition; pray tell me also what he then did when he was sick?

Wise. Did! he did many things which, I am sure, he never thought to have done; and which, to be sure, was not looked for of his wife and children. In this fit of sickness, his thoughts were quite altered about his wife; I say his thoughts, so far as could be judged by his words and carriages to her. For now she was his good wife, his godly wife, his honest wife, his duck and dear, and all. Now he told her that she had the best of it; she having a good life to stand by her, while his debaucheries and ungodly life did always stare him in the face. Now he told her the counsel that she often gave him was good; though he was so bad as not to take it.

Now he would hear her talk to him, and he would lie sighing by her while she so did. Now he would bid her pray for him, that he might be delivered from hell. He would also now consent that some of her good ministers might come to him to comfort him; and he would seem to show them kindness when they came, for he would treat kindly with words, and hearken diligently to what they said: only he did not care that they should talk much of his ill-spent life, because his conscience was clogged with that already. He cared not now to see his old companions, the thoughts of them were a torment to him; and now he would speak kindly to that child of his that took after its mother's steps, though he could not at all abide it before.

He also desired the prayers of good people, that God of his mercy would spare him a little longer; promising that if God would but let him recover this once, what a new, what a penitent man he would be toward God, and what a loving husband he would be to his wife; what liberty he would give her, yea, how he would go with her himself, to hear her ministers, and how they should go hand in hand in the way to heaven together.

Atten. Here was a fine show of things; I'll warrant you, his wife was glad for this.

Wise. His wife! aye, and a many good people besides. It was noised all over the town what a great change there was wrought upon Mr. Badman: how sorry he was for his sins, how he began to love his wife, how he desired good men should pray to God to spare him; and what promises he now made to God, in his sickness, that if ever he should raise him from his sick-bed to health again, what a new penitent man he would be towards God, and what a loving husband to his good wife. Well, ministers prayed, and good people rejoiced, thinking verily that they now had gotten a man from the devil; nay, some of the weaker sort did not stick to say that God had begun a work of grace in his heart; and his wife, poor woman, you cannot think how apt she was to believe it so; she rejoiced, and she hoped as she would have it. But, alas! alas! in little time things all proved otherwise.

After he had kept his bed a while, his distemper began to abate, and he to feel himself better; so he in a little time was so finely mended, that he could walk about the house, and also obtained a very fine stomach to his food; and now did his wife and her good friends stand gaping to see Mr. Badman fulfil his promise of becoming new towards God, and loving to his wife; but the contrary only showed itself. For, so soon as ever he had hopes of mending, and found that his strength began to renew, his trouble began to go off his heart, and he grew as great a stranger to his frights and fears, as if he never had them.

But verily, I am apt to think, that one reason of his no more regarding or remembering of his sick-bed fears, and of being no better for them, was some words that the doctor

that supplied him with physic said to him when he was
mending. For as soon as Mr. Badman began to mend, the
doctor comes and sits him down by him in his house, and
there fell into discourse with him about the nature of his
disease; and among other things they talked of Badman's
trouble, and how he would cry out, tremble, and express
his fears of going to hell when his sickness lay pretty hard
upon him. To which the doctor replied, that those fears
and outcries did arise from the height of his distemper; for
that disease was often attended with lightness of the head,
by reason the sick party could not sleep, and for that the
vapours disturbed the brain: but you see, sir, quoth he,
that so soon as you got sleep and betook yourself to rest,
you quickly mended, and your head settled, and so those
frenzies left you. And it was so indeed, thought Mr. Badman;
was my troubles only the effects of my distemper, and because ill vapours got up into my brain? Then surely, since
my physician was my saviour, my lust again shall be my
god. So he never minded religion more, but betook him
again to the world, his lusts and wicked companions: and
there was an end of Mr. Badman's conversion.

Atten. I thought, as you told me of him, that this would
be the result of the whole; for I discerned, by your relating
of things, that the true symptoms of conversion were wanting
in him, and that those that appeared to be anything like
them, were only such as reprobates may have.

Wise. You say right, for there wanted in him, when he
was most sensible, a sense of the pollution of his nature;
he only had guilt for his sinful actions, the which Cain, and
Pharaoh, and Saul, and Judas, those reprobates, have had
before him (Gen. iv. 13, 14; Exod. ix. 27; 1 Sam. xv. 24;
Matt. xxvii. 3–5).

Besides, the great things that he desired, were to be
delivered from going to hell, and who would, willingly? and
that his life might be lengthened in this world. We find not,
by all that he said or did, that Jesus Christ the Saviour was
desired by him, from a sense of his need of his righteousness
to clothe him, and of his Spirit to sanctify him. His own
strength was whole in him, he saw nothing of the treachery
of his own heart: for had he, he would never have been so
free to make promises to God of amendment. He would

rather have been afraid, that if he had mended, he should have turned with the dog to his vomit, and have begged prayers of the saints, and assistance from heaven upon that account, that he might have been kept from doing so. It is true he did beg prayers of good people, and so did Pharaoh of Moses and Aaron, and Simon Magus of Simon Peter (Exod. ix. 28; Acts viii. 24). His mind also seemed to be turned to his wife and child; but, alas! it was rather from conviction that God had given him concerning their happy estate over his, than for that he had any true love to the work of God that was in them. True, some shows of kindness he seemed to have for them, and so had rich Dives when in hell, to his five brethren that were yet in the world: yea, he had such love as to wish them in heaven, that they might not come thither to be tormented (Luke xvi. 27, 28).

Atten. Sick-bed repentance is seldom good for anything.

Wise. You say true, it is very rarely good for anything indeed. Death is unwelcome to nature, and usually when sickness and death visit the sinner; the first taking of him by the shoulder, and the second standing at the bed-chamber door to receive him; then the sinner begins to look about him, and to bethink with himself, these will have me away before God; and I know that my life has not been as it should, how shall I do to appear before God! Or if it be more the sense of the punishment, and the place of the punishment of sinners, that also is starting to a defiled conscience, now roused by death's lumbering at the door. And hence usually is sick-bed repentance, and the matter of it; to wit, to be saved from hell, and from death, and that God will restore again to health till they mend, concluding that it is in their power to mend, as is evident by their large and lavishing promises to do it. I have known many that, when they have been sick, have had large measures of this kind of repentance, and while it has lasted, the noise and sound thereof has made the town to ring again. But, alas! how long has it lasted? ofttimes scarce so long as until the party now sick has been well. It has passed away like a mist or a vapour, it has been a thing of no continuance. But this kind of repentance is by God compared to the howling of a dog. "And they have not cried unto me with their heart, when they howled upon their beds" (Hos. vii. 14).

K 815

Atten. Yet one may see by this the desperateness of man's heart; for what is it but desperate wickedness to make promise to God of amendment, if he will but spare them; and yet, so soon as they are recovered, or quickly after, fall to sin as they did before, and never to regard their promise more?

Wise. It is a sign of desperateness indeed; yea, of desperate madness (Deut. i. 34, 35). For, surely, they must needs think that God took notice of their promise, that he heard the words that they spake, and that he hath laid them up against the time to come; and will then bring out, and testify to their faces, that they flattered him with their mouth, and lied unto him with their tongue, when they lay sick, to their thinking, upon their death-bed, and promised him that if he would recover them they would repent and amend their ways (Ps. lxxviii. 34–7). But thus, as I have told you, Mr. Badman did. He made great promises that he would be a new man, that he would leave his sins and become a convert, that he would love, etc., his godly wife, etc. Yea, many fine words had Mr. Badman in his sickness, but no good actions when he was well.

Atten. And how did his good wife take it, when she saw that he had no amendment, but that he returned with the dog to his vomit, to his old courses again?

Wise. Why, it broke her heart, it was a worse disappoint- ment to her than the cheat that he gave her in marriage. At least she laid it more to heart, and could not so well grapple with it. You must think that she had put up many a prayer to God for him before, even all the time that he had carried it so badly to her, and now, when he was so affrighted in his sickness, and so desired that he might live and mend; poor woman, she thought that the time was come for God to answer her prayers; nay, she did not let with gladness, to whisper it out amongst her friends, that it was so: but when she saw herself disappointed by her husband turning rebel again, she could not stand up under it, but falls into a languishing distemper, and in a few weeks gave up the ghost.

Atten. Pray how did she die?

Wise. Die! she died bravely; full of comfort of the faith of her interest in Christ, and by him, of the world to come.

She had many brave expressions in her sickness, and gave
to those that came to visit her many signs of her salvation;
the thoughts of the grave, but especially of her rising again,
were sweet thoughts to her. She would long for death, because she knew it would be her friend. She behaved herself like to some that were making of them ready to go meet
their bridegroom. Now, said she, I am going to rest from
my sorrows, my sighs, my tears, my mournings, and com-
plaints: I have heretofore longed to be among the saints,
but might by no means be suffered to go, but now I am
going, and no man can stop me, to the great meeting, "to
the general assembly, and church of the firstborn, which
are written in heaven" (Heb. xii. 22–4). There I shall have
my heart's desire; there I shall worship without temptation
or other impediment; there I shall see the face of my Jesus,
whom I have loved, whom I have served, and who now I
know will save my soul. I have prayed often for my husband,
that he might be converted, but there has been no answer
of God in that matter. Are my prayers lost? are they forgotten? are they thrown over the bar? No: they are hanged
upon the horns of the golden altar, and I must have the
benefit of them myself, that moment that I shall enter into
the gates, in at which the righteous nation that keepeth
truth shall enter: I say, I shall have the benefit of them.
I can say as holy David; I say, I can say of my husband, as
he could of his enemies: "As for me, when they were sick,
my clothing *was* sackcloth; I humbled my soul with fasting,
and my prayer returned into mine own bosom" (Ps. xxxv.
13). My prayers are not lost, my tears are yet in God's bottle;
I would have had a crown and glory for my husband,
and for those of my children that follow his steps; but so
far as I can see yet, I must rest in the hope of having all
myself.

Atten. Did she talk thus openly?

Wise. No: this she spake but to one or two of her most
intimate acquaintance, who were permitted to come and see
her when she lay languishing upon her death-bed.

Atten. Well but pray go on in your relation, this is good;
I am glad to hear it, this is as a cordial to my heart while
we sit thus talking under this tree.

Wise. When she drew near her end, she called for her

husband, and when he was come to her she told him that now he and she must part, and, said she, God knows, and thou shalt know, that I have been a loving, faithful wife unto thee; my prayers have been many for thee; and as for all the abuses that I have received at thy hand, those I freely and heartily forgive, and still shall pray for thy conversion, even as long as I breathe in this world. But, husband, I am going thither, where no bad man shall come, and if thou dost not convert, thou wilt never see me more with comfort; let not my plain words offend thee; I am thy dying wife, and of my faithfulness to thee, would leave this exhortation with thee; break off thy sins, fly to God for mercy while mercy's gate stands open; remember that the day is coming, when thou, though now lusty and well, must lie at the gates of death as I do; and what wilt thou then do, if thou shalt be found with a naked soul, to meet with the cherubims with their flaming swords? Yea, what wilt thou then do, if death and hell shall come to visit thee, and thou in thy sins, and under the curse of the law?

Atten. This was honest and plain; but what said Mr. Bad-man to her?

Wise. He did what he could to divert her talk, by throw-ing in other things; he also showed some kind of pity to her now, and would ask her what she would have? and with various kind of words put her out of her talk; for when she saw that she was not regarded, she fetched a deep sigh, and lay still. So he went down, and then she called for her children, and began to talk to them. And first she spake to those that were rude, and told them the danger of dying before they had grace in their hearts. She told them also that death might be nearer them than they were aware of; and bid them look when they went through the churchyard again, if there were not little graves there. And, ah, children, said she, will it not be dreadful to you if we only shall meet at the day of judgment, and then part again, and never see each other more? And with that she wept, the children also wept: so she held on her discourse. Children, said she, I am going from you; I am going to Jesus Christ, and with him there is neither sorrow, nor sighing, nor pain, nor tears, nor death (Rev. vii. 16; xxi. 3, 4). Thither would I have you go also, but I can neither carry you nor fetch you thither;

but if you shall turn from your sins to God, and shall beg mercy at his hands by Jesus Christ, you shall follow me, and shall, when you die, come to the place where I am going, that blessed place of rest; and then we shall be for ever together, beholding the face of our Redeemer, to our mutual and eternal joy. So she bid them remember the words of a dying mother when she was cold in her grave, and themselves were hot in their sins, if perhaps her words might put check to their vice, and that they might remember and turn to God.

Then they all went down but her darling, to wit, the child that she had most love for, because it followed her ways. So she addressed herself to that. Come to me, said she, my sweet child, thou art the child of my joy; I have lived to see thee a servant of God; thou shalt have eternal life. I, my sweet heart, shall go before, and thou shalt follow after, if thou shalt "hold the beginning of thy confidence stedfast unto the end" (Heb. iii. 14). When I am gone, do thou still remember my words. Love thy Bible, follow my ministers, deny ungodliness still, and if troublesome times shall come, set a higher price upon Christ, his word, and ways, and the testimony of a good conscience, than upon all the world besides. Carry it kindly and dutifully to thy father, but choose none of his ways. If thou mayest go to service, choose that rather than to stay at home; but then be sure to choose a service where thou mayest be helped forwards in the way to heaven; and that thou mayest have such a service, speak to my minister, he will help thee, if possible, to such a one.

I would have thee also, my dear child, to love thy brothers and sisters, but learn none of their naughty tricks. "Have no fellowship with the unfruitful works of darkness, but rather reprove *them*" (Eph. v. 11). Thou hast grace, they have none; do thou therefore beautify the way of salvation before their eyes, by a godly life and conformable conversation to the revealed will of God, that thy brothers and sisters may see and be the more pleased with the good ways of the Lord. If thou shalt live to marry, take heed of being served as I was; that is, of being beguiled with fair words and the flatteries of a lying tongue. But first be sure of godliness, yea, as sure as it is possible for one to be in this world. Trust not thine own eyes, nor thine own judgment, I mean as to that person's godliness that thou art invited to marry. Ask counsel of good men, and do nothing therein, if he lives, without my minister's advice. I have also myself desired him to look after thee. Thus she talked to her children, and gave them counsel; and after she had talked to this a little longer, she kissed it, and bid it go down.

Well, in short, her time drew on, and the day that she must die. So she died, with a soul full of grace, a heart full of comfort, and by her death ended a life full of trouble. Her husband made a funeral for her, perhaps because he was glad he was rid of her, but we will leave that to be manifest at judgment.

Atten. This woman died well. And now we are talking of the dying of Christians, I will tell you a story of one that died some time since in our town. The man was a godly old Puritan, for so the godly were called in time past. This man, after a long and godly life, fell sick, of the sickness whereof he died. And as he lay drawing on, the woman that looked to him thought she heard music, and that the sweetest that ever she heard in her life, which also continued until he gave up the ghost. Now when his soul departed from him the music seemed to withdraw, and to go farther and farther off from the house, and so it went until the sound was quite gone out of hearing.

Wise. What do you think that might be?

Atten. For aught I know the melodious notes of angels that were sent of God to fetch him to heaven.

Wise. I cannot say but that God goes out of his ordinary road with us poor mortals sometimes. I cannot say this of this woman, but yet she had better music in her heart than sounded in this woman's ears.

Atten. I believe so; but pray tell me, did any of her other children hearken to her words, so as to be bettered in their souls thereby?

Wise. One of them did, and became a very hopeful young man. But for the rest I can say nothing.

Atten. And what did Badman do after his wife was dead?

Wise. Why, even as he did before; he scarce mourned a fortnight for her, and his mourning then was, I doubt, more in fashion than in heart.

Atten. Would he not sometimes talk of his wife when she was dead?

Wise. Yes, when the fit took him, and could commend her too extremely, saying she was a good, godly, virtuous woman. But this is not a thing to be wondered at. It is common with wicked men to hate God's servants while alive, and to commend them when they are dead. So served the Pharisees the prophets. Those of the prophets that were dead they commended, and those of them that were alive they condemned (Matt. xxiii.).

Atten. But did not Mr. Badman marry again quickly?

Wise. No, not a good while after; and when he was asked the reason he would make this slighty answer, Who would keep a cow of their own that can have a quart of milk for a penny? Meaning, who would be at the charge to have a wife that can have a whore when he listeth? So villainous, so abominable did he continue after the death of his wife. Yet at last there was one was too hard for him. For getting of him to her upon a time, and making of him sufficiently drunk, she was so cunning as to get a promise of marriage of him, and so held him to it, and forced him to marry her. And she, as the saying is, was as good as he at all his vile and ranting tricks. She had her companions as well as he had his, and she would meet them too at the tavern and ale-house more commonly than he was aware of. To be plain, she was a very whore, and had as great resort come to her, where time and place was appointed, as any of them all. Aye, and he smelt it too, but could not tell how to help it. For if he began to talk, she could lay in his dish the whores that she knew he haunted, and she could fit him also with cursing and swearing, for she would give him oath for oath, and curse for curse.

Atten. What kind of oaths would she have?

Wise. Why, damn her, and sink her, and the like.

Atten. These are provoking things.

Wise. So they are; but God doth not altogether let such things go unpunished in this life. Something of this I have showed you already, and will here give you one or two instances more.

There lived, saith one, in the year 1551, in a city of Savoy, a man who was a monstrous curser and swearer, and though he was often admonished and blamed for it, yet would he by no means mend his manners. At length a great plague happening in the city, he withdrew himself with his wife and a kinswoman into a garden, where being again admonished to give over his wickedness, he hardened his heart more, swearing, blaspheming God, and giving himself to the devil. And immediately the devil snatched him up suddenly, his wife and kinswoman looking on, and carried him quite away. The magistrates, advertised hereof, went to the place and examined the woman, who justified the truth of it.

Also at Oster, in the duchy of Magalapole, saith Mr. Clark, a wicked woman used in her cursing to give herself body and soul to the devil, and being reproved for it, still continued the same; till, being at a wedding-feast, the devil came in person, and carried her up into the air, with most horrible outcries and roarings; and in that sort carried her round about the town, that the inhabitants were ready to die for fear. And by and by he tore her in four pieces, leaving her four quarters in four several highways; and then brought her bowels to the marriage-feast, and threw them upon the table before the mayor of the town, saying, Behold these dishes of meat belong to thee, whom the like destruction waiteth for if thou dost not amend thy wicked life.

Atten. Though God forbears to deal thus with all men that thus rend and tear his name, and that immediate judgments do not overtake them, yet he makes their lives by other judgments bitter to them, does he not?

Wise. Yes, yes, and for proof, I need go no farther than to this Badman and his wife; for their railing, and cursing, and swearing ended not in words. They would fight and fly at each other, and that like cats and dogs. But it must be looked upon as the hand and judgment of God upon him for his villainy; he had an honest woman before, but she would not serve his turn, and therefore God took her away, and gave him one as bad as himself. Thus that measure that he meted to his first wife, this last did mete to him again. And this is a punishment wherewith sometimes God will punish wicked men. So said Amos to Amaziah, "Thy wife shall be a harlot in the city" (Amos vii. 17). With this last wife Mr. Badman lived a pretty while; but, as I told you before, in a most sad and hellish manner. And now he would bewail his first wife's death; not of love that he had to her godliness, for that he could never abide, but for that she used always to keep home, whereas this would go abroad; his first wife was also honest, and true to that relation, but this last was a whore of her body. The first woman loved to keep things together, but this last would whirl them about as well as he. The first would be silent when he chid, and would take it patiently when he abused her; but this would give him word for word, blow for blow, curse for curse; so that now Mr. Badman had met with his match. God had a mind to make him see the baseness of his own life in the wickedness of his wife's. But all would not do with Mr. Badman, he would be Mr. Badman still. This judgment did not work any reformation upon him, no, not to God nor man.

Atten. I warrant you that Mr. Badman thought when his wife was dead, that next time he would match far better.

Wise. What he thought I cannot tell, but he could not hope for it in this match. For here he knew himself to be catched, he knew that he was by this woman entangled, and would therefore have gone back again, but could not. He knew her, I say, to be a whore before, and therefore could not promise himself a happy life with her. For he or she that will not be true to their own soul, will neither be true to husband nor wife. And he knew that she was not true to her own soul, and therefore could not expect she should be true to him. But Solomon says, "A whore is a deep ditch," and Mr. Badman found it true. For when she had caught him in her pit, she would never leave him till she had got him to promise her marriage; and when she had taken him so far, she forced him to marry indeed. And after that, they lived that life that I have told you.

Atten. But did not the neighbours take notice of this alteration that Mr. Badman had made?

Wise. Yes; and many of his neighbours, yea, many of those that were carnal said, It is a righteous judgment of God upon him for his abusive carriage and language to his other wife: for they were all convinced that she was a virtuous woman, and that he, vile wretch, had killed her, I will not say with, but with the want of kindness.

Atten. And how long, I pray, did they live thus together?

* K 815

Wise. Some fourteen or sixteen years, even until, though she also brought something with her, they had sinned all away, and parted as poor as howlets. And, in reason, how could it be otherwise? he would have his way, and she would have hers; he among his companions, and she among hers; he with his whores, and she with her rogues; and so they brought their noble to ninepence.

Atten. Pray of what disease did Mr. Badman die, for now I perceive we are come up to his death?

Wise. I cannot so properly say that he died of one disease, for there were many that had consented, and laid their heads together to bring him to his end. He was dropsical, he was consumptive, he was surfeited, was gouty, and, as some say, he had a tang of the pox in his bowels. Yet the captain of all these men of death that came against him to take him away, was the consumption, for it was that that brought him down to the grave.

Atten. Although I will not say but the best men may die of a consumption, a dropsy, or a surfeit; yea, that these may meet upon a man to end him; yet I will say again, that many times these diseases come through man's inordinate use of things. Much drinking brings dropsies, consumptions, surfeits, and many other diseases; and I doubt that Mr. Badman's death did come by his abuse of himself in the use of lawful and unlawful things. I ground this my sentence upon that report of his life that you at large have given me.

Wise. I think verily that you need not call back your sentence; for it is thought by many that by his cups and his queans he brought himself to this his destruction: he was not an old man when he died, nor was he naturally very feeble, but strong and of a healthy complexion. Yet, as I said, he moultered away, and went, when he set a-going, rotten to his grave. And that which made him stink when he was dead, I mean, that made him stink in his name and fame, was, that he died with a spice of the foul disease upon him. A man whose life was full of sin, and whose death was without repentance.

Atten. These were blemishes sufficient to make him stink indeed.

Wise. They were so, and did do it. No man could speak well of him when he was gone. His name rotted above ground, as his carcase rotted under. And this is according to the saying of the wise man, "The memory of the just is blessed, but the name of the wicked shall rot" (Prov. x. 7).

This text, in both the parts of it, was fulfilled upon him and the woman that he married first. For her name still did flourish, though she had been dead almost seventeen years; but his began to stink and rot before he had been buried seventeen days.

Atten. That man that dieth with a life full of sin, and with a heart void of repentance, although he should die of the most golden disease, if there were any that might be so called, I will warrant him his name shall stink, and that in heaven and earth.

Wise. You say true; and therefore doth the name of Cain, Pharaoh, Saul, Judas, and the Pharisees, though dead thousands of years ago, stink as fresh in the nostrils of the world as if they were but newly dead.

Atten. I do fully acquiesce with you in this. But, sir, since you have charged him with dying impenitent, pray let me see how you will prove it; not that I altogether doubt it, because you have affirmed it, but yet I love to have proof for what men say in such weighty matters.

Wise. When I said he died without repentance, I meant so far as those that knew him could judge, when they compared his life, the Word, and his death together.

Atten. Well said, they went the right way to find out whether he had, that is, did manifest that he had repentance or no. Now then show me how they did prove he had none.

Wise. So I will. And first, this was urged to prove it. He had not in all the time of his sickness a sight and sense of his sins, but was as secure, and as much at quiet, as if he had never sinned in all his life.

Atten. I must needs confess that this is a sign he had none. For how can a man repent of that of which he hath neither sight nor sense? But it is strange that he had neither sight nor sense of sin now, when he had such a sight and sense of his evil before; I mean when he was sick before.

Wise. He was, as I said, as secure now as if he had been as sinless as an angel; though all men knew what a sinner he was, for he carried his sins in his forehead. His debauched life was read and known of all men; but his repentance was read and known of no man; for, as I said, he had none. And for aught I know, the reason why he had no sense of his sins now was, because he profited not by that sense that he had of them before. He liked not to retain that knowledge of God then, that caused his sins to come to remembrance. Therefore God gave him up now to a reprobate mind, to hardness and stupidity of spirit; and so was that scripture fulfilled upon him, "He hath blinded their eyes" (Is. vi. 10). And that, "Let their eyes be darkened that they may not see" (Rom. xi. 10). O, for a man to live in sin, and to go out of the world without repentance for it, is the saddest judgment that can overtake a man.

Atten. But, sir, although both you and I have consented that without a sight and sense of sin there can be no repentance, yet that is but our bare say so; let us therefore now see if by the Scripture we can make it good.

Wise. That is easily done. The three thousand that were converted (Acts ii.), repented not till they had sight and sense of their sins. Paul repented not till he had sight and sense of his sins (Acts ix.). The jailer repented not till he had sight and sense of his sins; nor could they (Acts xvi.). For of what should a man repent? The answer is, Of sin. What is it to repent of sin? The answer is, To be sorry for it, to turn from it. But how can a man be sorry for it, that has neither sight nor sense of it? (Ps. xxxviii. 18). David did not only commit sins, but abode impenitent for them, until Nathan the prophet was sent from God to give him a sight and sense of them; and then, but not till then, he indeed repented of them (2 Sam. xii.). Job, in order to his repentance, cries unto God, "Shew me wherefore thou contendest with me" (Job x. 2). And again, "That which I see not teach thou me, I have borne chastisement, I will not offend *any more*" (Job xxxiv. 32). That is, not in what I know, for I will repent of it; nor yet in what I know not, when thou shalt show me it. Also Ephraim's repentance was after he was turned to the sight and sense of his sins, and after he was instructed about the evil of them (Jer. xxxi. 18–20).

Atten. These are good testimonies of this truth, and do, if matter of fact, with which Mr. Badman is charged, be true, prove indeed that he did not repent, but as he lived so he died in his sin (Job xx. 11). For without repentance a man is sure to die in his sin; for they will lie down in the dust with him, rise at the judgment with him, hang about his neck like cords and chains when he standeth at the bar of God's tribunal (Prov. v. 22). And go with him, too, when he goes away from the judgment-seat, with a "Depart from me, ye cursed, into everlasting fire, prepared for the devil and his angels" (Matt. xxv. 41). And there shall fret and gnaw his conscience, because they will be to him a never-dying worm (Mark ix. 44; Is. lxvi. 24).

Wise. You say well, and I will add a word or two more to what I have said. Repentance, as it is not produced without a sight and sense of sin, so every sight and sense of sin cannot produce it; I mean every sight and sense of sin cannot produce that repentance, that is repentance unto salvation; repentance never to be repented of. For it is yet fresh before us, that Mr. Badman had a sight and sense of sin, in that fit of sickness that he had before, but it died without procuring any such godly fruit; as was manifest by his so soon returning with the dog to his vomit. Many people think also that repentance stands in confession of sin only, but they are very much mistaken; for repentance, as was said before, is a being sorry for, and returning from transgression to God by Jesus Christ. Now, if this be true, that every sight and sense of sin will not produce repentance, then repentance cannot be produced there where there is no sight and sense of sin. That every sight and sense of sin will not produce repentance, to wit, the godly repentance that we are speaking of, is manifest in Cain, Pharaoh, Saul, and Judas, who all of them had sense, great sense of sin, but none of them repentance unto life.

Now I conclude that Mr. Badman did die impenitent, and so a death most miserable.

Atten. But pray now, before we conclude our discourse of Mr. Badman, give me another proof of his dying in his sins.

Wise. Another proof is this, he did not desire a sight and sense of sins, that he might have repentance for them. Did I say he did not desire it, I will add, he greatly desired to remain in his security, and that I shall prove by that which follows. First, he could not endure that any man now should talk to him of his sinful life, and yet that was the way to beget a sight and sense of sin, and so of repentance from it, in his soul. But I say he could not endure such discourse. Those men that did offer to talk unto him of his ill-spent life, they were as little welcome to him, in the time of his last sickness, as was Elijah when he went to meet with Ahab as he went down to take possession of Naboth's vineyard. "Hast thou found me," said Ahab, "O mine enemy?" (1 Kings xxi. 17–21). So would Mr. Badman say in his heart to and of these that thus did come to him, though indeed they came even of love to convince him of his evil life, that he might have repented thereof and have obtained mercy.

Atten. Did good men then go to see him in his last sickness?

Wise. Yes. Those that were his first wife's acquaintance, they went to see him, and to talk with him, and to him, if perhaps he might now, at last, bethink himself and cry to God for mercy.

Atten. They did well to try now at last if they could save his soul from hell. But pray how can you tell that he did not care for the company of such?

Wise. Because of the differing carriage that he had for them from what he had when his old carnal companions came to see him. When his old companions came to see him he would stir up himself as much as he could, both by words and looks, to signify they were welcome to him; he would also talk with them freely and look pleasantly upon them, though the talk of such could be none other but such as David said carnal men would offer to him when they came to visit him in his sickness. "If he come to see me," says he, "he speaketh vanity, his heart gathereth iniquity to itself" (Ps. xli. 6). But these kind of talks, I say, Mr. Badman better brooked than he did the company of better men.

But I will more particularly give you a character of his carriage to good men, and good talk, when they came to see him. (1) When they were come he would seem to fail in his spirits at the sight of them. (2) He would not care to answer them to any of those questions that they would at times put to him, to feel what sense he had of sin, death, hell, and judgment. But would either say nothing or answer them by way of evasion, or else by telling of them he was so weak and spent that he could not speak much. (3) He would never show forwardness to speak to or talk with them, but was glad when they held their tongues. He would ask them no question about his state and another world, or how he should escape that damnation that he had deserved. (4) He had got a haunt at last to bid his wife and keeper, when these good people attempted to come to see him, to tell them that he was asleep, or inclining to sleep, or so weak for want thereof that he could not abide any noise. And so they would serve them time after time, till at last they were discouraged from coming to see him any more. (5) He was so hardened now in this time of his sickness, that he would talk, when his companions came unto him, to the disparagement of those good men, and of their good doctrine too, that of love did come to see him, and that did labour to convert him. (6) When these good men went away from him he would never say, Pray, when will you be pleased to come again, for I have a desire to more of your company and to hear more of your good instruction? No, not a word of that, but when they were going would scarce bid them drink, or say, Thank you for your good company and good instruction. (7) His talk in his sickness with his companions would be of the world, as trades, houses, lands, great men, great titles, great places, outward prosperity or outward adversity, or some such carnal thing. By all which I conclude that he did not desire a sense and sight of his sin, that he might repent and be saved.

Atten. It must needs be so as you say, if these things be true that you have asserted of him. And I do the rather believe them, because I think you dare not tell a lie of the dead.

Wise. I was one of them that went to him and that beheld his carriage and manner of way, and this is a true relation of it that I have given you.

Atten. I am satisfied. But pray, if you can, show me now, by the Word, what sentence of God doth pass upon such men.

Wise. Why, the man that is thus averse to repentance, that desires not to hear of his sins that he might repent and be saved, is said to be a man that saith unto God, "Depart from me, for I desire not the knowledge of thy ways" (Job xxi. 14). He is a man that says in his heart and with his actions, "I have loved strangers (sins), and after them will I go" (Jer. ii. 25). He is a man that shuts his eyes, stops his ears, and that turneth his spirit against God (Zech. vii. 11, 12; Acts xxviii. 26, 27). Yea, he is the man that is at enmity with God, and that abhors him with his soul.

Atten. What other sign can you give me that Mr. Badman died without repentance?

Wise. Why, he did never heartily cry to God for mercy all the time of his affliction. True, when sinking fits, stitches, or pains took hold upon him, then he would say, as other carnal men used to do, Lord, help me; Lord, strengthen me; Lord, deliver me, and the like. But to cry to God for mercy, that he did not, but lay, as I hinted before, as if he never had sinned.

Atten. That is another bad sign indeed, for crying to God for mercy is one of the first signs of repentance. When Paul lay repenting of his sin upon his bed, the Holy Ghost said of him, "Behold he prayeth" (Acts ix. 11). But he that hath not the first signs of repentance, it is a sign he hath none of the other, and so indeed none at all. I do not say but there may be crying where there may be no sign of repentance. "They cried," says David, "unto the Lord, but he answered them not"; but that he would have done if their cry had been the fruit of repentance (Ps. xviii. 41). But, I say, if men may cry and yet have no repentance, be sure they have none that cry not at all. It is said in Job, "They cry not when he bindeth them" (Job xxxvi. 13); that is, because they have no repentance; no repentance, no cries; false repentance, false cries; true repentance, true cries.

Wise. I know that it is as possible for a man to forbear crying that hath repentance, as it is for a man to forbear groaning that feeleth deadly pain. He that looketh into the book of Psalms, where repentance is most lively set forth even in its true and proper effects, shall there find that crying, strong crying, hearty crying, great crying, and incessant crying, hath been the fruits of repentance; but none of this had this Mr. Badman, therefore he died in his sins.

That crying is an inseparable effect of repentance, is seen in these scriptures: "Have mercy upon me, O God; according unto the multitude of thy tender mercies, blot out my transgressions" (Ps. li. 1). "O Lord, rebuke me not in thine anger, neither chasten me in thy hot displeasure. Have mercy upon me, O Lord, for I am weak: O Lord, heal me, for my bones are vexed. My soul is also sore vexed, but thou, O Lord, how long? Return, O Lord, deliver my soul: O save me for thy mercies' sake" (Ps. vi. 1-4). "O Lord, rebuke me not in thy wrath, neither chasten me in thy hot displeasure; for thine arrows stick fast in me, and thy hand presseth me sore. *There is* no soundness in my flesh because of thine anger, neither *is there any* rest in my bones, because of my sin. For mine iniquities are gone over mine head; as a heavy burden they are too heavy for me. My wounds stink *and* are corrupt, because of my foolishness. I am troubled, I am bowed down greatly, I go mourning all the day long. My loins are filled with a loathsome *disease*, and *there is* no soundness in my flesh. I am feeble and sore broken; I have roared by reason of the disquietness of my heart" (Ps. xxxviii. 1-8).

I might give you a great number more of the holy sayings of good men whereby they express how they were, what they felt, and whether they cried or no when repentance was wrought in them. Alas, alas, it is as possible for a man, when the pangs of guilt are upon him, to forbear praying, as it is for a woman, when pangs of travail are upon her, to forbear crying. If all the world should tell me that such a man hath repentance, yet if he is not a praying man I should not be persuaded to believe it.

Atten. I know no reason why you should, for there is nothing can demonstrate that such a man hath it. But pray, sir, what other sign have you by which you can prove that Mr. Badman died in his sins, and so in a state of damnation?

Wise. I have this to prove it. Those who were his old and sinful companions in the time of his health, were those whose company and carnal talk he most delighted in in the time of his sickness. I did occasionally hint this before, but now I make it an argument of his want of grace, for where there is indeed a work of grace in the heart, that work doth not only change the heart, thoughts, and desires, but the conversation also; yea, conversation and company too. When Paul had a work of grace in his soul he essayed to join himself to the disciples. He was for his old companions in their abominations no longer. He was now a disciple, and was for the company of disciples. "And he was with them coming in and going out at Jerusalem" (Acts ix. 27, 28).

Atten. I thought something when I heard you make

mention of it before. Thought I, this is a shrewd sign that he had not grace in his heart. Birds of a feather, thought I, will flock together. If this man was one of God's children he would herd with God's children, his delight would be with and in the company of God's children. As David said, "I *am* a companion of all *them* that fear thee, and of them that keep thy precepts" (Ps. cxix. 63).

Wise. You say well, for what fellowship hath he that believeth with an infidel? And although it be true that all that join to the godly are not godly, yet they that shall inwardly choose the company of the ungodly and open profane, rather than the company of the godly, as Mr. Bad-man did, surely are not godly men, but profane. He was, as I told you, out of his element when good men did come to visit him; but then he was where he would be, when he had his vain companions about him. Alas! grace, as I said, altereth all, heart, life, company, and all; for by it the heart and man is made new. And a new heart and a new man must have objects of delight that are new, and like himself; "Old things are passed away"; why? For "all things are become new" (2 Cor. v. 17). Now, if all things are become new, to wit, heart, mind, thoughts, desires, and delights, it followeth by consequence that the company must be answerable; hence it is said that they "that believed were together"; that "they went to their own company"; that they were "added to the church"; that they "*were* of one heart and of one soul"; and the like (Acts ii. 44–7; iv. 23, 32). Now if it be objected that Mr. Badman was sick, and so could not go to the godly, yet he had a tongue in his head, and could, had he had a heart, have spoken to some to call or send for the godly to come to him. Yea, he would have done so; yea, the company of all others, especially his fellow-sinners, would, even in every appearance of them before him, have been a burden and a grief unto him. His heart and affection standing bent to good, good companions would have suited him best. But his companions were his old associates, his delight was in them, therefore his heart and soul were yet ungodly.

Atten. Pray, how was he when he drew near his end? for I perceive, that what you say of him now hath reference to him and to his actions at the beginning of his sickness.

Then he could endure company and much talk; besides, perhaps then he thought he should recover and not die, as afterwards he had cause to think, when he was quite wasted with pining sickness, when he was at the grave's mouth. But how was he, I say, when he was, as we say, at the grave's mouth, within a step of death, when he saw and knew, and could not but know, that shortly he must die, and appear before the judgment of God?

Wise. Why, there was not any other alteration in him than what was made by his disease upon his body. Sickness, you know, will alter the body, also pains and stitches will make men groan; but for his mind he had no alteration there. His mind was the same, his heart was the same. He was the self-same Mr. Badman still. Not only in name but conditions, and that to the very day of his death; yea, so far as could be gathered, to the very moment in which he died

Atten. Pray, how was he in his death? Was death strong upon him? or did he die with ease, quietly?

Wise. As quietly as a lamb. There seemed not to be in it, to standers by, so much as a strong struggle of nature. And as for his mind, it seemed to be wholly at quiet. But, pray, why do you ask me this question?

Atten. Not for mine own sake, but for others. For there is such an opinion as this among the ignorant, that if a man dies, as they call it, like a lamb, that is, quietly, and without that consternation of mind that others show in their death, they conclude, and that beyond all doubt, that such a one is gone to heaven, and is certainly escaped the wrath to come.

Wise. There is no judgment to be made by a quiet death, of the eternal state of him that so dieth. Suppose that one man should die quietly, another should die suddenly, and a third should die under great consternation of spirit, no man can judge of their eternal condition by the manner of any of these kinds of deaths. He that dies quietly, suddenly, or under consternation of spirit, may go to heaven, or may go to hell; no man can tell whither a man goes, by any such manner of death. The judgment, therefore, that we make of the eternal condition of a man must be gathered from another consideration, to wit, Did the man die in his sins? did he die in unbelief? did he die before he was born again? then he has gone to the devil and hell, though he died never so quietly. Again, Was the man a good man? had he faith and holiness? was he a lover and a worshipper of God by Christ, according to his Word? Then he is gone to God and heaven, how suddenly, or in what consternation of mind soever he died. But Mr. Badman was naught, his life was evil, his ways were evil, evil to his end. He therefore went to hell and to the devil, how quietly soever he died.

Indeed there is, in some cases, a judgment to be made of a man's eternal condition by the manner of the death he dieth. As, suppose now a man should murder himself, or live a wicked life, and after that die in utter despair; these men, without doubt, do both of them go to hell. And here I will take an occasion to speak of two of Mr. Badman's brethren, for you know I told you before that he had brethren, and of the manner of their death. One of them killed himself, and the other, after a wicked life, died in utter despair. Now, I should not be afraid to conclude of both these, that they went by and through their death to hell.

Atten. Pray tell me concerning the first, how he made away with himself?

Wise. Why, he took a knife and cut his own throat, and immediately gave up the ghost and died. Now, what can we judge of such a man's condition, since the Scripture saith, "No murderer hath eternal life," etc., but that it must be concluded that such a one is gone to hell? He was a murderer, a self-murderer; and he is the worst murderer, one that slays his own body and soul. Nor do we find mention made of any but cursed ones that do such kind of deeds. I say, no mention made in Holy Writ of any others, but such that murder themselves.

And this is a sore judgment of God upon men, when God shall, for the sins of such, give them up to be their own executioners, or rather to execute his judgment and anger upon themselves. And let me earnestly give this caution to sinners: Take heed, sirs, break off your sins, lest God serves you as he served Mr. Badman's brother; that is, lest he gives you up to be your own murderers.

Atten. Now you talk of this; I did once know a man, a barber, that took his own razor and cut his own throat, and then put his head out of his chamber window, to show the neighbours what he had done, and after a little while died.

Wise. I can tell you a more dreadful thing than this; I mean as to the manner of doing the fact. There was, about twelve years since, a man that lived at Brafield, by Northampton, named John Cox, that murdered himself; the manner of his doing of it was thus. He was a poor man, and had for some time been sick, and the time of his sickness was about the beginning of hay-time, and taking too many thoughts how he should live afterwards, if he lost his present season of work, he fell into deep despair about the world, and cried out to his wife the morning before he killed himself, saying, We are undone. But quickly after, he desired his wife to depart the room, because, said he, I will see if I can get any rest; so she went out; but he, instead of sleeping, quickly took his razor, and therewith cut up a great hole in his side, out of which he pulled and cut off some of his guts, and threw them, with the blood, up and down the chamber. But this not speeding of him so soon as he desired, he took the same razor and therewith cut his own throat. His wife, then hearing of him sigh and fetch his wind short, came again into the room to him, and seeing what he had done, she ran out and called in some neighbours, who came to him where he lay in a bloody manner, frightful to behold. Then said one of them to him, Ah! John, what have you done? Are you not sorry for what you have done? He answered roughly, It is too late to be sorry. Then said the same person to him again, Ah! John, pray to God to forgive thee this bloody act of thine. At the hearing of which exhortation he seemed much offended, and in an angry manner said, Pray! and with that flung himself away to the wall, and so, after a few gasps, died desperately. When he had turned him of his back to the wall, the blood ran out of his belly as out of a bowl, and soaked quite through the bed to the boards, and through the chinks of the boards it ran pouring down to the ground. Some said that when the neighbours came to see him, he lay groping with his hand in his bowels, reaching upward, as was thought, that he might have pulled or cut out his heart. It was said, also, that some of his liver had been by him torn out and cast upon the boards, and that many of his guts hung out of the bed on the side thereof;

but I cannot confirm all particulars; but the general of the story with these circumstances above mentioned, is true. I had it from a sober and credible person, who himself was one that saw him in this bloody state, and that talked with him, as was hinted before.

Many other such dreadful things might be told you, but these are enough, and too many too, if God, in his wisdom, had thought necessary to prevent them.

Atten. This is a dreadful story. And I would to God that it might be a warning to others, to instruct them to fear before God, and pray, lest he gives them up to do as John Cox hath done. For surely self-murderers cannot go to heaven: and, therefore, as you have said, he that dieth by his own hands, is certainly gone to hell. But speak a word or two of the other man you mentioned.

Wise. What? of a wicked man dying in despair?

Atten. Yes, of a wicked man dying in despair.

Wise. Well then. This Mr. Badman's other brother was a very wicked man, both in heart and life; I say in heart, because he was so in life, nor could anything reclaim him; neither good men, good books, good examples, nor God's judgments. Well, after he had lived a great while in his sins, God smote him with a sickness, of which he died. Now in his sickness his conscience began to be awakened, and he began to roar out of his ill-spent life, insomuch that the town began to ring of him. Now, when it was noised about, many of the neighbours came to see him, and to read by him, as is the common way with some; but all that they could do, could not abate his terror, but he would lie in his bed gnashing of his teeth, and wringing of his wrists, concluding upon the damnation of his soul, and in that horror and despair he died; not calling upon God, but distrusting in his mercy, and blaspheming of his name.

Atten. This brings to my mind a man that a friend of mine told me of. He had been a wicked liver; so when he came to die, he fell into despair; and having concluded that God had no mercy for him, he addressed himself to the devil for favour, saying, Good devil, be good unto me.

Wise. This is almost like Saul, who being forsaken of God, went to the witch of Endor, and so to the devil for help (1 Sam. xxviii.). But, alas, should I set myself to collect these dreadful stories, it would be easy in little time to present you with hundreds of them. But I will conclude as I began; they that are their own murderers, or that die in despair, after they have lived a life of wickedness, do surely go to hell. And here I would put in a caution. Every one that dieth under consternation of spirit, that is, under amazement and great fear, do not therefore die in despair. For a good man may have this for his bands in his death, and yet go to heaven and glory (Ps. lxxiii. 4). For, as I said before, he that is a good man, a man that hath faith and holiness, a lover and worshipper of God by Christ, according to his Word, may die in consternation of spirit; for Satan will not be wanting to assault good men upon their death-bed, but they are secured by the Word and power of God; yea, and are also helped, though with much agony of spirit, to exercise themselves in faith and prayer, the which he that dieth in despair can by no means do. But let us return to Mr. Badman, and enter further discourse of the manner of his death.

Atten. I think you and I are both of a mind; for just now I was thinking to call you back to him also. And pray now, since it is your own motion to return again to him, let us discourse a little more of his quiet and still death.

Wise. With all my heart. You know we were speaking before of the manner of Mr. Badman's death; how that he died still and quietly; upon which you made observation that the common people conclude, that if a man dies quietly, and as they call it, like a lamb, he is certainly gone to heaven; when, alas, if a wicked man dies quietly, if a man that has all his days lived in notorious sin, dieth quietly; his quiet dying is so far off from being a sign of his being saved, that it is an uncontrollable proof of his damnation. This was Mr. Badman's case, he lived wickedly even to the last, and then went quietly out of the world; therefore Mr. Badman is gone to hell.

Atten. Well, but since you are upon it, and also so confident in it, to wit, that a man that lives a wicked life till he dies, and then dies quietly, is gone to hell; let me see what show of proof you have for this your opinion.

Wise. My first argument is drawn from the necessity of repentance. No man can be saved except he repents, nor can he repent that sees not, that knows not that he is a sinner; and he that knows himself to be a sinner will, I will warrant him, be molested for the time by that knowledge. This, as it is testified by all the Scriptures, so it is testified by Christian experience. He that knows himself to be a sinner is molested, especially if that knowledge comes not to him until he is cast upon his death-bed; molested, I say, before he can die quietly. Yea, he is molested, dejected, and cast down, he is also made to cry out, to hunger and thirst after mercy by Christ, and if at all he shall indeed come to die quietly, I mean with that quietness that is begotten by faith and hope in God's mercy, to the which Mr. Badman and his brethren were utter strangers, his quietness is distinguished by all judicious observers by what went before it, by what it flows from, and also by what is the fruit thereof.

I must confess I am no admirer of sick-bed repentance, for I think verily it is seldom good for anything. But I say, he that hath lived in sin and profaneness all his days, as Mr. Badman did, and yet shall die quietly, that is, without repentance steps in betwixt his life and death, he is assuredly gone to hell, and is damned.

Atten. This does look like an argument indeed; for repentance must come, or else we must go to hell-fire; and if a lewd liver shall, I mean that so continues till the day of his death, yet go out of the world quietly, it is a sign that he died without repentance, and so a sign that he is damned.

Wise. I am satisfied in it, for my part, and that from the necessity and nature of repentance. It is necessary, because God calls for it, and will not pardon sin without it. "Except ye repent, ye shall all likewise perish." (Luke xiii. 1–7). This is that which God hath said, and he will prove but a foolhardy man that shall yet think to go to heaven and glory without it. Repent, for "the axe is laid unto the root of the trees, therefore every tree which bringeth not forth good fruit," but no good fruit can be where there is not sound repentance, shall be "hewn down, and cast into the fire" (Matt. iii. 10). This was Mr. Badman's case, he had attending of him a sinful life, and that to the very last, and yet died quietly, that is, without repentance; he is gone to hell and is damned. For the nature of repentance, I have touched upon that already, and showed that it never was where a quiet death is the immediate companion of a sinful life; and therefore Mr. Badman is gone to hell.

Secondly. My second argument is drawn from that blessed word of Christ, While the strong man armed keeps the house, "his goods are in peace," till a stronger than he comes (Luke xi. 21). But the strong man armed kept Mr. Badman's house, that is, his heart, and soul, and body, for he went from a sinful life quietly out of this world. The stronger did not disturb by intercepting with sound repentance betwixt his sinful life and his quiet death. Therefore Mr. Badman is gone to hell.

The strong man armed is the devil, and quietness is his security. The devil never fears losing of the sinner, if he can but keep him quiet. Can he but keep him quiet in a sinful life, and quiet in his death, he is his own. Therefore he saith, "his goods are in peace"; that is, out of danger. There is no fear of the devil's losing such a soul, I say, because Christ, who is the best judge in this matter, saith, "his goods are in peace," in quiet, and out of danger.

Atten. This is a good one too; for, doubtless, peace and quiet with sin is one of the greatest signs of a damnable state.

Wise. So it is. Therefore, when God would show the greatness of his anger against sin and sinners in one word, he saith, They are "joined to idols; let them alone" (Hos. iv. 17). Let them alone, that is, disturb them not; let them go on without control; let the devil enjoy them peaceably, let him carry them out of the world unconverted quietly. This is one of the sorest of judgments, and bespeaketh the burning anger of God against sinful men. See also when you come home, the fourteenth verse of the fourth chapter of Hosea, "I will not punish your daughters when they commit whoredom." I will let them alone, they shall live and die in their sins. But,

Thirdly. My third argument is drawn from that saying of Christ, "He hath blinded their eyes, and hardened their heart; that they should not see with their eyes, nor understand with *their* heart, and be converted, and I should heal them" (John xii. 40). There are three things that I will take notice of from these words.

1. The first is, that there can be no conversion to God where the eye is darkened, and the heart hardened. The eye must first be made to see, and the heart to break and relent under and for sin, or else there can be no conversion. "He hath blinded their eyes, and hardened their heart, lest they should see and understand, and" so "be converted." And this was clearly Mr. Badman's case; he lived a wicked life, and also died with his eyes shut, and heart hardened, as is manifest, in that a sinful life was joined with a quiet death; and all for that he should not be converted, but partake of the fruit of his sinful life in hell-fire.

2. The second thing that I take notice of from these words is, that this is a dispensation and manifestation of God's anger against a man for his sin. When God is angry with men, I mean, when he is so angry with them, this among many is one of the judgments that he giveth them up unto, to wit, to blindness of mind, and hardness of heart, which he also suffereth to accompany them till they enter in at the gates of death. And then, and there, and not short of then and there, their eyes come to be opened. Hence it is said of the rich man mentioned in Luke, "He died, and in hell he lifted up his eyes" (Luke xvi. 22). Implying that he did not lift them up before; he neither saw what he had done, nor whither he was going, till he came to the place of execution, even into hell. He died asleep in his soul; he died besotted, stupefied, and so consequently for quietness like a child or lamb, even as Mr. Badman did. This was a sign of God's anger; he had a mind to damn him for his sins, and therefore would not let him see nor have a heart to repent for them, lest he should convert; and his damnation, which God had appointed, should be frustrate. "Lest they should be converted, and I should heal them."

3. The third thing I take notice of from hence is, that a sinful life and a quiet death annexed to it is the ready, the open, the beaten, the common highway to hell: there is no surer sign of damnation than for a man to die quietly after a sinful life. I do not say that all wicked men that are molested at their death with a sense of sin and fears of hell do therefore go to heaven, for some are also made to see, and are left to despair, not converted by seeing, that they might go roaring out of this world to their place. But I say there

is no surer sign of a man's damnation than to die quietly after a sinful life; than to sin and die with his eyes shut, than to sin and die with an heart that cannot repent. "He hath blinded their eyes, and hardened their heart, that they should not see with *their* eyes, nor understand with *their* heart" (John xii. 40). No, not so long as they are in this world, "Lest they should see with *their* eyes, and understand with *their* heart, and should be converted, and I should heal them" (Acts xxviii. 26, 27; Rom. ii. 1–5).

God has a judgment for wicked men; God will be even with wicked men. God knows how to reserve the ungodly to the day of judgment to be punished (2 Pet. ii.). And this is one of his ways by which he doth it. Thus it was with Mr. Badman.

4. Fourthly, it is said in the book of Psalms, concerning the wicked, "*There are* no bands in their death, but their strength *is* firm" (Ps. lxxiii. 4–6). By no bands he means no troubles, no gracious chastisements, no such corrections for sin as fall to be the lot of God's people for theirs; yea, that many times falls to be theirs at the time of their death. Therefore he adds concerning the wicked, "They *are* not in trouble (then) as *other* men, neither are they plagued like *other* men"; but go as securely out of the world as if they had never sinned against God, and put their own souls into danger of damnation. "There is no bands in their death." They seem to go unbound, and set at liberty out of this world, though they have lived notoriously wicked all their days in it. The prisoner that is to die at the gallows for his wickedness, must first have his irons knocked off his legs; so he seems to go most at liberty, when indeed he is going to be executed for his transgressions. Wicked men also have no bands in their death, they seem to be more at liberty when they are even at the wind-up of their sinful life, than at any time besides.

Hence you shall have them boast of their faith and hope in God's mercy when they lie upon their death-bed; yea, you shall have them speak as confidently of their salvation as if they had served God all their days; when the truth is, the bottom of this their boasting is because they have no bands in their death. Their sin and base life comes not into their mind to correct them, and bring them to repentance;

but presumptuous thoughts, and a hope and faith of the spider's, the devil's, making, possesseth their soul, to their own eternal undoing (Job viii. 13, 14).

Hence wicked men's hope is said to die, not before, but with them; they give up the ghost together. And thus did Mr. Badman. His sins and his hope went with him to the gate, but there his hope left him, because he died there; but his sins went in with him, to be a worm to gnaw him in conscience for ever and ever.

The opinion, therefore, of the common people concerning this kind of dying is frivolous and vain; for Mr. Badman died like a lamb, or, as they call it, like a chrisom-child, quietly and without fear. I speak not this with reference to the struggling of nature with death, but as to the struggling of the conscience with the judgment of God. I know that nature will struggle with death. I have seen a dog and sheep die hardly. And thus may a wicked man do, because there is an antipathy betwixt nature and death. But even while, even then, when death and nature are struggling for the mastery, the soul, the conscience, may be as besotted, as benumbed, as senseless and ignorant of its miserable state, as the block or bed on which the sick lies. And thus they may die like a chrisom-child in show, but indeed like one who by the judgment of God is bound over to eternal damnation; and that also by the same judgment is kept from seeing what they are, and whither they are going, till they plunge down among the flames.

And as it is a very great judgment of God on wicked men that so die, for it cuts them off from all possibility of repentance, and so of salvation, so it is as great a judgment upon those that are their companions that survive them, for by the manner of their death, they dying so quietly, so like unto chrisom-children, as they call it, they are hardened, and take courage to go on in their course.

For comparing their life with their death, their sinful, cursed lives, with their childlike, lamblike death, they think that all is well, that no damnation is happened to them; though they lived like devils incarnate, yet they died like harmless ones. There was no whirlwind, no tempest, no band or plague in their death. They died as quietly as the most godly of them all, and had as great faith and hope of salvation, and would talk as boldly of salvation as if they had assurance of it. But as was their hope in life, so was their death; their hope was without trial, because it was none of God's working, and their death was without molestation, because so was the judgment of God concerning them.

But I say, at this their survivors take heart to tread their steps, and to continue to live in the breach of the law of God; yea, they carry it stately in their villainies; for so it follows in the Psalm: "*There are* no bands in their death, but their strength *is* firm," etc. "Therefore pride compasseth them," the survivors, "about as a chain, violence covereth them *as* a garment" (Ps. lxxiii. 6). Therefore they take courage to do evil, therefore they pride themselves in their iniquity. Therefore, wherefore? Why, because their fellows died, after they had lived long in a most profane and wicked life, as quietly and as like to lambs as if they had been innocent.

Yea, they are bold, by seeing this, to conclude that God either does not, or will not, take notice of their sins. They "speak wickedly, and speak loftily" (Ps. lxxiii. 8). They speak wickedly of sin, for that they make it better than by the Word it is pronounced to be. They speak wickedly, concerning oppression that they commend, and count it a prudent act. They also speak loftily. "They set their mouth against the heavens," etc. "And they say, How doth God know? and is there knowledge in the Most High?" (Ps. lxxiii. 11). And all this, so far as I can see, ariseth in their hearts from the beholding of the quiet and lamblike death of their companions. "Behold these *are* the ungodly who prosper in the world," that is, by wicked ways; "they increase *in* riches" (Ps. lxxiii. 12).

This therefore is a great judgment of God, both upon that man that dieth in his sins, and also upon his companion that beholdeth him so to die. He sinneth, he dieth in his sins, and yet dieth quietly. What shall his companion say to this? What judgment shall he make how God will deal with him, by beholding the lamblike death of his companion? Be sure he cannot, as from such a sight, say, Woe be to me, for judgment is before him. He cannot gather that sin is a dreadful and a bitter thing, by the childlike death of Mr. Badman. But must rather, if he judgeth according to what he sees, or according to his corrupted reason, conclude with the wicked ones of old, that "every one that doeth evil *is* good in the sight of the Lord, and he delighteth in them; or, Where *is* the God of judgment?" (Mal. ii. 17).

Yea, this is enough to puzzle the wisest man. David himself was put to a stand by beholding the quiet death of ungodly men. "Verily," says he, "I have cleansed my heart *in* vain, and washed my hands in innocency" (Ps. lxxiii. 13). They, to appearance, fare better by far than I: "Their eyes stand out with fatness," they have more than heart could wish. But "all the day long have I been plagued, and chastened every morning." This, I say, made David wonder, yea, and Job and Jeremiah too. But he goeth into the sanctuary, and then he understands their end, nor could he understand it before. "I went into the sanctuary of God." What place was that? Why there where he might inquire of God, and by him be resolved of this matter; "*Then,*" says he, "understood I their end." Then I saw that thou hast "set them in slippery places," and that "thou castedst them down to destruction." Castedst them down, that is, suddenly, or, as the next words say, "As in a moment they are utterly consumed with terrors"; which terrors did not seize them on their sick-bed, for they had "*no bands*" in their death. The terrors, therefore, seized them there, where also they are holden in them for ever. This he found out, I say, but not without great painfulness, grief, and pricking in his reins; so deep, so hard, and so difficult did he find it rightly to come to a determination in this matter.

And, indeed, this is a deep judgment of God towards ungodly sinners; it is enough to stagger a whole world, only the godly that are in the world have a sanctuary to go to, where the oracle and Word of God is, by which his judgments and a reason of many of them are made known to, and understood by them.

Atten. Indeed this is a staggering dispensation. It is full of the wisdom and anger of God. And I believe, as you have said, that it is full of judgment to the world. Who would have imagined, that had not known Mr. Badman, and yet had seen him die, but that he had been a man of an holy life and conversation, since he died so stilly, so quietly, so like a lamb or a chrisom-child? Would they not, I say, have con-

cluded that he was a righteous man? or that if they had
known him and his life, yet to see him die so quietly, would
they not have concluded that he had made his peace with
God? Nay farther, if some had known that he had died in
his sins, and yet that he had died so like a lamb, would they
not have concluded that either God doth not know our sins,
or that he likes them; or that he wants power, or will, or
heart, or skill, to punish them; since Mr. Badman himself
went from a sinful life so quietly, so peaceable, and so like
a lamb as he did?

Wise. Without controversy, this is a heavy judgment of
God upon wicked men; one goes to hell in peace, another
goes to hell in trouble; one goes to hell, being sent thither
by his own hands; another goes to hell, being sent thither
by the hand of his companion; one goes thither with his
eyes shut, and another goes thither with his eyes open; one
goes thither roaring, and another goes thither boasting of
heaven and happiness all the way he goes (Job xxi. 23). One
goes thither like Mr. Badman himself, and others go thither
as did his brethren. But above all, Mr. Badman's death, as
to the manner of dying, is the fullest of snares and traps
to wicked men; therefore, they that die as he are the greatest
stumble to the world. They go, and go, they go on peaceably
from youth to old age, and thence to the grave, and so to
hell, without noise. "They go as an ox goeth to the slaughter,
or as a fool to the correction of the stocks"; that is, both
senselessly and securely. O! but being come at the gates of
hell. O! but when they see those gates set open for them. O!
but when they see that that is their home, and that they
must go in thither, then their peace and quietness flies away
for ever. Then they roar like lions, yell like dragons, howl
like dogs, and tremble at their judgment, as do the devils
themselves. O! when they see they must shoot the gulf and
throat of hell! when they shall see that hell hath shut her
ghastly jaws upon them, when they shall open their eyes
and find themselves within the belly and bowels of hell!
Then they will mourn, and weep, and hack, and gnash their
teeth for pain. But this must not be, or if it must, yet very
rarely, till they are gone out of the sight and hearing of those
mortals whom they do leave behind them alive in the world.

Atten. Well, my good neighbour Wiseman, I perceive that

the sun grows low, and that you have come to a conclusion with Mr. Badman's life and death; and, therefore, I will take my leave of you. Only first, let me tell you, I am glad that I have met with you to-day and that our hap was to fall in with Mr. Badman's state. I also thank you for your freedom with me, in granting of me your reply to all my questions. I would only beg your prayers that God will give me much grace, that I may neither live nor die as did Mr. Badman.

Wise. My good neighbour Attentive, I wish your welfare in soul and body; and if aught that I have said of Mr. Badman's life and death may be of benefit unto you, I shall be heartily glad; only I desire you to thank God for it, and to pray heartily for me, that I with you may be kept by the power of God through faith unto salvation.

Atten. Amen. Farewell.

Wise. I wish you heartily farewell.